PROPHECY
Made Easy

EXPERIENCE THE FUTURE NOW!

Glen Walker

PROPHECY PRESS

Editing and page design by Ken McFarland
Cover art direction and design by Ed Guthero

The author assumes full responsibility for the accuracy of all facts, quotations, and references as cited in this book.

ISBN: 0-615-11356-7

Contents

Dedication

To my wife Idalmi, my son David, and my daughter Liz,
each of whom has inspired me—and in memory of my loving parents,
Dave and Seena Walker.

Foreword

The future.

Does anyone really know with absolute certainty what is going to happen in the days, months, or years ahead? Can you be sure what is going to happen in your life tomorrow—or even an hour from now? Do any of us even have any guarantees that we'll still be here for the next sunrise?

From history, we know much of what has happened in years and centuries gone by. And if our memories serve us reliably, each of us can remember most of what's happened in our own lifetime. But the future?

Attempting to predict the future is the province of supermarket-tabloid psychics, of gambling oddsmakers, of meteorologists, of astrologers, of Wall Street forecasters. And these predictions run the gamut from hunches and "educated" guesses to outright flim-flam.

But predicting the future is also the province of prophets. And because genuine prophets have prophesied, counterfeit and false prophets have also flourished. The "batting average" for the predictions of pseudo-prophets through time has repeatedly proven that they see the future no more clearly than anyone else. But the prophecies of true Bible prophets continue to be fulfilled with pinpoint accuracy.

Are you curious about where this world is headed? Would you really like to know what tomorrow's headlines are going to be? Does anything the Bible prophets predicted centuries ago have anything to do with YOUR life?

Prophecy Made Easy is a book about the future. It's about what God Himself wants you to know about what's just ahead in time. Through His prophets, God offers you and everyone else on earth a preview of what is coming up fast as we move ahead into the unknown of this new millennium.

Just as you've already experienced the past—and are at this very moment experiencing the present—you can also experience the future, NOW! By focusing on Bible prophecy as set forth clearly and simply in this book, you will learn all that God so fervently wants you to know about the future.

Many books make Bible prophecy seem almost impossibly complex and difficult to understand. Some even take the position that many Bible prophecies aren't even *meant* to be understood. That is certainly not true of the book you hold in your hand—the very title of which promises that you can easily learn the basics of Bible prophecy. This book, of course, is a beginning—a launching place for your own new or continued study of God's prophetic messages to you.

May God enlighten and bless you as the author of *Prophecy Made Easy* shares with you the results and insights of his own study of Bible prophecy. And may the future lose its mystery as you explore God's Word to find what He says about tomorrow.

—Ken McFarland

Introduction

Experience the Future Now!

The future is bright!

The last book of the Bible, Revelation, reveals God's great love for you as no other book can! It reveals God's love to you in both history and prophecy.

In order to understand the future, the great Bible prophecies, we must understand the past. History and prophecy are bound tightly together. They are twins. History is prophecy in reverse, and prophecy is history in advance. It is impossible to have a correct understand of either when separated from its twin.

In Revelation 1:3, Jesus says, "Blessed is the one who reads and hears and takes to heart what is written in it, because the time is near."

You can now go behind the headlines. *Prophecy Made Easy* reveals what is really happening! It reveals "the rest of the story." It allows you to experience the future before it happens! It reveals the story that newspapers can't tell you! Haven't you ever wanted to get tomorrow's news today? That is exactly what you are getting in *Prophecy Made Easy!* Don't miss reading this exciting book! Don't miss understanding, for the first time, what the newspapers can't tell you.

Discover the real story behind the movies "Star Wars" and "Raiders of the Lost Ark"! What is "the ark," and what does it have to do with prophecy? You will be amazed as you find the answers to these questions in *Prophecy Made Easy.*

You will also be amazed as you discover the true meaning of life! What is actually going to happen the moment you die?

Discover the real story behind the television show "Touched by an Angel." Who are the angels? And who is the devil? Is he real? You will discover for yourself whether the devil is real or just a made-up fictitious character designed to scare people. Does he really wear red pajamas? Does he really have horns, a tail, and a pitchfork?

What is the story behind the "mark of the beast"? *Prophecy Made Easy* reveals the true identity of the "beast" of Revelation and the true identity of its "mark." What many people are unaware of is that there are two different "beasts" or powers that are working together. Read about it in Revelation 13. *Prophecy Made Easy* takes you "behind the scenes"! You will discover facts in both history and prophecy that these powers do not want you to know. You will not only discover the identity of these two powers; you will know how to be victorious over them. Now, go ahead, be amazed—read tomorrow's news, today!

God knows what is going to happen before it happens! Through the prophet Daniel, He predicted in the Bible the exact year Christ would be baptized and the exact year He would be crucified, hundreds of years ahead of time! That is just one of the amazing prophecies that provides real evidence for the reality of God.

God is real. He loves you and has an exciting plan for your life. The future is bright for everyone who will invest time in preparing for it! If you have invested in the stock market, if you have invested in your future, and are unsure of what your future holds, I urge you to invest time with Jesus Christ. The stock market may fail you, but Jesus Christ never will. Invest your time today! Read *Prophecy Made Easy.* It will easily prove to be the best and most exciting investment you have ever made!

God Loves You!

If you were walking down the road and saw someone walking barefoot and about to step on a big piece of broken glass, what would you do? You would probably shout to the person, "Watch out for the broken glass!" This book looks into the future and reveals to you, the reader, the hidden dangers and exciting choices! You will have a "behind the scenes" knowledge to be able to make the best choices. You will walk into the future more securely. Jesus Christ will be by your side, and the knowledge of a bright, secure future will put a smile on your face. Why not help a friend make this discovery today? Share this book with friends. Help them find greater success and power.

The Secret of a Life of Super Power

Do you want a life filled with real success and real power? Take a look at the very small corn kernel. Within that kernel is a huge stalk of corn just waiting to burst out and produce ears of corn. Look at the lowly watermelon seed. Within the watermelon seed are huge watermelons just waiting to burst out of the seed once it is planted.

We human beings sometimes think we have great power, yet with all our huge laboratories and scientists, we have never been able to produce an ear of corn or a watermelon without the lowly seed. God has placed huge watermelons within the lowly seed and ears of corn within the tiny kernel. Now that is power! Just imagine! Huge watermelons weighing forty pounds are just waiting to burst out of the little seed. Those little seeds planted in a garden produce wonderful vegetables and fruits of a variety of colors and tastes.

There is miraculous life in planting those tiny seeds. Those tiny seeds can turn a garden into a wonderful place of beauty and enjoyment and nourishment. We eat the product of the seeds, and we are benefited by receiving strength and health and *power!* Stop eating the products of seeds, and see how healthy and how powerful you really are!

Nature teaches us that real power comes from seeds. Did you know that God calls the words of the Bible "seed"? Luke 8:11. "The seed is the word of God." God has put His very creative power in the Bible "seed." If you really want power, you must "plant" God's "seed"—His Word—in your mind. The power of God's Word, the Bible, is released as you meditate on God's promises and the great messages of power within God's Word. You will never be a real power in this world without it! Jesus knew that. He is called the Word of God in the first chapter of the gospel of John.

"Superpower" is an illusion. The nation of Rome was the superpower that ruled the world when Christ walked the earth as a humble carpenter. Jesus Christ preached for three and a half years and then was put to death.

Who was the real superpower? The nation of Rome, with all its military hardware—or the humble carpenter, Jesus of Nazareth? It appeared that Rome was more powerful. Rome had the power of life or death. The Jewish leaders and the Romans thought they were more powerful than Christ when they put Him to death on the cross. He was put in the tomb, and they gloried in their great power over Christ.

One question must be asked. How many of those strong Roman soldiers are walking around today? How many of the Jewish religious leaders who condemned Christ are alive today? And what about Christ? He walked out of the tomb Sunday morning after resting in the tomb on the Sabbath day. It is His voice that will bring these Roman soldiers from their graves to see the one they laughed at coming again in majesty and glory and wrapped in "flaming fire."

Appearances were deceiving. They are still deceiving. Who is the real superpower? The billionaires? The United States? Those countries that are part of the nuclear club? Or the lowly person who has Jesus Christ in his heart? What are you seeking for? Are you seeking the illusory goal of success? The lowly carpenter, Jesus, said, "What does it profit a person if he gain the whole world and lose his own soul?"

Life is strange! It is like a thirsty person lost in the desert who is sure he sees water, but it turns out to be a mirage—the illusion of water. When you are thirsty, you sometimes can see water where there is no water. It is the same way with power. We chase after power and success. We may reach the heights of success only to lose it all to the enemy known as death.

Who is successful—the billionaire who can buy anything he wants, or the lowly Christian who often faces hardships? How many of those billions of dollars would the billionaire spend if he could buy eternal life? Only one heartbeat separates the billionaire from his vast riches and eternal poverty. Don't waste your time chasing mirages—illusions of power. Choose living power. Choose Jesus Christ!

Christ still has power over the grave. When you read the Bible with spiritual hunger, you are planting God's power, God's "seed," in your mind. Just as a watermelon seed planted in the ground produces forty-pound watermelons from one seed, God's seeds will produce their own gifts. You will become a different person—a happier person—with less fear. You will no longer fear death. You will trust Christ, who still has power over death. The grave will not be able to hold you. You will be able to help others discover this very same power in their lives. You will live forever in a world made new. Your power then will be as the power of the angels.

Read in chapter 3 on angels about the tremendous physical powers they have. Your powers will increase mentally, physically, socially, and spiritually. You will not see maximum power in this life, but you will see a definite increase in power over the fear of death. You will have power over the grave.

As we noted, within a lowly watermelon seed are huge watermelons weighing forty pounds. Within the seed we call the Word of God is eternal life. The Word of God appears tiny and insignificant. Yet the tiny seed has a power within it that not all the scientists and laboratories of earth can duplicate. Plant the seed, the Word of God, in your mind, and reap the harvest now and eternally.

Today the grave has power over all people everywhere. But I tell you that with Jesus in your heart, with His Word in your mind, you too will conquer the grave. You too will be filled with super power! "The harvest is the end of the world and the angels are the reapers." Get ready for that day when everyone will finally realize that God's Word was the only real superpower! God offers you His word, His super power! Matthew 13:39.

Fill your life with His Word, and you will have "super power." You will one day have a "super life," and you will have powers that not even the comic book character "Superman" dreamed possible. The apostle Paul tells us that we can not even imagine how wonderful it is going to be! Have you ever surprised someone you loved with a gift? How did you feel? I imagine you felt happy about giving them that gift. God has gone to prepare homes for us, and He tells us that they will be better than our wildest imagination. John 14:1-3; Isaiah 65:21.

God is looking forward to seeing the astonishment on your face as He gives you the gift of eternal life, without the headaches of pain and death. There will be adventure and joy and new discoveries to be made each and every day throughout all the time of eternity! The apostle Paul wrote: "No eye has seen, no ear has heard, no mind has conceived what God has prepared for those who love him." 1 Corinthians 2:9. Here the apostle Paul is quoting the prophet Isaiah—Isaiah 64:4.

Isaiah continues in the next chapter, talking about the future glories of the earth made new. "I will create new heavens and a new earth. The former things will not be remembered. They will build houses and dwell in them; they will plant vineyards and eat their fruit. The wolf and the lamb will feed together and the lion will eat straw like the ox. . . They will neither harm nor destroy on all my holy mountain, says the Lord." Isaiah 65:17, 21, 25.

Experience the New Birth!

Every person has a God-shaped "hole" in their soul! Everyone seeks to fill that hole with something. Some try to fill it with smoking, sex, drugs, movies, wild parties, crime—or even a life of honor, glory, adventure, and excitement, but the hole remains as big as ever! Only God can fill that hole. Our attempt to fill the hole just makes it bigger. Why not accept Christ into your life to fill that hole for you today?

God offers to fill the "hole in your soul" and make you completely whole. He offers you a way out of the mess you are in—a way out of sin. The results of sin are death. God lowered Himself and chose to became a human, to live a sinless life, and to experience the most painful death possible to make a bridge across the chasm of death. Christ is that bridge, and He is a ladder out of the pit of unhappiness and pain.

Have you ever felt weak? Christ felt weak when the weight of your sins and mine was crushing out His life in the garden of Gethsemene. Have you ever felt guilt, or darkness, or depression, or pain, or loneliness, or the hatred of others? Christ felt it all—and so much more than we have. He felt it so much that great drops of blood and sweat were forced from the pores of His skin, rolled down His face, and fell to the earth as He prayed in the garden the night before He was crucified.

Christ felt it when He was brought, under the direction of the jealous religious leaders, to the Judgment Hall and then to the cross. His back was ripped open by the whips of the soldiers. Blood ran down His back. Blood also ran down His face as the crown of thorns was beaten into His head—and from His hands and feet as the nails were pounded through them.

He was nailed to the cruel instrument of torture, the cross. Strong Roman soldiers lifted the cross and let it drop into the hole prepared for it. The tremendous jolt of the cross hitting the bottom of that hole caused the most extreme pain. But the worst pain He felt was the mental anguish, the sense of separation from God His Father, when He cried out, "My God, My God, why have you forsaken me?"

Why did the King of the universe leave His home to come to Planet Earth? Why did He choose to become a human—a little baby boy—and then grow up with the religious leaders hating Him? Why did He allow His enemy, Lucifer, to bring Him pain and suffering? Why did He allow those He made to spit on Him without retaliation? Why did He suffer the ultimate humiliation of dying naked on two pieces of wood—on "The Old Rugged Cross"—hanging between heaven and earth? It was out of love for you. And it was out of love for me. If you had been the only sinner who needed a bridge over "the valley of death," God would have done it for you alone.

What would it be worth to you to have Jesus Christ in your home today? I mean to have Him really come walking up to your door and knock on it? What would you do if Jesus Christ, who loves you personally so very, very much, walked up to your door and offered you a crown? What if He said, "_____," (imagine your name in the blank—He knows you by name!) "I just stopped by to bring you this crown. It is a much finer crown than has ever been worn by any king. Also, I am inviting you to come to my house—to my mansion. I have a special place of honor for you."

"To him who overcomes I will give the right to sit with me on my throne, just as I overcame, and sat down with my Father on his throne." Revelation 3:21. "In My Father's house are many mansions." John 14:2, NKJV.

What would you do? I know what I would do. I would shout with joy! I would be excited! If you accept Jesus as your bridge over "the valley of death," He will one day be just that physically close. The Bible, God's Word, says that every person is a sinner. It says that sin is disobedience to God's Ten Commandment law. It also says that everyone must die, because the just penalty for sin is death. There is a law that says that weight keeps an object on the ground. That law is the law of gravity. But we have discovered another law—the law of aerodynamics—that overcomes the law of gravity and allows very heavy objects, like airplanes, to fly through the sky.

Sin holds us down, just as gravity holds us down. The power that overcomes gravity is the power of aerodynamics. The only power that overcomes sin is Jesus Christ! People are trying every other option. Many of the other attempts to overcome sin have good-sounding religious names. But the only problem is, they don't work. The only one that works is Jesus Christ. It was Jesus who said, "I am the way, the truth, and the life. No one comes to the Father but by me." If you want to go to California, you had better get on the right highway. If you want to get eternal life, Jesus Christ is that highway. If it is truth you are after, you will find truth when you choose Christ. If it is life that you want, you will find that in knowing Christ. It is Christ who says, "I am the way, the truth and the life."

Jesus says, "For God so loved_____[say your own name here] that He gave His one and only Son, that" by believing in Him you should not die "but have eternal life." John 3:16.

Won't you invite Jesus Christ into your life right now? You can pray this prayer: "Jesus, I am a sinner, and I need Your help. I need Your forgiveness. Thank You for dying for me so that I can live with You forever. Please forgive me for the wrongs I have done. Enter my heart, be my Saviour from sin, be my Master and my King. And please teach me day by day. In Jesus' name, Amen."

Prayer is not big words. Prayer is not a lot of words. Prayer is talking to God as to a friend. When you sign a check that somebody gives you, it does not require a lot of words, but unless you sign that check, the check is no good. So if somebody gives you a check, sign it and put it in the bank.

God's checkbook is the Bible. God has thousands of checks made out to you. God's checks are His promises. Why not sign some of God's checks today? Take each promise personally. That is like signing a check made out in your name. Just as a check that is never signed and never cashed is worthless, so God's promises are powerless until you personally accept them.

Two thousand years ago, Christ was nailed to the cross. Two thieves were dying on crosses on either side of Him. One of them watched and listened and became convinced that Christ was truly the King of kings, the King of the universe, and would live again and rule the universe again. He turned his head toward Christ and said, "Lord, remember me when You come into your kingdom."

In those few words, he was asking for the gift of eternal life. He was asking for forgiveness. He was asking for the new birth. Jesus turned and said, "You will be with me in Paradise!" The promise Christ made to that dying thief that day is a promise, a check, made out to you too! If you come to Christ and ask Him to remember you when He comes again, just as the dying thief asked Christ, His answer will be the same. He is saying to you—just as He said to the dying thief—that you too will be with Christ in paradise. You will be with Him in the beautiful earth made new. Luke 23:43; see John 14:1-3; see Revelation 21 and 22.

God's promises are meant for you individually. He says, "For God loved the world so much that he gave his only Son, that everyone who has faith in him may not die but have eternal life." If you put your name in this check—this promise—eternal life begins now. You are on the way. You are on the right highway. Read the road map, the Bible, often, and you can continue your journey with Christ right into eternal life.

The Bible is your road map. Satan will try to get you to take a detour. So read your Bible, your road map, often, and talk to God as if talking to a friend, because He *is* your best friend. He loves you enough to bleed and suffer in your place. Continue following Jesus wherever He leads. You will find strength and healing and forgiveness and love in the Bible, and in prayer and in sharing this marvelous plan with others.

If you have trouble understanding your road map, the Bible, read *Prophecy Made Easy* and take the free Bible study course offered at the end of this book. This book was designed to act like a magnifying glass, making it easier for you to read and understand the road map, your Bible, and help you avoid Satan's detours.

God Bless You, Child of God!

The author freely borrows material and thoughts from the books of Daniel and Revelation, other books of the Bible, the book *The Great Controversy*, and Emilio Knechtle's oral presentation, "Eden to Eden." I have also used several Bible versions and translations in making the prophecies come alive for the reader.

Prophecy Made Easy has been written in part to help fulfill the prophecy of Habakkuk, who wrote, "Write the vision, and make it plain, . . . that he may run that reads it." Habakkuk 2:2, NKJV.

God called John to "write the vision" in the last book of the Bible, Revelation. God has called me, and others, to help "make it plain." And once you understand God's last message of love, God is calling you to "run" with this vision. When God says "run," He means He is calling you to rapidly help your loved ones, your friends, and your neighbors to find the freedom and joy you are finding from understanding the "vision"—the book of Revelation. One way to do that is to share this very book with someone special, and then with yet another person.

Jesus said, "You shall know the truth, and the truth shall set you free." You will be able to see through the popular false prophecies that are sweeping across the country. You will know a freedom to teach the Word of God. You will know more about the true God of the Bible in a short amount of time than many theologians know in a lifetime.

Ask God to guide you as you read *Prophecy Made Easy*. God will answer your prayer with finer teachers than have ever taught from any theological seminary! God will send angels and the Holy Spirit to guide you and teach you and give you a new freedom you have never felt before. You will not need a Ph.D. in theology to understand *Prophecy Made Easy*. It was not written for the theologian. It was written with you in mind. God is calling you. God expects ordinary men and women to teach others the Word of God. This is a job Jesus never ever left to "religious experts."

For Those Unfamiliar With the Bible

Don't be fooled by T.V. preachers who refer to Bible texts fast as a machine gun. Don't be fooled by those who tell you what the Bible says in this book or that book of the Bible but don't allow you time to look up the text. If they don't put the texts on the screen so you can see them, be careful what you accept from that individual. Those who teach the Word should not be afraid to let you examine the Bible texts they refer to. Those who teach the Word should teach truths that are in complete harmony with the entire Bible.

Prophecy Made Easy has many Bible quotations all through the book. If you are unfamiliar with your Bible, let me explain. I will give you the quotation as in the following example: John 3:16.

That means the Book of John, chapter 3 and verse 16. The book name always comes first. That is followed by the chapter number. And that is followed by the verse number. The Bible is like a library of 66 different books. Let's say you do not know where the book of John is located. You can open up your Bible to one of the beginning pages and usually find a list of the books of the Bible and the page number for that particular book.

The Bible is divided into two sections: The Old Testament (written before Christ's birth) and the New Testament (written after Christ's birth). If you were looking for the book of John, you would notice that it is the fourth book of the New Testament. You would turn to it and then to the appropriate chapter and verse. You can do that with any verse quoted in *Prophecy Made Easy*.

This book was written to reveal what God says in the great prophecies of the Bible. God talks about organizations. He uses strong words in reference to some of the organizations of which we—the common man and woman—might be members. Remember that God loves the members, even when He speaks strong words about the direction the organization is going. Remember the story of Jonah? God sent him to Nineveh with a message. It was not a "happy" message, and Jonah did not want to carry an "unhappy" warning message to anyone. He tried to avoid his duty and took a trip by boat in the opposite direction of Nineveh.

But God still wanted Jonah to carry His message to Nineveh. God created a terrible storm so that everyone on the boat was close to death. Jonah told the people on the boat that He had run away from telling the people of Nineveh that God was planning to destroy the city. Jonah said, "Throw me over the ship into the water, and you will be safe." They did—and they were safe—but Jonah was swallowed by a large fish or whale. The whale got near land and spit him out, and Jonah went to Nineveh to warn the city of coming destruction.

Conditional prophecy has two tracks on which it can travel. We see this in the words of Moses in the book of Deuteronomy (11:26-28). "I am setting before you today a blessing and a curse—the blessing if you obey the commands of the Lord your God that I am giving you today; the curse if you disobey the commands of the Lord your God and turn from the way that I command you today by following other gods, which you have not known."

Ezekiel the prophet gives a foundation for conditional prophecy. He writes: "If a wicked man turns away from all the sins he has committed and keeps all my decrees and does what is just and right, he will surely live; he will not die. . . . But if a righteous man turns from his righteousness and commits sin and does the same detestable things the wicked man does, will he live? None of the righteous things he has done will be remembered." Ezekiel 18:21, 24.

You remember that the people then turned to God for forgiveness, and the city was spared. This is what we call "conditional prophecy." Some prophecies have conditions attached to them. God's great love is behind prophecy. His love is a combination of His great mercy and His great justice. If God prophesies destruction upon a sinful people, and they repent, God will display His great mercy. If they do not repent, prophetic justice will prevail. If, on the other hand, God prophesies blessings on a people, and they choose to turn their backs on God, justice will prevail, and the promised prophecy will result in justice instead of blessings. The prophecy of Ninevah's destruction was changed as a result of the repentance of the people. It was not destroyed. God's message through Jonah was not a "happy" message, but the results were "happy" results.

I sympathize with Jonah's feeling, as God has called me also to be faithful and tell you exactly what will happen in your lifetime. There are "happy" parts and "unhappy" parts—but I must tell you the whole story. The truth is not always pleasant at first, so there is a natural desire to "sugar coat" the truth to make it more appetizing. God won't let me do that, even though that is my natural tendency.

The prophecies of the book of Revelation, as discussed in *Prophecy Made Easy,* will come to pass. The choice is yours. You may choose to ignore these prophecies. The results of that are revealed in the pages ahead. Or you may choose to believe the prophecies. The benefits from choosing to believe these prophecies and to ask God to change your life and fill you with HIS

GREAT POWER are also foretold in the pages ahead. The choice is yours.

Warning!

If you want everything to sound sweet and "sugar coated" and are unwilling to put away your preconceived opinions and pray that God will send you His Holy Spirit to understand the great prophecies of Daniel and Revelation, I would not recommend this book for you. But if you are sincere with God and willing to learn what He thinks is important, this book is for you.

Are the prophecies of the Holy Bible trustworthy? In Chapter 1 of *Prophecy Made Easy*—"The Messianic Prophecies"—we will look at how dependable Bible prophecy really is. Can the true Messiah of prophecy be identified by the clues that the prophets give us in their great prophecies? Find out who the Messiah of prophecy is! This chapter is the anchor chapter for the rest of the book. When you see how, with pinpoint precision, the Messianic prophecies were fulfilled, you will be able to trust the God of all biblical prophecy. It will give you an assurance that *Prophecy Made Easy* will provide you with answers to all the important questions of life! Questions such as "Where did I come from?" "Why am I here?" And "Where am I going?"

The ancient truths within this book have been known to God's children from Adam and Eve, our great grandparents, on down through every generation that has ever lived. Many of these truths have been lost sight of to a large extent by our present generation. It is my desire to share with you what prophecy has to say about these truths, the future, and God's message for those living here on Earth today.

1

Prelude to Star Wars: The Messianic Prophecies

P rophecy is like the rudder on a ship. The rudder gives the ship direction, and prophecy gives our lives direction and purpose. Where did I come from? Why am I here? And where am I going? It seems as if the majority of people never get these questions answered in their entire lifetime.

I too had these questions as a child. I asked them over and over, and God listened and answered my questions. I did not know God, but God knew me and answered the cry of my heart.

At the age of eighteen, I got a job as a salesman and met many people. One of these people led me to a knowledge of God and the Messiah through the biblical prophecies—something I will be eternally grateful for.

The answers to these three basic questions of life are vitally connected to prophecy. God knows where you and I came from, why we are here, and where we are going! He is the Author of all true prophecies—the non-tabloid prophecies—of His book, the Holy Bible!

All true prophecy is connected to the first major prophecy of the Bible, Genesis 3:15. This is the first prophecy dealing with the promised Messiah. The promises of the coming Messiah were made throughout the Old Testament portion of God's holy book, the Bible.

This chapter is divided into three parts. Part One deals with the prophecies of the Messiah as given by King David in the book of Psalms. Part Two deals with the prophecies of the Messiah as given by the prophet Isaiah in the book of Isaiah. And Part Three deals with the messianic prophecies of other Old Testament prophets.

In our search to find what life is all about, we will start by examining the prophecies of two books of the Bible—the book of Psalms and the book of Isaiah. King David wrote his prophecies of the Messiah in the book of Psalms nearly three thousand years ago. Isaiah wrote his prophecies of the Messiah over two thousand seven hundred years ago. Let's find out who the Messiah of Psalms and Isaiah is.

Who Does the Prophet King David, in the Book of Psalms, Identify as the Messiah of Prophecy?

Just as a detective gathers clues to find out who committed a particular crime, the Bible, in contrast, *gives* us prophetic clues of who the Messiah of the world would be. Let's examine those clues that David wrote down for our benefit. David foretold many different characteristics of the Messiah so that everyone who would read his words would know beyond the shadow of a doubt who the real Messiah would be.

Jesus of Nazareth quoted more frequently from Psalms and Isaiah than from any of the other Old Testament books. No other Old Testament books are so frequently quoted in the New Testament as the books of Psalms and Isaiah.

The prophet King David wrote psalms about 950 B.C. In the book of Psalms he tells us that the Messiah would be born into this world to one of his own direct descendants. David predicts that the Messiah would be rejected, like the huge stone that the builders of the temple rejected in building it.

An immense stone was taken to the building site of the temple in Solomon's day. The builders took one look at it and wondered why on earth anyone would bring such a stone to their building site. They pushed the stone aside. They rejected it. That huge stone was in their way and was very annoying.

Finally the day came when the workmen needed a very large and very strong stone that would serve as the cornerstone of the foundation to the temple. They looked everywhere and could not find a stone that was strong enough and of the right size and shape to be the cornerstone for the foundation of the temple. Days dragged by and then weeks as they searched for the right-sized stone with the right amount of strength.

Finally someone suggested the rejected stone. They found it to be exactly the right size and shape. The rejected stone became the most important stone in the building of the temple. David predicted that the Messiah would be rejected by most people just as the stone was at first rejected that was used in building the Temple in King Solomon's day.

The Prophet King David predicted about 950 B.C. that the future Messiah would:

1. Be rejected like the rejected stone.

2. Be a teacher of parables.

3. Be welcomed to Jerusalem by people shouting, "Blessed is he who comes in the name of the LORD."

4. Be betrayed by a trusted friend after they ate together.

5. Be judged unfairly by earthly rulers.

6. Be offered a drink containing gall.

7. Die naked on a cross.

8. Be stared at.

9. Have part of his clothing divided between those at the cross.

10. Lose the other part of His clothing to those who would gamble for it.

11. Be ridiculed by people shaking their heads and saying, "He trusted in the Lord—let Him rescue Him; Let Him deliver Him."

12. Cry out. "My God, My God, why have you forsaken Me" before dying.

13. Speak these last words: "Into Your hand I commit my spirit."

14. Die without any broken bones.

15. Be raised from the dead before His body started to decay.

16. Bring others to life and take them home with Him after being resurrected.

From these many clues from the prophet King David in the book of Psalms, who then is the promised Messiah?

CLUE #1

The Messiah would be in the descendant line of King David.

The Prophecy

"The LORD swore an oath to David, a sure oath that he will not revoke: 'One of your own descendants I will place on your throne.'" Psalm 132:11.

The Fulfillment of Prophecy

"A record of the genealogy of Jesus Christ the son of David, the son of Abraham. . . . David was the father of Solomon, Solomon the father of Rehoboam. . . . and Jacob the father of Joseph, the husband of Mary, of who was born Jesus, who is called Christ [Messiah]." Matthew 1:1-16.

CLUE #2

The Messiah would be rejected by most people like the stone that was at first rejected in building the temple in King Solomon's day. It later was found to be the perfect size for the most important part of the foundation— the cornerstone.

The Prophecy

"The stone which the builders rejected has become the chief cornerstone." Psalm 118:22, NKJV.

The Fulfillment of Prophecy

"Jesus said to them, Have you never read in the Scriptures: The stone which the builders rejected has become the chief cornerstone." Matthew 21:42, NKJV.

CLUE #3

The Messiah would be a teacher of parables.

The Prophecy

"I will open my mouth in parables." Psalm 78:2.

The Fulfillment of Prophecy

"Jesus spoke all these things to the crowd in parables; he did not say anything to them without using a parable." Matthew 13:34.

CLUE #4

The common people would use the words, "Blessed is he who comes in the name of the Lord" to welcome Jesus.

The Prophecy

" Blessed is he who comes in the name of the LORD." Psalm 118:26.

The Fulfillment of Prophecy

"The crowds that went ahead of him and those that followed shouted, 'Hosanna to the Son of David. Blessed is he who comes in the name of the Lord!'" Matthew 21:9.

CLUE #5

The true Messiah would be betrayed by a trusted friend after they had eaten together.

The Prophecy

"Even my close friend whom I trusted, He who shared my bread, has lifted up his heel against me." Psalm 41:9.

The Fulfillment of Prophecy

"Then one of the Twelve—the one called Judas Iscariot—went to the chief priests, and said, What are you willing to give me if I hand him over to you?" Matthew 26:14-16.

CLUE #6

The betrayer of the Messiah would be replaced by another person.

The Prophecy

"May his days be few; may another take his place of leadership." Psalm 109:8.

The Fulfillment of Prophecy

"Then they cast their lots, and the lot fell to Matthias; so he was added to the eleven apostles." Acts 1:26.

CLUE #7

The Messiah would be judged unfairly by earthly rulers.

The Prophecy

"The kings of the earth take their stand and the rulers gather together against the LORD and against his Anointed One." Psalm 2:2.

The Fulfillment of Prophecy

"The chief priests and the whole Sanhedrin were looking for false evidence against Jesus so that they could put him to death." Matthew 26:59.

"Early in the morning, all the chief priests and the elders of the people came to the decision to put Jesus to death." Matthew 27:1.

"Indeed Herod and Pontius Pilate met together with the Gentiles and the people of Israel in this city to conspire against your holy servant Jesus, whom you anointed." Acts 4:27-31.

CLUE #8

King David, around the year 950 B.C., predicted that the true Messiah would die the death of the cross.

The Prophecy

"They have pierced My hands and My feet." Psalm 22:16. Remember that David wrote nearly a thousand years before Jesus, the Messiah, was born into this world.

The Fulfillment of Prophecy

"They crucified Him." Mark 15:24.

CLUE #9

The type of drink to be offered to the dying Messiah was foretold.

The Prophecy

"They also gave me gall for my food, and for my thirst they gave me vinegar to drink." Psalm 69:21, NKJV.

The Fulfillment of Prophecy

"They gave Him sour wine mingled with gall to drink. But when He had tasted it, He would not drink." Matthew 27:34, NKJV.

CLUE #10

The people would stare at Jesus.

The Prophecy

"People stare and gloat over me." Psalm 22:17.

The Fulfillment of Prophecy

"Sitting down, they kept watch over Him there." Matthew 27:36.

CLUE #11

David, in the book of Psalms, predicted that some at the cross would divide up part of His clothing to keep and gamble over the other part.

The Prophecy

"They divide my garments among them, and cast lots for my clothing." Psalm 22:18.

The Fulfillment of Prophecy

"When the soldiers crucified Jesus, they took his clothes, dividing them into four shares, one for each of them, with the undergarment remaining. This garment was seamless, woven in one piece from top to bottom. 'Let's not tear it,' they said to one another. 'Let's decide by lot who will get it.'" John 19:23, 24.

CLUE #12

King David predicted that the Messiah would be ridiculed by people, saying, "He trusted in the Lord . . . let Him deliver Him."

The Prophecy

"All those who see Me ridicule Me; they shoot out the lip, they shake the head, saying. 'He trusted in the Lord, let Him rescue Him; let Him deliver Him'." Psalm 22:7, 8.

The Fulfillment of Prophecy

"He trusted in God; let Him deliver Him now if He will have Him; for He said, I am the Son of God." Matthew 27:43, NKJV.

CLUE #13

The Messiah would be insulted by people who were shaking their heads.

The Prophecy

"I am an object of scorn to my accusers; when they see me, they shake their heads." Psalm 109:25.

The Fulfillment of Prophecy

"Those who passed by hurled insults at Him, shaking their heads and saying, 'You who are going to destroy the temple and build it in three days, save yourself!'" Matthew 27:39, 40.

CLUE #14

The Messiah would cry out "My God, My God, why have you forsaken Me" before dying.

The Prophecy

"My God, My God, why have you forsaken me?" Psalm 22:1.

The Fulfillment of Prophecy

"And about the ninth hour Jesus cried out with a loud voice, saying, . . . My God, my God, why have you forsaken me?" Matthew 27:46; Mark 15:34.

CLUE #15

The final words of the Messiah on the cross were foretold by David in the book of Psalms.

The Prophecy

"Into your hands I commit my spirit." Psalm 31:5.

The Fulfillment of Prophecy

"Jesus called out with a loud voice, 'Father, into your hands I commit my spirit.' When he had said this, he breathed his last." Luke 23:46.

CLUE #16

The Passover lamb was not to have any broken bones. The Messiah was to die, like the passover lamb, without any broken bones.

The Prophecy

"He protects all his bones, not one of them will be broken." Psalm 34:20.

The Fulfillment of Prophecy

"The soldiers therefore came and broke the legs of the first man who had been crucified with Jesus, and then those of the other. But when they came to Jesus and found that he was already dead, they did not break His legs." John 19:32, 33.

CLUE #17

The Messiah would be killed but raised before His body started to decay.

The Prophecy

"I have set the LORD always before me. Because he is at my right hand, I will not be shaken. Therefore my heart is glad and my tongue rejoices; my body also will rest secure, because you will not abandon me to the grave, nor will you let your Holy One see decay." Psalm 16:8-11.

The Fulfillment of Prophecy

" Seeing what was ahead, he spoke of the resurrection of the Christ, that he was not abandoned to the grave, nor did his body see decay. God has raised this Jesus to life, and we are all witnesses of the fact." Acts 2:31, 32.

CLUE #18

The Messiah would take others with Him after being resurrected.

The Prophecy

"When you ascended on high, you led captives in your train." Psalm 68:18.

The Fulfillment of Prophecy

"And when Jesus had cried out again in a loud voice, he gave up his spirit. At that moment the curtain of the temple was torn in two from top to bottom; the earth shook, and the rocks split. The tombs broke open and the bodies of many holy people who had died were raised to life." Matthew 27:50-53.

"After he said this, he was taken up before their very eyes, and a cloud hid him from their sight." Acts 1:9.

Who Is the Messiah, As Identified by the Prophet Isaiah in the Book of Isaiah?

Isaiah the prophet wrote the book of Isaiah around 700 B.C. He tells us that the Messiah would be born to a virgin and born as a direct descendant of King David. Isaiah uses the same story that David uses in the book of Psalms to describe the predicted rejection of the Messiah. He reminds the people of the story they all knew—the story of the rejected stone.

The prophet Isaiah predicted that the future Messiah would:

1. Be rejected like the rejected stone in the building of the temple.

2. Have His way prepared by a wilderness prophet.

3. Spend time in Galilee teaching the people of Galilee.

4. Warn others to avoid hypocrisy.

5. Restore eyesight to the blind and hearing to the deaf.

6. Make the lame walk.

7. Be a gentle, Spirit-filled servant.

8. Teach both Jews and Gentiles.

9. Teach people to take care of the hungry and care for the needs of others.

10. Preach to the poor and would do a work of healing to comfort those in sorrow and to bring discomfort to the careless.

11. Be taken a prisoner and be unjustly given the death penalty.

12. Be silent in His own defense when others would seek to kill Him.

13. Go through suffering that would change His appearance.

14. Allow others to whip His back.

15. Allow others to spit in His face.

16. Die, not from the mistreatment of the people, but rather from the weight of the sins of the entire world crushing out His life. The Messiah would be "crushed" to death by the weight of your sins and mine—the sins of the world.

17. Die with criminals.

18. Have a burial site provided for by a rich person.

From these many clues from the prophet Isaiah in the book of Isaiah, who is the promised Messiah?

CLUE #1

Isaiah tells us that the Messiah, God with us, would be born of a virgin.

The Prophecy

"Therefore the Lord himself will give you a sign: The virgin will be with child and will give birth to a son, and will call him Immanuel [God with us]." Isaiah 7:14.

The Fulfillment of Prophecy

"In the sixth month, God sent the angel Gabriel to Nazareth, a town in Galilee, to a virgin pledged to be married to a man named Joseph, a descendant of David. . . . You will be with child and give birth to a son, and you are to give him the name Jesus." Luke 1:26, 27, 31.

CLUE #2

The Messiah was to be a born into the descendants of David and reign as King.

The Prophecy

"Of the increase of his government and peace there will be no end. He will reign on David's throne and over his kingdom, establishing and upholding it with justice and righteousness from that time on and forever. The zeal of the LORD Almighty will accomplish this." Isaiah 9:7.

The Fulfillment of Prophecy

"A record of the genealogy of Jesus Christ the son of David, the son of Abraham: and Jesse the father of King David. David was the father of Solomon. . . ." Matthew 1:1, 6.

CLUE #3

Isaiah lets us know that the Messiah would be rejected by most people, like the stone that was at first rejected in building the temple in King Solomon's day. It later was found to be the perfect size for the most important part of the foundation—the cornerstone. Trust this Messiah. He will never let you down.

The Prophecy

"So this is what the Sovereign LORD says: 'See, I lay a stone in Zion, a tested stone, a precious cornerstone for a sure foundation; the one who trusts will never be dismayed.'" Isaiah 28:16.

The Fulfillment of Prophecy

"As it is written: 'See, I lay in Zion a stone that causes men to stumble and a rock that makes them fall, and the one who trusts in him will never be put to shame.'" Romans 9:33.

"As the Scripture says, 'Anyone who trusts in him will never be put to shame.'" Romans 10:11.

CLUE #4

Isaiah tells us that the Messiah would not draw attention to Himself. To many people He would be as unnoticed as an unseen stone that people stumble over.

The Prophecy

"He will be a stone that causes men to stumble and a rock that makes them fall. And for the people of Jerusalem he will be a trap and a snare. Many of them will stumble; they will fall and be broken, they will be snared and captured." Isaiah 8:14, 15.

The Fulfillment of Prophecy

"Then Simeon blessed them and said to Mary, his mother: 'This child is destined to cause the falling and rising of many in Israel, and to be a sign that will be spoken against.'" Luke 2:34.

Matthew 21:44 "He who falls on this stone will be broken to pieces, but he on whom it falls will be crushed." Matthew 21:44.

CLUE #5

Someone living in the wilderness would prepare the way for the coming Messiah.

The Prophecy

"A voice of one calling: In the desert prepare the way for the Lord; make straight in the wilderness a highway for our God. Every valley shall be raised up, every mountain and hill made low; the rough ground shall become level, the rugged places a plain. And the glory of the Lord will be revealed. . . . For the mouth of the Lord has spoken." Isaiah 40:3-5.

The Fulfillment of Prophecy

"John the Baptist came, preaching in the wilderness of Judea, and saying, 'Repent, for the kingdom of heaven is at hand!' For this is he who was spoken of by the prophet Isaiah, saying, "The voice of one crying in the wilderness: 'Prepare the way of the Lord; make His paths straight'."'" Matthew 3:1-3.

CLUE #6

The Messiah would spend time teaching the people of Galilee.

The Prophecy

"Nevertheless, there will be no more gloom for those who were in distress. In the past he humbled the land of Zebulun and the land of Naphtali, but in the future he will honor Galilee of the Gentiles, by the way of the sea, along the Jordan—the people walking in darkness have seen a great light; on those living in the land of the shadow of death a light has dawned." Isaiah 9:1, 2.

The Fulfillment of Prophecy

"Leaving Nazareth, he went and lived in Capernaum, which was by the lake in the area of Zebulun and Naphtali—to fulfill what was said through the prophet Isaiah: 'Land of Zebulun and land of Naphtali, the way to the sea, along the Jordan, Galilee of the Gentiles—the people living in darkness have seen a great light; on those living in the land of the shadow of death a light has dawned.'" Matthew 4:13-16.

"On His robe and on His thigh he has this name written: King of Kings and Lord of Lords." Revelation 19:16.

CLUE #7

Isaiah predicted that the Messiah would restore eyesight to the blind and hearing to the deaf—and that the lame would walk.

The Prophecy

"In that day the deaf will hear the words of the scroll, and out of gloom and darkness the eyes of the blind will see." Isaiah 29:18.

"Then will the eyes of the blind be opened and the ears of the deaf unstopped. Then will the lame leap like a deer, and the mute tongue shout for joy." Isaiah 35:5, 6.

The Fulfillment of Prophecy

"Which is easier: to say, 'Your sins are forgiven,' or to say, 'Get up and walk'? Then he said to the paralytic, 'Get up, take your mat and go home.' And the man got up and went home. As Jesus went on from there, two blind men followed him, calling out, 'Have mercy on us, Son of David!' When he had gone indoors, the blind men came to him, and he asked them, 'Do you believe that I am able to do this?' 'Yes, Lord,' they replied. Then he touched their eyes and said, 'According to your faith will it be done to you'; and their sight was restored. Jesus warned them sternly, 'See that no one knows about this.'" Matthew 9:5-7, 27-30.

CLUE #8

The Messiah would teach people to take care of the hungry and to care for the needs of others.

The Prophecy

"Is it not to share your food with the hungry and to provide the poor wanderer with shelter— when you see the naked, to clothe him, and not to turn away from your own flesh and blood?" Isaiah 58:7.

The Fulfillment of Prophecy

"For I was hungry and you gave me something to eat, I was thirsty and you gave me something to drink, I was a stranger and you invited me in, I needed clothes and you clothed me, I was sick and you looked after me, I was in prison and you came to visit me. Then the righteous will answer him, 'Lord, when did we see you hungry and feed you, or thirsty and give you something to drink? When did we see you a stranger and invite you in, or needing clothes and clothe you? When did we see you sick or in prison and go to visit you?' The King will reply, 'I tell you the truth, whatever you did for one of the least of these brothers of mine, you did for me.'" Matthew 25:35-40.

CLUE #9

The Messiah would preach to the poor and would do a work of healing to comfort those in sorrow and to bring discomfort to the careless.

The Prophecy

"The Spirit of the Sovereign LORD is on me, because the LORD has anointed me to preach good news to the poor. He has sent me to bind up the brokenhearted, to proclaim freedom for the captives and release from darkness for the prisoners, to proclaim the year of the LORD's favor and the day of vengeance of our God, to comfort all who mourn." Isaiah 61:1, 2.

The Fulfillment of Prophecy

"As soon as Jesus was baptized, he went up out of the water. At that moment heaven was opened, and he saw the Spirit of God descending like a dove and lighting on him. And a voice from heaven said, 'This is my Son, whom I love; with him I am well pleased.'" Matthew 3:16, 17.

"The Spirit of the Lord is on me, because he has anointed me to preach good news to the poor. He has sent me to proclaim freedom for the prisoners and recovery of sight for the blind, to release the oppressed, to proclaim the year of the Lord's favor." Luke 4:18, 19.

CLUE #10

The Messiah would be a gentle, Spirit-filled servant.

The Prophecy

"Here is my servant, whom I uphold, my chosen one in whom I delight; I will put my Spirit on him and he will bring justice to the nations. He will not shout or cry out, or raise his voice in the streets. A bruised reed he will not break, and a smoldering wick he will not snuff out. In faithfulness he will bring forth justice; he will not falter or be discouraged till he establishes justice on earth. In his law the islands will put their hope." Isaiah 42:1-4.

The Fulfillment of Prophecy

"Here is my servant whom I have chosen, the one I love, in whom I delight; I will put my Spirit on him, and he will proclaim justice to the nations. He will not quarrel or cry out; no one will hear his voice in the streets." Matthew 12:18, 19.

"As soon as Jesus was baptized, he went up out of the water. At that moment heaven was opened, and he saw the Spirit of God descending like a dove and lighting on him. And a voice from heaven said, 'This is my Son, whom I love; with him I am well pleased.'" Matthew 3:16, 17.

"While he was still speaking, a bright cloud enveloped them, and a voice from the cloud said, 'This is my Son, whom I love; with him I am well pleased. Listen to him!'" Matthew 17:5.

CLUE #11

The Messiah was to teach both Jews and Gentiles.

The Prophecy

"I, the LORD, have called you in righteousness; I will take hold of your hand. I will keep you and will make you to be a covenant for the people and a light for the Gentiles." Isaiah 42:6.

The Fulfillment of Prophecy

"Now there was a man in Jerusalem called Simeon, who was righteous and devout. He was waiting for the consolation of Israel, and the Holy Spirit was upon him. It had been revealed to him by the Holy Spirit that he would not die before he had seen the Lord's Christ. Moved by the Spirit, he went into the temple courts. When the parents brought in the child Jesus to do for him what the custom of the Law required, Simeon took him in his arms and praised God, saying: 'Sovereign Lord, as you have promised, you now dismiss your servant in peace. For my eyes have seen your salvation, which you have prepared in the sight of all people, a light for revelation to the Gentiles and for glory to your people Israel.' The child's father and mother marveled at what was said about him." Luke 2:25-33.

CLUE #12

The teachings of the Messiah on hypocrisy are foretold.

The Prophecy

"The Lord says: 'These people come near to me with their mouth and honor me with their lips, but their hearts are far from me. Their worship of me is made up only of rules taught by men.'[" Isaiah 29:13.

The Fulfillment of Prophecy

"These people honor me with their lips, but their hearts are far from me. They worship me in vain; their teachings are but rules taught by men." Matthew 15:8, 9.

"He replied, 'Isaiah was right when he prophesied about you hypocrites; as it is written: "These people honor me with their lips, but their hearts are far from me. They worship me in vain; their teachings are but rules taught by men.""" Mark 7:6, 7.

CLUE #13

The Messiah would go through suffering that would change His appearance.

The Prophecy

"His appearance was so disfigured beyond that of any man." Isaiah 52:14.

The Fulfillment of Prophecy

"And being in anguish, he prayed more earnestly, and his sweat was like drops of blood falling to the ground." Luke 22:44.

CLUE #14

The Messiah would be rejected by the very people He would come to help. He would go through suffering in order to save us.

The Prophecy

"He is despised and rejected by men, a man of sorrows and familiar with suffering. Surely he . . . carried our sorrows." Isaiah 53:3, 4.

The Fulfillment of Prophecy

"Then the chief priests and the elders of the people assembled in the palace of the high priest, whose name was Caiaphas, and they plotted to arrest Jesus in some sly way and kill him." Matthew 26:3, 4.

"And being in anguish, he prayed more earnestly, and his sweat was like drops of blood falling to the ground." Luke 22:44.

The weight of the sins of all mankind was crushing out His life. He would have died right in the garden before being nailed to the cross if an angel had not come to give him strength to endure the weight of the sins of the world.

CLUE #15

The Messiah was to be taken as a prisoner and unjustly judged worthy of death. The real cause of death would not be the usual physical cause of death—the actual cause of death would be the weight of the sins of the entire world crushing out His life.

The Prophecy

"He was taken from prison and from judgment, and who will declare His generation? For He was cut off from the land of the living; for the transgressions of My people He was stricken." Isaiah 53:8, NKJV.

The Fulfillment of Prophecy

"Meanwhile Jesus stood before the governor, and the governor asked him, 'Are you the king of the Jews?' 'Yes, it is as you say,' Jesus replied. When he was accused by the chief priests and the elders, he gave no answer. Then Pilate asked him, 'Don't you hear the testimony they are bringing against you?' But Jesus made no reply, not even to a single charge—to the great amazement of the governor. Now it was the governor's custom at the Feast to release a prisoner chosen by the crowd.

At that time they had a notorious prisoner, called Barabbas. So when the crowd had gathered, Pilate asked them, 'Which one do you want me to release to you: Barabbas, or Jesus who is called Christ?' For he knew it was out of envy that they had handed Jesus over to him. While Pilate was sitting on the judge's seat, his wife sent him this message: 'Don't have anything to do with that innocent man, for I have suffered a great deal today in a dream because of him.' But the chief priests and the elders persuaded the crowd to ask for Barabbas and to have Jesus executed. 'Which of the two do you want me to release to you?' asked the governor. 'Barabbas,' they answered. 'What shall I do, then, with Jesus who is called Christ?' Pilate asked. They all answered, 'Crucify him!' 'Why? What crime has he committed?' asked Pilate. But they shouted all the louder, 'Crucify him!' When Pilate saw that he was getting nowhere, but that instead an uproar was starting, he took water and washed his hands in front of the crowd. 'I am innocent of this man's blood,' he said. 'It is your responsibility!' All the people answered, 'Let his blood be on us and on our children!' Then he released Barabbas to them. But he had Jesus flogged, and handed him over to be crucified." Matthew 27:11-26.

"For what I received I passed on to you as of first importance: that Christ died for our sins according to the Scriptures." 1 Corinthians 15:3.

CLUE #16

The Messiah would be silent in His own defense when others would seek to kill Him.

The Prophecy

"He was oppressed and He was afflicted, Yet He did not open His mouth; He was led like a lamb to the slaughter, and as a sheep before her shearers is silent, so He opened not His mouth." Isaiah 53:7.

The Fulfillment of Prophecy

"When he was accused by the chief priests and the elders, he gave no answer. Then Pilate asked him, 'Don't you hear the testimony they are bringing against you?' But Jesus made no reply, not even to a single charge—to the great amazement of the governor." Matthew 27:12-14.

"And he went back inside the palace. 'Where do you come from?' he asked Jesus, but Jesus gave him no answer." John 19:9.

CLUE #17

People would whip the back of the Messiah and spit in His face.

The Prophecy

"I offered my back to those who beat me, and my cheeks to those who pulled out my beard: I did not hide my face from mocking and spitting." Isaiah 50:6.

Remember that Isaiah wrote nearly 700 years before Jesus the Messiah was born into this world.

The Fulfillment of Prophecy

"Then they spit in His face and struck him with their fists. Others slapped him, and said, Prophesy to us, Christ! Who hit you?" Matthew 26:67.

"Then he released Barabbas to them. But he had Jesus flogged, and handed him over to be crucified." Matthew 27:26.

CLUE #18

The Messiah would be whipped. That whipping would bring healing to sinful mankind.

The Prophecy

"By His stripes [blows that cut in] we are healed." Isaiah 53:5, NKJV.

The Fulfillment of Prophecy

"For what I received I passed on to you as of first importance: that Christ died for our sins according to the Scriptures, that he was buried, that he was raised on the third day according to the Scriptures." 1 Corinthians 15:3, 4.

"He himself bore our sins in his body on the tree, so that we might die to sins and live for righteousness; by his wounds you have been healed. For you were like sheep going astray, but now you have returned to the Shepherd and Overseer of your souls." 1 Peter 2:24, 25.

"The eunuch was reading this passage of Scripture: 'He was led like a sheep to the slaughter, and as a lamb before the shearer is silent, so he did not open his mouth. In his humiliation he was deprived of justice. Who can speak of his descendants? For his life was taken from the earth.' The eunuch asked Philip, 'Tell me, please, who is the prophet talking about. . . ? Then Philip began with that very . . . Scripture and told him the good news about Jesus." Acts 8:32-35.

CLUE #19

The Messiah would die with criminals, and a burial site would be provided by a rich person.

The Prophecy

"And they made His grave with the wicked—but with the rich at His death." Isaiah 53:9, NKJV.

The Fulfillment of Prophecy

"Two robbers were crucified with Him, one on his right and one on his left." Matthew 27:38.

"As evening approached, there came a rich man from Arimathea, named Joseph, who had himself become a disciple of Jesus. Going to Pilate, he asked for Jesus' body, and Pilate ordered that it be given to him. Joseph took the body, wrapped it in a clean linen cloth, and placed it in his own new tomb that he had cut out of the rock. He rolled a big stone in front of the entrance to the tomb and went away." Matthew 27:57-60.

CLUE #20

The Messiah would be "crushed" to death by the weight of the sins of the world.

The Prophecy

"Yet it was the Lord's will to crush him [bruise him] and cause him to suffer, and though the Lord makes his life a guilt offering, he will see his offspring and prolong his day, and the will of the Lord will prosper in his hand. After the suffering of his soul, he will see the light of life and be satisfied; by his knowledge my righteous servant will justify many and he will bear their iniquities. . . . he poured out his life unto death, and was numbered with the transgressors. For he bore the sin of many, and made intercession for the transgressors." Isaiah 53:10-12.

The Fulfillment of Prophecy

" He himself bore our sins in his body on the tree, so that we might die to sins and live for righteousness; by his wounds you have been healed." 1 Peter 2:24.

David, in Psalms, and Isaiah, in his prophetic book known as Isaiah, do enough detective work to pinpoint with absolute accuracy that Jesus Christ is this world's Messiah. In the next chapter, we will explore how the need for a Messiah, a Saviour from sin, came about. The author believes in the Word of God as our final authority. God loves us and has revealed the past, present, and future to us in His holy book, the Bible. In my attempts to clarify what I believe happened, from my extensive study of God's Word, I will take the reader with me on a journey that will involve both the infallible Word of God and my conclusions of those specific events.

Who is the true Messiah of Bible prophecy, according to other prophets?

Other prophets predicted that the future Messiah would:

1. Come to Planet Earth to restore communication between heaven and earth.

2. Be born in a certain small town called Bethlehem.

3. Be born into the Jewish race.

4. Have His way prepared by a powerful prophet like Elijah (John the Baptist).

5. Be baptized ("anointed") in the year A.D. 27.

6. Enter Jerusalem riding on the back of a donkey.

7. See His followers run away when He was mistreated.

8. Die a bloody death like a sacrificial lamb.

9. Die ("be cut off") in the year A.D. 31.

10. Not have any broken bones.

11. Allow His body to be "pierced" by those He came to save.

12. Die, and that afterward, some of the inhabitants of Jerusalem would grieve over what they had done.

CLUE #1

Moses tells us in Genesis that the true Messiah would be "bruised."

The Prophecy

"He shall bruise your head, and you shall bruise His heel." Genesis 3:15, NKJV.

The Fulfillment of Prophecy

Jesus' "heel" was wounded at the cross—a wound type that is survivable. The devil will receive a "head wound." He will lose his life and be reduced to ashes, as revealed in Ezekiel 28:18, 19: "I reduced you to ashes on the ground . . . you . . . will be no more."

CLUE #2

The Messiah would come from the Jewish race.

The Prophecy

"In you [Abram] all the families of the earth shall be blessed." Genesis 12:3.

The Fulfillment of Prophecy

"A record of the genealogy of Jesus Christ, the son of David, the son of Abraham." Matthew 1:1.

CLUE #3

The Messiah was to restore communication between heaven and earth!

The Prophecy

Jacob "dreamed, and behold a ladder was set up on the earth, and its top reached to heaven; and there the angels of God were ascending and descending on it. . . . in your seed all the families of the earth shall be blessed." Genesis 28:12-14, NKJV.

Jesus claims to have fulfilled this prophecy. Read what Jesus said!

The Fulfillment of Prophecy

"Hereafter you shall see heaven open, and the angels of God ascending and descending upon the Son of Man." John 1:51, NKJV.

In claiming to fulfill this prophecy, was Jesus a liar, a lunatic, or was He, and is He, Lord of all creation?

CLUE #4

The Messiah would come to Planet Earth to give His life and shed His blood as a gift to each and every individual. Through accepting the Messiah as the Saviour from sin, man can find victory over death.

Every death of every lamb in the sacrificial service was to represent the future death of the Messiah, the Saviour of the world. Because the Messiah was sinless, He could pay the penalty for our sinful lives and give us the gift of eternal life. A plague of death would come to Egypt in Moses' day. The only safety was to kill the lamb representing the death of their future Messiah and paint the door frames of their houses with the blood. Those who did not do it had death in their family, and those who did had safety. This is a prophecy that the Messiah would shed His blood to save His people from death. Many have claimed to be the Messiah, but if they did not fulfill these pinpoint prophecies, they were not. Only one individual in history has made such a claim and has fulfilled these prophecies. That individual is Jesus Christ!

The Prophecy

"When He sees the blood the Lord will pass over the door and not allow the destroyer to come into your houses. At midnight the Lord struck all the firstborn in the land of Egypt." Exodus 12:23, 29, NKJV.

The Fulfillment of Prophecy

"For Christ, our Passover lamb, has been sacrificed." 1 Corinthians 5:7.

John the Baptist said "Look! The Lamb of God who takes away the sin of the world!" John 1:29.

CLUE #5

The Passover lamb, a symbol of the Messiah, was to have no broken bones in its death. In the same way, the Messiah was to have no broken bones in His death.

The Prophecy

"It must be eaten inside one house; take none of the meat outside the house. Do not break any of the bones." Exodus 12:46.

"Moses then took the blood, sprinkled it on the people and said, 'This is the blood of the covenant that the LORD has made with you in accordance with all these words.'" Exodus 24:8.

"The Lord's Passover. They shall eat it with unleavened bread and bitter herbs. They shall leave none of it until morning, nor break one of its bones." Numbers 9:10-12.

The Fulfillment of Prophecy

"The soldiers therefore came and broke the legs of the first man who had been crucified with Jesus, and then those of the other. But when they came to Jesus and found that he was already dead, they did not break his legs." John 19:32, 33.

CLUE #6

The Messiah would be mistreated and beaten and would submit to it.

The Prophecy

"Let him offer his cheek to the one who would strike him." Lamentations 3:30.

The Fulfillment of Prophecy

"'Look, now, you have heard the blasphemy! What do you think?' 'He is worthy of death,' they answered. Then they spit in his face and struck him with their fists. Others slapped him and said, 'Prophesy to us, Christ, Who hit you?'" Matthew 26:65-68.

CLUE #7

The word *Messiah* means "anointed one." The true Messiah would be baptized or "anointed" in the year A.D. 27 and be "cut off," or killed, in the year A.D. 31. This time prophecy of Daniel, written over 600 years before it happened, foretold the exact year of the coming Messiah's death.

The Prophecy

Read about this amazing, precisely accurate time prophecy in chapter 9 of *Prophecy Made Easy.*

CLUE #8

The Messiah would be born into the human race in Bethlehem.

The Prophecy

"But you, Bethlehem Ephrathah, though you are little among the thousands of Judah, yet out of you shall come forth to Me the One to be Ruler in Israel." Micah 5:2, NKJV.

The Fulfillment of Prophecy

"After Jesus was born in Bethlehem in Judea during the time of King Herod, Magi from the East came to Jerusalem." Matthew 2:1.

CLUE #9

The Messiah would enter Jerusalem riding on the back of a donkey.

The Prophecy

"Rejoice greatly, O Daughter of Zion! Shout, Daughter of Jerusalem! See, your king comes to you righteous and having salvation, gentle and riding on a donkey, on a colt, the foal of a donkey." Zechariah 9:9.

The Fulfillment of Prophecy

"As they approached Jerusalem and came to Bethphage on the Mount of Olives, Jesus sent two disciples, saying to them, 'Go to the village ahead of you, and at once you will find a donkey tied there, with her colt by her. Untie them and bring them to me. If anyone says anything to you, tell him that the Lord needs them, and he will send them right away.' This took place to fulfill what was spoken through the prophet: Say to the Daughter of Zion, 'See, your king comes to you, gentle and riding on a donkey, on a colt, the foal of a donkey.'

"The disciples went and did as Jesus had instructed them. They brought the donkey and the colt, placed their cloaks on them, and Jesus sat on them. A very large crowd spread their cloaks on the road, while others cut branches from the trees and spread them on the road. The crowds that went ahead of him and those that followed shouted, 'Hosanna to the Son of David!' 'Blessed is he who comes in the name of the Lord!' 'Hosanna in the highest!'" Matthew 21:1-10.

CLUE #10

The Messiah would be "pierced" by "the inhabitants of Jerusalem." Some of these "inhabitants of Jerusalem" would grieve over what had taken place.

The Prophecy

"And I will pour on the house of David and on the inhabitants of Jerusalem a Spirit of grace and supplication; They will look on me, the one they have pierced, and they will mourn for Him as one mourns for his only son, and grieve bitterly for Him as one grieves for a firstborn son." Zechariah 12:10.

The Fulfillment of Prophecy

"Instead one of the soldiers pierced Jesus' side with a spear, bringing a sudden flow of blood and water." John 19:34.

Peter said, "You with the help of wicked men, put him to death by nailing him to the cross. But God raised him from the dead. . . . When the people heard this, they were cut to the heart and said to Peter and the other apostles, 'Brothers, what shall we do?' Peter replied, 'Repent and be baptized every one of you in the name of Jesus Christ for the forgiveness of your sins. And you will receive the gift of the Holy Spirit.'" Acts 2:23, 24, 37, 38.

CLUE #11

Zechariah the prophet predicted that people would oppose the Messiah physically and wound Him. When that would happen, His followers would run away.

The Prophecy

"If someone asks him, 'What are these wounds on your body?' he will answer, 'The wounds I was given at the house of my friends.' 'Awake, O sword, against my shepherd, against the man who is close to me!' declares the LORD Almighty. 'Strike the shepherd, and the sheep will be scattered.'" Zechariah 13:6, 7.

The Fulfillment of Prophecy

"Then Jesus told them, 'This very night you will all fall away on account of me, for it is written: "I will strike the Shepherd, and the sheep of the flock will be scattered."'" Matthew 26:31.

"Then all the disciples deserted him and fled." Matthew 26:56.

CLUE #12

A powerful prophet like Elijah would prepare the way for the Messiah.

The Prophecy

"Behold, I send My messenger, and he will prepare the way before Me." Malachi 3:1.

"See, I will send you the prophet Elijah before that great and dreadful day of the LORD comes. He will turn the hearts of the fathers to their children, and the hearts of the children to their fathers; or else I will come and strike the land with a curse." Malach 4:5, 6.

The Fulfillment of Prophecy

"For this is the one about whom it is written: I will send my messenger ahead of you, who will prepare your way before You." Matthew 11:10.

"Jesus replied, 'I tell you, Elijah has already come, and they did not recognize him, but have done to him everything they wished. In the same way the Son of Man is going to suffer at their hands.' Then the disciples understood that he was talking to them about John the Baptist." Matthew 17:12, 13.

John the Baptist called the nation to repentance several months before Jesus Christ was baptized. Christ was baptized by John in the Jordan River, and the Spirit came down on Christ in the form of a dove.

Old Testament Bible prophets made the following predictions concerning the promised Messiah.

The Old Testament prophets predicted that the future Messiah would:

1. Be born a Jewish male child to a Jewish virgin in Bethlehem.

2. Be an unpretentious man who taught both Jewish and Gentile people in parables.

3. Live in Galilee and often teach in Galilee.

4. Restore eyesight to the blind, hearing to the deaf, and make the lame to walk.

5. Have the gentle spirit of a servant.

6. Be introduced to others by a great wilderness prophet.

7. Be baptized in A.D. 27.

8. Enter Jerusalem riding on the back of a donkey while people shouted "Blessed is he who comes in the name of the Lord."

9. Be betrayed by a friend.

10. Be rejected and judged unfairly by earthly rulers.

11. Be silent in His own defense.

12. Be beaten with a whip.

13. Allow people to spit in His face.

14. Be nailed to a cross in the year A.D. 31.

15. Be stripped naked, nailed to the cross, and watched as others divided up part of His clothing and gambled for the other part.

16. Be laughed at by people coming up and shaking their heads and saying, "He trusted in the Lord; let Him rescue Him; let Him deliver Him."

17. Carry the weight of the sins of the world until they crushed out His life.

18. Cry out on that cross: "My God, My God, why have you forsaken Me?"

19. Cry out: "Into Your hands I commit my spirit."

20. Be beaten and die without any broken bones.

21. Be raised from the dead before His body had begun to decay.

22. Take many back to heaven with Him who were specially resurrected from the dead.

Jesus Christ Is the Only Individual in All of History Who Fulfills All of These Prophecies!

BIRTH

Between 2,500 and 6,000 years ago, the ancient prophets, including Moses, Isaiah, David, Daniel, Micah, Solomon, Zechariah, Malachi, and others predicted that a Messiah, a Saviour, a King, would come. The prophets predicted that He would be born a male Jewish descendant of King David to a virgin in the little town of Bethlehem.

LIFE

They predicted that He would live in Galilee and that the Messiah would be introduced to the world by a great wilderness prophet. They said that the Messiah would be baptized in the year A.D. 27 and would restore eyesight to the blind, hearing to the deaf, and make the lame walk. He would be a gentle, Spirit-filled servant and be rejected by the majority.

TEACHINGS

These prophets also predicted that the Messiah would be an unpretentious man. He would teach both Jewish and Gentile people in parables and warn the religious people to avoid the religious hypocrisy of saying one thing and doing another. He would teach people to take care of the hungry and those in need. He would preach to the poor and would do a work of healing to comfort those in sorrow and bring discomfort to the careless.

LAST WEEK

The ancient prophets further predicted He would announce Himself a king by entering Jerusalem riding on the back of a donkey while people shouted "Blessed is he who comes in the name of the Lord." And they predicted that He would be betrayed by a trusted friend for thirty pieces of silver, after they ate together

LAST DAY

These ancient prophets predicted that the Messiah would go through suffering that would change His appearance. They predicted that He would be taken a prisoner and unjustly judged by earthly rulers as guilty of death, that He would say nothing in His own defense, and that He would allow others to whip His back and spit in His face.

DEATH

They predicted the exact year in which He would be crucified. They accurately predicted that to be the year A.D. 31. He would be stripped naked and nailed to a cross while others stared at Him. They predicted what would happen to the very clothes worn by the Messiah on that day. They predicted that some of His clothing would be divided up between those who were there, and another part of His clothing would be gambled for.

They said He would be offered a drink containing gall. They predicted that people would pass by, shaking their heads and saying, "He trusted in the Lord; let Him rescue Him; let Him deliver Him." Not only were the words of the people foretold, but the actual dying words of the Messiah were also foretold. They predicted that the Messiah would cry out on that cross, "My God, My God, why have you forsaken Me?"—and also the words "Into Your hands I commit my spirit." They predicted that He would die without any broken bones.

His death, they predicted, would not be from the mistreatment of the people, but rather from the weight of the sins of the entire world crushing out His life. The Messiah would be "crushed" to death by the weight of your sins and mine—the sins of the world. He would die with criminals, and He would have a burial site provided for by a rich person.

RESURRECTION

The ancient prophets predicted that He would be raised from the dead before His body started to decay and would bring others to life and take them home with Him after being resurrected.

Were these prophecies fulfilled in Jesus Christ? Did everything the prophets predicted would happen, happen? Absolutely! Everything they said would happen to the Messiah happened to Jesus Christ. Read the first four books of the New Testament and see the fulfillment of all the Messianic prophecies of Jesus Christ. These are just some of the Messianic prophecies that convince me that Jesus Christ is the true Messiah. Do you know of another Jewish person, in all of history, who was baptized in A.D. 27 and crucified in A.D. 31 and was born of a virgin in Bethlehem?

There are many Messianic prophecies in the Holy Bible, but there is no other person in history who fulfills even these five Messianic prophecies. No one else fulfills all the many prophecies mentioned in this book—*Prophecy Made Easy*—or even just the five mentioned in the previous paragraph. Jesus Christ is the only one who meets every one of these pinpoint prophecies exactly. He came to live a sinless life and to love and teach and reestablish His church on correct principles. But most of all, He came to carry your sins and mine and to pay the penalty for our sins. Sin separated everyone from eternal life. The Messiah, Jesus Christ, came to bridge the gulf that sin makes with His own broken, bleeding body.

God loves you and me. He wants us to have evidence for our faith in Him. The evidence for God's existence and His love is GIGANTIC. The Messianic prophecies and their fulfillments are irrefutable evidence! They constitute evidence that cannot be overthrown by reason! Only our sinful desires can overcome this evidence. Reason alone would have to be on the side of the overwhelming evidence that Jesus Christ is the promised Messiah.

Those who are out of harmony with God can choose not to believe this evidence by ignoring it, neglecting it, or by choosing to close their eyes for fear of the cost of following Jesus Christ. This choice is a foolish choice, however, because the Messiah will return the second time. He will then invite us to sit with Him upon His throne. We will explore the universe with greater powers than Superman ever dreamed of—powers similar to that of the angels of God. We will build houses that will last forever—and we will plant and eat and travel. We will never know pain or suffering or loneliness ever again. What will you do with this evidence? The choice is yours. You can accept Jesus Christ as your Messiah, your Saviour from sin, and live forever—or you can choose not to believe. You can choose death. See Revelation 3:21.

What stronger evidence could you have for God's existence and His love but these great Messianic prophecies? God gave pinpoint-accurate prophecies of how the promised Messiah would be born—how He would live and teach and heal and serve and suffer and die and be resurrected. Prophecy predicted when it would happen, where it would happen, where He would be born, where He would live, what He would teach, what year He would be baptized, what year He would be crucified, how people would treat Him, and how a friend would betray Him. Also how much money the friend would get for betraying Him, what the people around him would do and say, and what the Messiah Himself would say. Prophecy predicted how His burial costs would be taken care of, when He would be resurrected, and what would happen after that. What more could God do to prove His existence and His love?

Every one of these Messianic prophecies was fulfilled in Jesus Christ. This chapter has limited itself to just some of the Messianic prophecies. There are others. They all point to Jesus Christ as the Messiah of Bible prophecy as well.

All of this information is given by the prophets, predicting the coming Messiah over 600 years in advance. These are all Old Testament prophecies. Not one of these identifying pieces of prophetic information came from the New Testament. We include the New Testament only to show how each prophecy was fulfilled in Jesus Christ.

The blindness of the people who lived during Christ's appearance on earth as the Messiah should not surprise us. It is not a question of race—it is a question of human nature. God says that modern man is no less blind to spiritual truth than the people who lived at that time. God says to modern man, "You say, I am rich; I have acquired wealth and do not need a thing. But you do not realize that you are wretched, pitiful, poor, blind and naked. I counsel you to buy from me gold refined in the fire, so you can become rich; and white clothes to wear so you can cover your shameful nakedness; and salve to put on your eyes, so you can see." Revelation 3:17, 18.

The prophets Moses, Isaiah, David, Daniel, Micah, Zechariah, and Malachi are a few of the prophets God used to pass on clues as to the true identity of the Messiah. God expects us to gather these clues like a detective. When we do, the overwhelming evidence points with absolute accuracy to Jesus Christ as this world's Messiah.

In his book *Science Speaks*, Professor Peter W. Stoner says that by using the modern science of probability in reference to just eight of the scores of Messianic prophecies, "We find that the chance that any man might have lived down to the present time and fulfilled all eight prophecies is 1 in 10^{17}." That would be 1 in 100,000,000,000,000,000. In order to help us understand these amazing odds, Stoner explains it by imagining that "we take 10^{17} silver dollars and lay them on the face of Texas. They will cover all of the state two feet deep. Now mark one of these silver dollars and stir the whole mass thoroughly, all over the state. Blindfold a man and tell him that he can travel as far as he wishes, but he must pick up one silver dollar and say that this is the right one. What chance would he have of getting the right one? Just the same chance that the prophets would have had of writing these eight prophecies and having them all come true in any one man, from their day to the present time, providing they wrote them in their own wisdom." And remember, that is using just eight of the scores of Messianic prophecies that are found in the Old Testament part of the Bible!

The overwhelming weight of fulfilled prophetic evidence leads to no other option. Prophecy speaks and says that Jesus Christ is the true Messiah. He loves you. Won't you choose to let Him be your Messiah, your Lord, and your Master today? Read about the way to accept Him as your Messiah, your Lord, and your Master in the Introduction to *Prophecy Made Easy.*

Why did our world need a Messiah? Why do we need a Messiah? *Star Wars*—the next chapter—will provide the answer to that question. The reconstructed conversations found in the *Star Wars* chapter are based on the biblical evidence documented in this book, *Prophecy Made Easy.*

2

Star Wars!

In imagination, let's travel back in time to the beginning of creation. God the Father, God the Son, and God the Holy Spirit were then—and still are—equal. One was not inferior. God wanted to have many children upon whom to shower their infinite love and gifts, so they began an enormous experiment—to create intelligent beings.

A major challenge they faced was to decide what these beings would be like. Shall we create them to be like robots who have no choice but to obey us, they considered, or shall we give them free will? The idea of free will carried an enormous risk. What if any of those beings, they pondered—on one of those planets where they will live—turn against us and choose to disobey us? What if they try to set up their own government, bringing certain chaos to the universe? What would we do? Would we just wipe them off the map the moment even one thought of rebellion enters their minds?

In the heart of God, the plan of salvation was born. God knew a crisis would come. Yet the Father, Son, and Holy Spirit decided that the coming crisis would give them the only real opportunity to prove their love for those they had created. Words were not enough. It was not enough to say to created beings, "I love you, I love you—just believe me that I love you!"

No, that was not enough. They knew that a crisis would come. They knew that the crisis would even lead to violence. Yet they knew too that they would prove that they loved their created beings more than their own lives.

The first person of the Godhead turned to the second person of the Godhead, whom we call Jesus Christ.

"If such a revolution should happen on any of the planets we are going to create," He asked, "are You willing to carry out this tremendous experiment fully by going there to save them? Are You willing to become one of them, giving up the form You have now? Are You willing to become weak, laying all Your power at my feet, and live there only by the power I will give You through the Holy Spirit?

"You will accomplish nothing by Your own strength for yourself. You will become obedient to me in everything, proving that the laws we have created are only for the good of the universe. Our law is not for evil—not to set up a tyranny, not to make a slave camp—but is for everyone's good.

"And are You willing to go even farther? Are You willing that I shall put the sin, the rebellion of that planet, upon You, to punish You instead of them and give them a second chance?"

"Yes, Father, I am willing to carry out this beautiful plan," Jesus replied. "Then if You are willing to become my Son and humble Yourself to that degree," the Father continued, "then You will be the only spokesperson between the whole universe and me. They will only see You.

"You are the one that should create, not I. I will go into the background, You will go into the foreground. You deal with every intelligent being that we create."

This is why, after Jesus came to earth, He said, "The Father loves me because I lay down my life."

Jesus Christ, the Creator of "All Things"!

John put it this way: "He was in the world, and the world was made through Him and the world did not know Him. He came to His own, and His own did not receive Him. But as many as received Him, to them He gave the right to become children of God, to those who believe in His name." John 1:10-12, NKJV.

"He was in the world, and the world was made by Him, and the world knew him not." John 1:10, KJV.

Paul says of Jesus: "He is the image of the invisible God. For by Him all things were created: things in heaven and on earth, visible and invisible, whether thrones or powers or rulers or authorities; all things were created by Him and for Him. He is before all things and in Him all things hold together." Colossians 1:15-17.

God the Son created world after world. He populated those worlds with intelligent beings such as you and me. There is one big difference between us and all other created beings, however. We are sinners, and they are not. They never age, never get sick, and never die. They have never experienced pain, sickness, or death.

The Son of God referred to these sinless worlds and to Planet Earth in the story He told of the man who owned a hundred sheep, one of which got lost. "Does he not leave the ninety-nine in the open country and go after the lost sheep until he finds it? And when he finds it, he joyfully puts it on his shoulders and goes home. Then he calls his friends and neighbors together and says, Rejoice with me; I have found my lost sheep." Luke 15:3-7.

Jesus was here referring, primarily, to one lost person, but secondarily to Earth—the one lost planet. Planet Earth is the only world—of the vast number God has created—that has a sin problem, an aging problem, or a death problem. This is the planet where the Son of God, the Shepherd, came.

God paid an enormous price. He spent the resources of the universe to remove the curse of sin, aging, and death from Earth. And He will be successful: "Rejoice with me; I have found my lost sheep." One day, Planet Earth will be free of sin, pain, aging, and death—and you and I can be part of that exciting life.

God is a God of order. He established first a government with beings of supreme intelligence, beauty, and power. They became the seat of the government, to rule over the whole universe. The leader? A supreme being. The most wonderful creature God ever made. His name was Lucifer, "Son of the morning." Lucifer had the seal of God, which meant that all that God did passed through his hands. Yet Lucifer is the same one whose name was later changed to Satan, or the Devil. In the book of Revelation he is even called the Dragon.

What Does the Devil Look Like?

Lucifer is a real being. He wears no red pajamas and carries no pitchfork. He was created a beautiful, wise, powerful, and perfect angel. He retains much of his former beauty, intelligence, and power, but none of his original perfection. God loved Lucifer. Lucifer and Christ, Lucifer and the Father, Lucifer and the Holy Spirit were intimate friends.

We do not know how long they were such friends. Lucifer stood on the left side of the throne of God and Christ on the right. Nevertheless, as Lucifer watched the Father, Son, and Holy Spirit meet occasionally in secret council, he began to wonder. "Why can't I be part of that inner circle? Am I not as powerful as they are?"

He began to eye the Son of God with jealousy. "Couldn't I uphold the universe with my own strength?" he asked himself.

The Lord God said of Lucifer, "You were the seal of perfection, full of wisdom, and perfect in beauty. You were in Eden the garden of God; every precious stone was your covering. You were the anointed" covering angel. "You were on the holy mountain of God. You walked back and forth in the midst of fiery stones. You were perfect in your ways from the day that you were created, until" you chose sin. Ezekiel 28:12-15, NKJV.

The Devil Has "I" Problems

"Your heart became proud on account of your beauty, and you corrupted your wisdom because of your splendor."

"How you are fallen from heaven O Lucifer, son of the morning!" "You said in your heart, I will ascend to heaven; I will raise my throne above the stars of God; I will sit enthroned on the mount of assembly, on the utmost heights of the sacred mountain. I will ascend above the tops of the clouds; I will make myself like the Most High." Ezekiel 28:17, 6; Isaiah 14:12, NKJV; 14:13, 14.

Jesus often approached Lucifer. "Son," He would say, "I made you. I love you. I put great wisdom and ability into you. No one is like you anywhere. You have the highest privileges. So son, please do not be jealous of me. You are a created being. We, on the other hand, have existed from eternity—with no beginning. There is a difference. Please be satisfied with the power and authority I have given you. Do not be jealous. Do not think rebellious thoughts."

But Lucifer was headstrong. He approached the other created beings stationed at the seat of God's government, pretending to want to honor God.

"I only have the best interest for God," he told them. "I want to honor Him, I want to improve His government and His laws, but to do so, I have to be part of that secret council."

Because he was so intelligent, loved, and respected, many sided with him, and that gave him a feeling of power.

Jesus came to him repeatedly. "Lucifer, I know what you're doing. I told you that I love you, I forgive everything you've said against us. I know what your plans are. Please stop—you are destroying yourself."

"Oh, no, I will not," Lucifer protested. "I want to be a part of that secret council. I want to be God, like You!"

Lucifer became bolder and bolder, because he found sympathetic hearers. "God's law is too rigid," he would say to the angels. "It is developing into tyranny. God is a stern Judge over His whole creation. He is merciless. God immediately destroys anyone who disagrees with His ideas. He is not willing to serve—He only commands. He demands that everyone serve Him like a slave."

"He also does not know anything about humility. He has the gall to say that we have free will, but He does not allow us to do what we want."

Lucifer put God on trial before the whole universe. Imagine—God on trial before the whole universe! God could have destroyed Lucifer instantly. Lucifer was a created being. So God could have withdrawn life immediately, in a split second, but what would have been the result? The whole universe would have said, "Oh, look—you say something against God, and He wipes you out! Maybe Lucifer was right after all."

Lucifer plunged the whole universe into a crisis. An atmosphere of fear would have filled the whole universe if God had then destroyed Lucifer. But God did not want to have a universe that would obey Him out of fear. He wants to be loved wholeheartedly.

Lucifer chose to rebel against the government of God. He convinced one third of the angels of heaven to join his rebellion against God, God's law, and His government. Lucifer thought he had it made. I do not know what weapons he had available. We know just a little now—having discovered hydrogen bombs and lasers—about what he could have used. However, he attacked God at headquarters with all the power that he had available. One third of God's government was with him.

Star Wars

The first revolution happened right where God is—at His headquarters. It was a foolish experiment. Of course, Lucifer lost. Here again, after Lucifer lost the battle, Christ could have destroyed him as a punishment. But no. That would be all wrong. All the rest of the universe would have been in fear. Was Lucifer right? Throughout eternity, they would have doubted and wondered, "Maybe Lucifer had a point." No, God would remove Lucifer's disguise. He would permit the whole universe to see Lucifer's real intent, his true nature, over a long period of time.

"And there was war in heaven. Michael and his angels fought against the dragon, and the dragon and his angels fought back. But he was not strong enough, and they lost their place in heaven. The great dragon was hurled down—that ancient serpent called the devil, or Satan, who leads the whole world astray. He was hurled to the earth, and his angels with him." Revelation 12:7-9.

"God said, 'Let us make man in our image, in our likeness." Genesis 1:26. Today, Lucifer is seeking to convince all of the human race to follow his rebellion. The book of Genesis tells us about his attempt to convince our first parents, Adam and Eve, to join his rebellion. The Son of God had warned Adam and Eve of Lucifer. They knew about his rebellion.

Jesus also told them of two special trees in the garden. One was the Tree of Life and the other was the Tree of the Knowledge of Good and Evil. God wanted Earth's first couple to be happy. Eating from the Tree of Life would bring them a happy, satisfying, everlasting life. But eating of the Tree of the Knowledge of Good and Evil would unite them in rebellion with Lucifer and result in death.

God asked them to avoid even getting near that tree. Jesus told them that only there would He permit Lucifer to tempt them into joining his rebellion. If they avoided that tree and stayed together, they would continue to enjoy everlasting life and happiness.

Lucifer knew that to get Adam and Eve to join his rebellion, he would have to use deception. He could not succeed in talking with them directly. Had he done so, they would have called for help from God, and Lucifer was no match for God.

Lucifer chose to disguise himself to Adam and Eve and used a snake as a puppet. He made it appear as if the snake could talk. Eve wandered away from Adam one day and found herself looking at the fruit tree from which Christ had warned her to stay away. She saw a snake in the tree eating the very fruit the Son of God had told her would bring death. Yet not only was the snake eating the fruit—he also spoke her name. This was truly amazing! She had never seen anything like this before. If Lucifer had spoken to her directly, she would have run away. This tree was the test of loyalty for the human race.

She Talked to the Devil

Adam and Eve would have run had they seen an angel talking to them at this tree, but this was no angel. This was something new and amazing! Eve spoke with the snake, who told her that she could have greater happiness!

"Look at what I, a snake, can do. I can talk with you. When have you ever seen a snake talk to either you or Adam? God has told you not to eat of this fruit, but look at me. I ate it, and I can talk. You eat it, and you will enter a world of endless opportunities. You will know as much as God knows." Today Lucifer is still making promises. He hides behind glamorous advertising, promising us happiness, social acceptance, and "coolness" if we will only drink this or smoke that. After losing our health to emphysema, cancer, cirrhosis of the liver, or any number of other diseases, we sometimes finally realize that all of Lucifer's promises are just an illusion.

We know the rest of the story. Eve joined Lucifer's rebellion and convinced Adam to join also. The result is that they died and brought death to the whole human race.

Christ Reveals the Plan of Salvation

Christ spoke to Satan and said, "I will put enmity [dislike] between you and the woman. And between your offspring and hers; he will crush your head, and you will strike his heel." Genesis 3:15.

This is the first Bible reference to the plan of salvation. This was the promise that Christ Himself would come, being born of one of Eve's descendents. He would wage war with Satan. In that war, Satan would "strike Christ's heel" (cause Him suffering) but Christ would "crush Satan's head" (eventually destroy Satan).

Perhaps what Christ said to Adam and Eve went something like this: "I love you—we love you—and though Lucifer has deceived you into choosing death, there is still hope."

He told them of the plan of salvation. They saw death for the first time when the Lord killed an animal and made clothes for them.

"Adam and Eve," Christ might have said, "just as you saw the animal die, I will come one day to suffer and die the death your sin deserves. In that way, you can have the life I deserve. You will have children. One day I will be born from one of those who will descend from them. I will become a helpless human baby. I will continue to grow until I become a little boy and then a man. I will live the life of obedience that you should have lived. I will prove to the universe that my law is just and fair and can be obeyed. I will live a sinless life, and I will die a terrible death to save you. I will pay the just claims of my law.

"By faith, you can have my sinless life credited to your account. After my death, I will return to heaven to prepare a home for you and your children who accept my substitute death, my forgiveness, and my love in their lives.

"But you must leave this Eden home now. You will see it again if you accept the forgiveness and changing power of my love. I can only offer this to you if you will have faith in my future sinless life, suffering, and death as a human.

"You can show your faith by confessing your sins over the head of an innocent lamb. 'The wages of sin is death.' You will then kill the innocent lamb. He will die in your place. In the death of each innocent lamb, you will see an example of my future suffering and death for you."

Adam and Eve were stunned! They now saw the immensity of their sin, and their love for God was great as they saw that God would suffer for them to save them.

Lucifer had won a major battle in his warfare against God. He had brought pain, suffering, and death into a pain-free, death-free, contented universe of worlds. Now Planet Earth had become the theater of the universe. God kept sin confined to Earth, and the Son of God was coming to win the battle. He was not coming to win it with force but with love. He was coming to unmask Lucifer and reveal to the universe what God is really like.

3

Angels

D o you need to see something in order to believe it? Do you believe in the power of electricity? I imagine that you do! I suspect you use the power of electricity to do numerous things to make your life more enjoyable. Do you believe in the power of the wind? Have you actually seen either electricity or the wind? No—because they are invisible. You see the effects of the wind, but not the wind itself. You see the effects of electricity, but not the electricity itself. Both wind and electricity are invisible but very powerful and sometimes deadly. What about angels? Angels also have a power we do not understand—the power to be either visible or invisible. The Bible says they are very real and are as much individual beings as you and I are.

After the fall of man, God sent angels to guard the tree of life before anyone had died. If angels are dead people, where did those angels come from? God created man "a little lower than the angels." Psalm 8:5; Hebrews 2:7. So angels are a higher life form than people. Not only a higher life form but a different life form. Angels are not dead people.

How Many Are There?

Daniel saw more than 100 million angels near God's throne. Daniel 7:10. "Thousands upon thousands of angels," says Hebrews 12:22.

59

How Strong Are They?

"Angels that excel in strength," "ministers of His, that do His pleasure." Psalm 103:19-21, KJV.

They have super strength! One angel killed 185,000 armed soldiers in one night. One angel is stronger than a whole army!

"That night the angel of the Lord went out and put to death a hundred and eighty-five thousand men in the Assyrian camp."2 Kings 19:35.

"And the Lord sent an angel, who annihilated all the fighting men and the leaders and officers in the camp of the Assyrian king. So he withdrew to his own land in disgrace." 2 Chronicles 32:21.

What Do Angels Look Like?

Angels can have the appearance of lightning. Their faces often look as bright as lightning.

Angels have "the appearance of a flash of lightning." They are overwhelmingly, blindingly bright and can travel faster then anything we can imagine. Ezekiel 1:14, KJV.

As for the angel that appeared at the Saviour's tomb, his face appeared "like lightning, and his" clothing "white as snow." The appearance of this angel so petrified the mighty Roman soldiers with fear that they fell down and "became as dead men." Matthew 28:3, 4.

Will They Protect Me?

God appoints a guardian angel to every follower of Christ. Does Job fear God for no reason? Satan asked. "Have You not put a hedge around him and his household and everything he has? You have blessed the work of his hands, so that his flocks and herds are spread throughout the land." Job 1:9, 10.

"The angel of the Lord encamps around those who fear Him, and he delivers them." Psalm 34:7.

"See that you do not look down on one of these little ones. For I tell you that their angels in heaven always see the face of my Father in heaven." Matthew 18:10.

Are There "Evil Angels"?

Lucifer and his angels are called demons or evil spirits. The New Testament clearly states the fact that men have been possessed by demons—evil angels.

"A woman whose little daughter was possessed by an evil spirit came and fell at His feet. The woman was a Greek, born in Syrian Phoenicia. She begged Jesus to drive the demon out of her daughter . . . Then He told her, . . . the demon has left your daughter. She went home and found her child lying on the bed, and the demon gone." Mark 7:25-30.

"Then they brought Him a demon-possessed man who was blind and mute [speechless], and Jesus healed him, so that he could both talk and see." Matthew 12:22.

"My name is Legion: for we are many." Mark 5:9.

"My son . . . is possessed by a spirit that has robbed him of speech. Whenever it seizes him, it throws him to the ground. He foams at the mouth, gnashes his teeth and becomes rigid. . . . When the spirit saw Jesus, it immediately threw the boy into a convulsion. He fell to the ground and rolled around, foaming at the mouth. . . . He rebuked the evil spirit. 'You deaf and mute spirit,' He said, 'I command you, come out of him and never enter him again.' The spirit shrieked, convulsed him violently and came out." Mark 9:17-26.

Who Is Stronger—Christ, or the Devil?

Somebody might ask, "Is the devil a real being, or is he make-believe?" If you are a Christian, you believe in Christ. If you believe in Christ, then you should believe in a very real being called the devil, because Christ not only believed he was real, but He actually spoke with the devil.

A man in church had "a spirit of an unclean devil." Luke 4:33-36. Christ spoke to the demon as an intelligent individual, commanding him to come out of his victim. "'Be quiet,' Jesus said sternly. 'Come out of him.' Then the demon came out without injuring the man. All the people were amazed and said to each other, 'What is this teaching? With authority and power he gives orders to evil spirits and they come out!'" Luke 4:36.

Those who possessed the spirit of witchcraft—such as Simon Magus, Elymus the sorcerer, and the woman who followed Paul and Silas at Philippi— welcomed satanic influence.

No one is in greater danger from the influence of evil spirits than those who deny the reality of the devil and his angels. Satan spreads everywhere the belief that he does not exist.

Satan can most readily control the minds of those who are unconscious of his power. Terrible is the condition of those who refuse to obey God and yield to Satan's temptations, until God gives them up to the control of evil spirits.

Those who follow Christ are always safe under His watchcare. Christ sends angels that excel in strength from heaven to protect them. Satan and his evil angels cannot break through the guard that God has put around His people.

4

Rebellion

S atan was the first to seek to do away with God's law. He promised those who followed him in rebellion a new freedom, a better life. He now seeks to convince man to join in the same rebellion, promising liberty through disobedience to God and His law.

Satan wants people to think of God as demanding and cruel. But the Lord says: "And he passed in front of Moses, proclaiming, 'the LORD, the LORD, the compassionate and gracious God, slow to anger, abounding in love and faithfulness, maintaining love to thousands, and forgiving wickedness, rebellion and sin. Yet he does not leave the guilty unpunished.'" Exodus 34:6, 7.

In the war between Christ and Satan during the Savior's earthly life, Lucifer's mask came off. He revealed his true feelings of hatred as he constantly tried to make Christ's life unhappy and kill Him. Satan used men as his agents to fill the Saviour's life with pain and sadness. The hatred and cruelty Lucifer put in the minds of his followers all sprang from deep-seated revenge.

Now Satan revealed his true character as a liar and a murderer. He had claimed that disobeying God's law would bring liberty and exaltation. However, disobedience instead resulted in pain, grief, and sorrow.

Satan had told the angels that while the Creator required sacrifice from all others, He Himself made no sacrifice. Now the loyal angels understood. For the salvation of a fallen and sinful people, the Ruler of the universe had made the greatest sacrifice that love could make. "God was in Christ, reconciling the world to Himself." 2 Corinthians 5:19, NKJV.

Christ came not only to save people from sin but also to prove to all the worlds of the universe that God's law is unchangeable. Could God have changed it; then the Son of God would not have had to suffer and die to pay the penalty for its violation, which is death. He chose to take the terrible risk, to suffer and die that we might have an opportunity to live again.

God Will Turn Lucifer Into Ashes!

Lucifer, Also Known as the Devil or Satan, Will Be Burned to Ashes

Lucifer had said, "I will exalt my throne above the stars of God: . . . I will be like the Most High." However, God looks into the future and says, "I made a fire come out from you, and it consumed you, and I reduced you to ashes on the ground in the sight of all who were watching. All the nations who knew you are appalled at you; you have come to a horrible end and will be no more." Isaiah 14:13, 14; Ezekiel 28:18, 19.

"'The day is coming; it will burn like a furnace. All the arrogant and every evildoer will be stubble, and that day that is coming will set them on fire,' says the Lord Almighty. 'Not a root or a branch will be left to them. Then you will trample down the wicked; they will be ashes under the soles of your feet on the day when I do these things,' says the Lord Almighty." "It will leave them neither root nor branch." Malachi 4:1-3.

Not a root or a branch will be left. Lucifer is the root and his followers are the branches. The fire that will one day burn up the earth will destroy both root and branches of Lucifer's rebellion. Rebellion will never arise again. Lucifer, Satan, and the Devil are three names for one individual. He will not be in charge of any superstitious "hell fire."

God will turn him into ashes in hell fire. This fire from God will destroy this evil angel and all his followers, and the results will be eternal. No eternal devil with red pajamas and a pitchfork will crank up the fires of hell. Just as God cleansed the earth with water in the days of Noah, He will again cleanse the earth. This time He will do it with fire. When the fire has gone out, sin and sinners will be no more.

The Devil, Lucifer, Satan, Evil Angel or Demon will not romp and play eternally in the fires of hell. No! The Devil, Lucifer, Satan, will not have eternal life! God will help him lose weight. He will reduce him to ashes! He will be blotted out of existence. He will be no more! He will never have an opportunity to tempt or trick another individual! No, not ever! "Affliction will not rise up a second time." "Trouble will not come a second time." Nahum 1:9, NKJV; Nahum 1:9, NIV.

True Christians realize that there are two principles demonstrated in the Bible. Christ teaches us that the cross must come before the crown. We learn, on the other hand, that self-exaltation comes before destruction. Self-exaltation comes before being turned into ashes. If you are planning to live with Christ forever and wear the crown He will give you as a king or queen, you must choose the life of self-denial as a soldier of Christ. He that is ashamed of inconvenience and the criticism that goes with being a Christian will not be recognized by Christ unless he repents and willingly follows his Master, accepting the life of the cross. Choosing self-exaltation is choosing death.

In Genesis 3:15, God spoke to Lucifer and told him that he would not have complete control of the human race. This is the first promise of salvation for the human race. It was the promise of a Messiah who would suffer. Symbolically, it says that Lucifer would "strike" the Messiah's "heel," but the Messiah would "crush" Lucifer's head—destroy Lucifer. "I will put enmity [dislike] between you and the woman, and between your seed and her seed; it will bruise your head, and you will bruise his heel."Genesis 3:15, NKJV.

"I will put enmity" (a dislike) between you, Lucifer and the human race. There exists naturally no enmity (dislike) between sinful man and the originator of sin. Satan heard God say that a dislike would exist between himself and the woman. He knew that by some means God would give man the power to resist his own satanic power. When people hate sin instead of loving it, when they resist sin and conquer their cravings, we can be sure that the power comes directly from above.

Christ revealed a life of sacrifice and sinless loyalty to God and to helping people. This felt uncomfortable, like a constant attack, to a proud sensual people. This discomfort encouraged hatred against the Son of God.

"In fact, everyone who wants to live a godly life in Christ Jesus will be persecuted." 2 Timothy 3:12.

All who do not choose to serve and follow Christ are servants of Satan. Temptations often come when we choose ungodly and unbelieving companions. The closer we are to sin, the more sin we see and hear, the less distasteful it will appear. If we place ourselves close to temptation, we will fall eventually.

Many individuals who have morals, culture, intelligence, and pleasant manners are but polished tools in the hands of Satan. "For our struggle is not against flesh and blood, but against the rulers, against the authorities, against the powers of this dark world and against the spiritual forces of evil in the heavenly realms." Ephesians 6:12.

"Be self-controlled and alert. Your enemy the devil prowls around like a roaring lion looking for someone to devour."
1 Peter 5:8.

"Put on the full armor of God, so that you can take your stand against the devil's schemes." Ephesians 6:11.

5

Traps

The Ten Commandments According to Satan

Satan's plan is to hold the people in darkness and disobedience until
Christ finishes His work as mediator and there is no longer a
sacrifice for sin.

SATAN'S TEN COMMANDMENTS

Satan hates Jesus, the Heavenly Father, the Holy Spirit, and every person that has ever been born. Satan is like a hunter stalking his prey. You are that prey, and he knows that the only way to get to you is to get you to turn your back on God and His protective care.

Many different traps are used to capture animals such as beaver and mink. Each trap is built especially for the type of animal being trapped. Satan has designed his trap to get us away from God and God's angels. He knows that he is no match for God and His angels

Since Satan hates God's Ten Commandments, let's call these ten traps the Ten Commandments According to Satan. The Bible clearly teaches that these are His principles and desires for you and me. His ultimate objective is to bring us as much pain, sorrow, and death as possible. These commandments, Satan's traps, when carried out in our lives, leave us entirely defenseless against his attacks and expose us to the ultimate in pain, sorrow, and death. If you avoid these ten traps, you will find security, peace, and ultimate happiness.

I. SATAN SAYS:

"You can be a Christian. Just don't invest any time
building a relationship with Christ."

Satan is afraid of a person who loves Jesus Christ. He knows we can easily defeat him if we place our confidence in Jesus. He tries to discourage us into not searching God's Word and into neglecting prayer. Satan knows that our connection to God is through these two avenues. He wants us to find anything else to do—anything else! "Wouldn't you rather watch a movie, rather than pray or study God's Word?" Satan whispers in our ear. He knows he is no match for a person who seeks to know God on a daily, hourly basis through prayer and Bible study and sharing these great truths with others. God's plan is to grant us, in answer to the prayer of faith, that which He would not give us if we didn't ask. No one is safe for a day or an hour without prayer. We should especially ask the Lord for wisdom to understand His Word. Praying regularly throughout the day is vitally important. During the day when others are around and you can't pray out loud, speak the words silently. Jesus will hear and send angels in answer to your prayer.

2. SATAN SAYS:

"Don't bother to search the Bible. It doesn't apply today."

But God's promise is, "Blessed is he that reads and they that hear the words of this prophecy, and keep those things which are written in it." Revelation 1:1-3, NKJV. Notice that this promise applies especially to the book of Revelation. *Prophecy Made Easy* will open up the book of Revelation for your understanding and enjoyment. You will receive the blessing that comes to those who "read and hear and do" the things written in the book of Revelation.

Satan knows very well that anyone whom he can lead to neglect prayer and the study of the Bible will fail and ultimately die without receiving eternal life. The Bible feeds your spiritual life just as food feeds your physical life. See how strong you are physically after you go several days without eating food. The same thing happens when we neglect to read or hear the Word of God. The greatest danger a Christian faces is not Satan, alias the devil. Our greatest danger is not communism! Our greatest danger is not atheism! Our greatest danger is *neglect.* The greatest danger we face is just ignoring God. "How shall we escape, if we ignore such a great salvation?" "How shall we escape if we neglect so great salvation?" Hebrews 2:3; NIV; Hebrews 2:3, KJV. More people will be eternally lost from neglecting God, from ignoring God, than from all other reasons combined! Your greatest danger will be that of neglecting to read God's Word with a spiritual hunger every day. Your greatest danger will be in neglecting to pray constantly throughout each day.

I challenge you to become a spiritual giant using these two avenues of strength. To avoid becoming spiritually fat and lazy, there is a third part to spiritual health. Reading God's Word compares to eating food. You eat two or three times a day. A good program is to read God's Word as often as you eat food. Prayer is compared to breathing fresh air. Talk with God in your thoughts all through the day, just like breathing. Exercise is also important to good physical health, and it is important to spiritual health as well. This is the third part of the "good spiritual health" triangle. Tell others about the great things you are learning. Help them find good spiritual health too. Sharing these things with others is "exercising your faith," and just as physical exercise helps make you strong, sharing the Word of God will help make you spiritually strong. Those who are ultimately lost will be lost from neglecting these three sources of power. May God guide you to strong spiritual health.

3. SATAN SAYS:

"What you believe is unimportant."

But Jesus Christ says, "For God so loved the world that He gave His one and only Son that whoever believes should not" die "but have eternal life" John 3:16. And "whoever believes and is baptized will be saved, but whoever does not believe will be condemned." Mark 16:16.

4. SATAN SAYS:

"Twist the Bible meaning to say anything you want it to say. Don't study too deeply, and prove your point by quoting just half of a single verse."

Jesus never depended on just half of a single Bible verse to prove anything. He used the whole Bible (what we call The Old Testament) to teach His disciples. "And beginning with *Moses* and all the *Prophets*, he explained to them what was said in all the Scriptures concerning himself." Luke 24:27.

The prophets of old foretold the coming of Christ with pinpoint accuracy. Look at the first chapter once again, if you wish, to see what Christ shared with His disciples after coming out of the grave. Paul also taught us the importance of Old Testament scripture, when he wrote to Timothy and to the whole world, telling Timothy and us that "All Scripture is given by inspiration of God, and is profitable for doctrine, for reproof, for correction, for instruction." 2 Timothy 3:16, NKJV.

The Scriptures here refered to were primarily what Christians call "The Old Testament." The part of the Bible we call "The Old Testament" was "The Bible" Christ taught from and "The Bible" Timothy taught from and said was "inspired of God." Let's use the whole Bible in our search for God. The whole Bible is in agreement on the plan of salvation. It is false teachers who discredit "The Old Testament." Study the Bible in its entirety.

5. SATAN SAYS:

"God's Ten Commandment law has been done away with. It does not matter what you do. Heaven is your future home."

Many reject the plain, cutting truths of the Bible because they involve a cross. They neglect the Word of God because it is inconvenient. They will be left to receive outrageous heresy for religious truth. "They perish because they refused to love the truth and so be saved." 2 Thessalonians 2:10.

Some, unwilling to obey God's requirements, attempt to overthrow God's authority. They become infidels to excuse their neglect of duty. Others choose not to believe because of their pride and laziness. Too lazy to distinguish themselves by accomplishing anything worthy of honor, which requires effort and self-denial, they aim to secure a reputation for superior wisdom by criticizing the Bible. Many enjoy finding something in the Bible to confuse the minds of others. Some at first criticize and reason on the wrong side, from a mere love of controversy. They do not realize that they are, in reality, getting caught in Satan's trap. Having openly spoken with disbelief, they feel that they must defend their position.

6. SATAN SAYS:

"Trust psychics, spirits, mediums, and miracles."

Jesus said that "false Christs and false prophets will appear and perform great signs and miracles to deceive." John wrote in Revelation that "they are spirits of demons performing miraculous signs . . ." Matthew 24:24; Revelation 16:14.

Isaiah wrote, "When men tell you to consult mediums and spiritists, who whisper and mutter, should not a people inquire of their God? Why consult the dead on behalf of the living?" Isaiah 8:19, 20.

These are an abomination to the Lord. They are a revival of the witch-craft of old under a new disguise. These things actually open channels of speaking, not with God, but with Lucifer and the fallen angels. In the days of the ancient prophets, they were forbidden under penalty of death. Today they have become entertainment and are promoted on television. Compare Numbers 25:1-3, Psalm 106:28, 1 Corinthinans 10:20, Revelation 16:14, and Leviticus 19:31; 20:27.

7. SATAN SAYS:

"You can believe that Jesus was a good man. Just *don't* believe that
He was God in human form."

Christ claimed, "I am the way and the truth and the Life. No one comes to the Father except through me." John 14:6. Christ here claims that there is no other way to find eternal life except through Himself.

One day the Jews asked Christ if He was greater than Abraham. Christ responded, "Your father Abraham saw my day and was glad." The Jews answered, "You are not yet fifty years old, and you have seen Abraham? 'I tell you the truth,' Jesus answered, 'Before Abraham was born, I AM!' At this, they picked up stones to stone him but Jesus slipped away." John 8:57, 58. The Jews understood His claims, and that is why they tried to kill Him with stones that day.

Either Jesus is "God in human flesh" just as He said He was, or He is the greatest liar of all time. He said that He knew Abraham, who, along with Isaac and Jacob, had been dead for hundreds of years. And then He said, "Before Abraham was, I AM." The words *I AM* are words that refer only to God.

At the burning bush Moses spoke with God, and "God said unto Moses I AM THAT I AM. This is what you are to say to the Israelites: I AM has sent me to you." Exodus 3:14. It was God who spoke with Moses at the burning bush. It was Jesus Christ who spoke with Moses at the burning bush. The entire Bible is a Revelation of Jesus Christ. "And beginning with *Moses* and all the *Prophets*, he explained to them what was said in all the Scriptures concerning himself." Luke 24:27. Either Christ was who He claimed to be, or He was a liar and a deceiver. A "good man" would not make such claims. Turn back to Chapter 1 for a confirmation of who the Messiah is.

8. SATAN SAYS:

"Don't be afraid of me. I am not a real person."

The New Testament clearly states that Jesus believed in a personal

Satan. He spoke face to face with him in the desert after His baptism. He forced Satan and the other evil angels to leave many of those whom they controlled, those who were demon possessed.

In Africa, the animals, such as zebras, that are in the greatest danger are the ones that do not know that the lion is stalking them. Those who either smell, hear, or see the lion are ready to run away. The others just keep eating until the lion seems to come out of nowhere and pounces on them. The Bible compares Satan to a lion. Satan seeks to convince man that He is not real. He wants people to picture Him with horns, a pitchfork, and red pajamas. This creates amusement and even laughter. But those who laugh loudest at the existence of a real devil are in the greatest danger.

9. SATAN SAYS:

"The second coming of Christ is His coming to each individual at death."

Jesus says, "In my Father's house are many mansions. I will come back and take you to be with me." "The harvest is the end of the world and the reapers [harvesters] are the angels." John 14:1-3, NKJV; Matthew 13:39, KJV. Jesus plainly states that He does not come for us until "the end of the world." Not until He comes in glory with all the heavenly angels and "the trumpet of God." That day is not far away.

"Write the vision, and make it plain, . . . that he may run who reads it." Habakkuk 2:2, NKJV.

"The natural man does not receive the things of the Spirit of God, for they are foolishness to him; nor can he know them, because they are spiritually discerned [understood]." 1 Corinthians 2:14. False doctrines and ideas without number are found in the many churches claiming to serve Christ. The errors of popular theology have driven many people to skepticism.

Read 2 Thessalonians 2:10-12. With such a warning before us, it is very important that we be on our guard about what doctrines we receive.

10. SATAN SAYS:

"Jesus is coming again in a secret rapture."

According to the dictionary, *rapture* means "the act of transporting or fact of being transported." The secret rapture belief is that Christ will return in secret when He comes the second time—and that those who are Christians (the dead and the living) at that time will be secretly transported out of this world before the tribulation—before the seven last plagues fall on Planet Earth. According to this theory, the followers of Christ will be in heaven while life goes on down here on the earth. The theory claims that the plagues of Revelation chapter 16 will be poured out on the world, but that Christians are safe in heaven. According to the secret rapture theory, those who follow Jesus will experience no cross, no persecution. Believers in this theory say that Christians will be taken out of this world before the time of crisis.

Many of God's children have been deceived by this wonderful-sounding doctrine. Believing in the secret rapture does not make a person "bad." But it does effectively stop them from preparing for the crisis ahead. Jesus said, "As it was in the days of Noah, so it will be at the coming of the Son of Man. For in the days before the flood, people were eating and drinking, marrying and giving in marriage, up to the day Noah entered the ark; and they knew nothing about what would happen until the flood came and took them all away. That is how it will be at the coming of the Son of Man." Jesus says that His second coming will be similar to the time of Noah. Noah and his family were not taken out of the storm—they went *through* the storm. Matthew 24:37-39.

God removes "wrinkles" from our characters through the "cross" of painful trials. When you iron your clothes and want to get out the wrinkles, what do you use—a hot iron, or a cold iron? A hot iron, of course. The apostle Paul says, "Christ loved the church and gave himself up for her to make her holy, cleansing her by the washing with water through the word, and to present her to himself as a radiant church without stain or wrinkle or any other blemish, but holy and blameless." Peter explains it like this: "Dear friends, do not be surprised at the painful trial you are suffering, as though something strange were happening to you. But rejoice that you participate in the sufferings of Christ." Ephesians 5:25-27; 1 Peter 4:12, 13. Peter was speaking from experience. Peter himself did not believe Jesus when Jesus told him that He would die on a cross. Peter was converted, and later, Peter himself died on a cross. And finally, Timothy says, "Everyone who wants to live a godly life in Christ Jesus will be persecuted." 2 Timothy 3:12.

Belief in the secret rapture conveniently takes away the cross—the trials—of those who live just before Christ comes again. The devil wants people to sleep on, unprepared for the "time of distress such as has not happened from the beginning of nations until then." "But at that time your people—everyone whose name is found written in the book—will be delivered. Multitudes who sleep in the dust of the earth will awake: some to everlasting life, others to shame and everlasting contempt." Daniel 12:1, 2.

God has always taken His children through the storm, through the trial. He says, "Take up your cross and follow me." Noah was not saved from the storm. He was saved *through* the storm. Daniel was not saved from the lions' den. He was saved *through* the lions' den. Shadrach, Meshach, and Abednego were not saved from the furnace of fire. They were saved *through* the furnace of fire.

"Nebuchadnezzar ordered the furnace heated seven times hotter than usual and commanded some of the strongest soldiers in his army to tie up Shadrach, Meshach and Abednego and throw them into the blazing furnace. So these men were bound and thrown into the blazing furnace." The king was amazed, as the furnace was so hot that it killed the soldiers who threw these three men in—but when he looked in to watch them die, he saw four men walking unhurt through the fire. The fourth was Christ Himself, protecting His three faithful servants. Daniel 3:19, 20.

Christ told the story of the wise man and the foolish man. He said, "Everyone who hears these words of mine and puts them into practice is like a wise man who built his house on the rock. The rain came down, the streams rose, and the winds blew and beat against that house; yet it did not fall, because it had its foundation on the rock. But everyone who hears these words of mine and does not put them into practice is like a foolish man who built his house on sand. The rain came down, the streams rose, and the winds blew and beat against that house, and it fell with a great crash." Matthew 7:24-27.

Notice that the two houses, on two different foundations, represent two types of people—two type of Christians. This parable tells us that those Christians who not only "hear" Christ's words but "put them into practice" are like a wise man. Both houses, representing all people, must go THROUGH the storm. The difference is that those who put Christ's words "into practice" go THROUGH the storm successfully.

Read in Exodus about the children of Israel. God delivered them from slavery to the king of Egypt through the use of plagues. They were on their way to "the promised land." Persecution will come to all who live obedient, Spirit-filled lives just before Christ comes to take His people to "the promised land." God will again use "plagues" to deliver His people. Read about it in Revelation, chapter 16. In the days of Moses, God's children were then protected from the plagues, and God's children now, just before Jesus comes to take us to "the promised land" will also be protected from the plagues. God did not rapture His people before the plagues fell then— and He will not rapture His people now before the plagues fall.

The lure of the secret rapture is that it promises no pain. If I were to offer you a journey that involved trials and suffering—or a journey that was entirely free from pain or trials, which would you take? Naturally, you would take the journey that is free from all trials and pain. That is the way my natural heart would rather have it. If you have been tricked by the false teaching of the secret rapture, I can certainly understand. This false teaching, the doctrine of the secret rapture, has its own type of magic.

Everyone I know would rather have a pain-free future. But the truth is that no one will have a pain-free future. If the secret rapture were true, I'd be the first to teach it, because my own natural heart prefers the easiest way. Satan tricked our first parents with a miracle and with lies. He has returned to this last generation to try and trick us into joining his rebellion. It is sad that he has tricked so very many. Won't you accept God's call to "set the captives free" from erroneous thinking? God's way is the best way! When the plagues fall, only those who have chosen to follow their self-denying Saviour will be safe! It is truly the best way! Many who have dreamed of the security of the secret rapture will be shocked awake when it is too late!

Christ tells us in Revelation about the people who are saved when He comes again and says, "These are they who have come out of the great tribulation; they have washed their robes and made them white in the blood of the Lamb." Revelation 7:14. Notice that God's children go *through* the tribulation. The tribulation is a refining process. Today we put iron ore into an intensely hot furnace to refine it—to make steel. The product is better for having gone through the heat. God wants to refine you and your character. The character of Christ will shine out of your life if you will submit patiently to the heated trials you will pass through, if you are truly a born-again, Spirit-filled Christian.

Those who believe in the secret rapture believe that Christ will come and take His children home before the tribulation—before the seven last plagues of Revelation 16 are poured out on Planet Earth. Notice that there are seven plagues. Read about the first six plagues in Revelation 16:1-17. During the outpouring of the sixth plague, Christ says He has not yet come. Christ says, "Behold I come like a thief! Blessed is he who stays awake." Revelation 16:15. It is during the sixth plague that Christ tells us that He still hasn't come yet but is coming soon.

What about the Bible texts that say, "the Lord will come like a thief" in the night? Doesn't that mean that Christ will come and slip into this world and take His children home without anyone else knowing He came? The Bible says: "But the day of the Lord will come like a thief. The heavens will disappear with a roar; the elements will be destroyed by fire, and the earth and everything in it will be laid bare. Since everything will be destroyed in this way, what kind of people ought you to be? You ought to live holy and godly lives as you look forward to the day of God and speed its coming. That day will bring about the destruction of the heavens by fire, and the elements will melt in the heat. But in keeping with his promise we are looking forward to a new heaven and a new earth, the home of righteousness." 2 Peter 3:10-14.

Notice that it is *when* He comes that is compared to "the thief" in the night, not the *way* He comes. Everyone will see the fiery coming of Christ when "the heavens . . . disappear with a roar and the elements melt in the heat." They will see Christ come. They will hear Christ come. They will feel Christ come. Thieves come unexpectedly and silently. Jesus is not emphasizing silence, but rather the unexpectedness and unpreparedness of the Christian world.

It is amazing that those who believe in the secret rapture use one of the "noisiest" passages in the Bible to teach the "secret" rapture theory!

1 Thessaloninans 4:16-18 speaks of Christ coming down through the skies. "For the Lord himself will come down from heaven with a loud command, with the voice of the archangel, and with the trumpet call of God, and the dead in Christ will rise first. After that, we who are still alive and are left will be caught up [raptured] together with them in the clouds to meet the Lord in the air." The King James Version says that Christ comes "with a shout, and with the trump [trumpet] of God." I have a very difficult time imagining my Creator "shouting," and angels blowing "the trumpet of God" in such a quiet way that it is "secret." This coming of Christ, and this rapture (taking His children up out of this world) will be no secret—it will be majestic, noisy, and visible to all.

6

Like a "Thief"!

How can I avoid the Satanic traps
that have been set for me?

Does the book of Revelation have anything that God wants me to know? How can I be ready for that wonderful time when there will be no more pain, aging, suffering, or death? The book of Revelation is the key for our generation.

Christ in Matthew 24 compares the days of Noah's generation, when the world was destroyed by a flood, to the last generation before Christ returns the second time. The world's fate was decided before the flood. Noah and his family were safe inside the ark for seven days before the flood came. God had shut the doors, and they could not be opened again until after the flood. The people did not know their fate was sealed, that their judgment had been decided seven days before there was any evidence of a flood.

Lucifer, alias the devil, does not want you and me to know certain Bible truths. He does not want you to know that God is in the work of judgment at this very moment! He has been successful in hiding this truth from most people so far. Keep an open mind and look at the evidence for this shocking truth.

The second coming of Christ is spoken of as being like a "thief in the night," meaning that He will come the second time when least expected. Not only is His second coming unexpected, like a thief in the night, but the judgment is also a shocking surprise. Before He comes, Christ begins and ends His work of judging those who have identified themselves as His followers. When He comes, He says, "my reward is with Me." Revelation 22:12. The sentencing, or rewarding, part of the judgment, in a courtroom, always occurs after the investigative part of the judgment.

When Christ comes, He sentences some to death and rewards others with life. Just as in an earthly courtroom, the investigative part of the judgment is over before the sentencing part of the judgment. Christ's coming is the sentencing part of the judgment. The investigative judgment is taking place right now. The decision as to who will be saved is made before He comes. The people in Noah's day did not know that when they chose not to get into the ark that, at that moment, it was too late. They did not know that for another seven days. The sun continued to shine, and life went on as usual. The separation of the saved and lost was made seven days before the actual flood. Their fate was sealed seven days before the first raindrops fell.

The thief comes when least expected. The vast majority of Christians have been taught that the judgment begins after death, which is true for most generations. It is, however, not true for the last generation before Jesus Christ returns. The judgment has begun for all who died claiming Christianity and will soon begin for all the living who claim to be Christians.

"I saw another angel flying in midair, and he had the eternal gospel to proclaim to those who live on the earth—to every nation, tribe, language and people. He said in a loud voice, 'fear God and give him glory, because the hour of his judgment has come.'" Revelation 14:6, 7.

The book of the century is the book of Revelation. The book of Revelation says that a warning message of the presence of God's judgment would be carried worldwide, just before Jesus Christ returns to Planet Earth the second time.

Revelation has a special warning to those people living just before Jesus Christ comes the second time. A special warning message prepares them for His return to Planet Earth. The fourteenth chapter of Revelation tells us of three warning messages. They are so important that the Bible pictures them as three angels shouting these three messages to each person in the world.

When Will God Judge Me?

"Then I saw another angel flying in midair and he had the eternal gospel to proclaim to those who live on the earth—to every nation, tribe, language and people. He said in a loud voice, 'Fear God and give him glory, because the hour of his judgment has come.'" Revelation 14:6, 7. In other words, he shouts to the people of the world that "the hour of His judgment is here now!" The words "loud voice" and "to every nation, tribe, language and people" suggest that God will use people to carry this message worldwide quickly! God is using this very book—both in print and on the Internet— as part of that "loud voice" to be carried to "every nation, tribe, language and people."

Will we see these three angels shouting these messages in the streets of our large cities, as Jonah did in the city of Nineveh? No! The Bible uses this wording to let the reader know that to be ready for Christ's second coming, there are three things he or she must understand. In the first message of love, Christ says, "God is judging you and me now." The judgment that is going on right now and the second coming of Christ are both unexpected. They are both part of "the thief in the night" experience the Bible warns us about. This is an unexpected truth, just as a thief slipping into your house at night would be an unexpected truth.

It is sad, but most Christians are spiritually "asleep." Matthew 25:5. They do not understand these three warning messages from Revelation. The first message is that the judgment, our day in court, is going on right now in heaven. We can be there, by faith. People can and must understand these three messages. Our future depends on it. God further explains these three messages in other parts of His Word, as well. It all fits together like a jigsaw puzzle.

Let us pray and ask God for help in understanding these three messages right now: "Father in heaven, help me understand how to be ready to meet Jesus Christ when He returns to take me home with Him. Help me to understand the book of Revelation, especially the three warning messages of the fourteenth chapter of Revelation. Please make them easy for me to understand. Use me to also help others understand, so that they also might be ready to meet Jesus Christ when He comes again. In Jesus' name, Amen."

Have you ever felt a need for greater spiritual growth?
Have you ever felt that the churches may have lost
something somewhere and need revival?

7

Babylon Is Fallen

The second angel's message says, "Babylon is fallen, is fallen, that great city that made all nations drink of the wine of the wrath of her fornication." Revelation 14:8. "Her fornication" is her false teachings. The church has rejected Bible truth and has made all nations accept her unscriptural beliefs.

"Babylon is fallen, is fallen, . . . Come out of her, my people, so you will not share in her sins and so that you will not receive her plagues." Revelation 14:8; 18:4. Many churches that claim to follow Christ have turned away from His teachings. In other words, Jesus Christ says, "God will pour out His plagues on the disobedient churches." Come out of them, my children, so that you will be safe.

Babylon has not yet completely fallen as of the writing of this book. It is in a falling condition. Babylon will be completely fallen when the church unites with the world governments to persecute those who "keep the commandments of God, and the faith of Jesus." Revelation 14:12, KJV.

Where does God say most of *His* people are?

In Babylon.

What does God say His people must do?

Come out of Babylon.

Notice God does not say GO out of Babylon.

If you hear a person calling you to come out of your house,
where is that person?

He is outside your house.

If you hear God calling you to *come* out of Babylon, where is God?

*God is withdrawing from those churches that are part of Babylon and
will soon be completely outside of Babylon. He is calling His people
to come out too!*

Listen to His voice and follow Your sacrificing Saviour!

Revelation 18:4: *"Come out* of her, My people, so that you will not share
in her sins, so that you will not receive any of her plagues."

Why did God say He is calling *His people* to come out of Babylon?

To protect them from the soon coming plagues and destruction.

God Says, "My People Are in Babylon"

God says, "Babylon is Fallen, is Fallen. Come out of her, My People." If
you recognize yourself as being in one of the churches that make up "spiritual" Babylon, you are saying, "I am God's child," because that is where
God says His children are. Who am I to argue with God? Praise the Lord
that you are His special child and that He cares enough for you to call you
out of Babylon. God sent two angels to Sodom to warn His child, Lot, to
leave Sodom. God is sending you the messages of three angels (see Revelation chapter 14) to call you out of Babylon.

You know the story as recorded in Genesis. Lot left Sodom, and his life
was spared. His wife turned back and lost her life. Jesus tells us to "remember Lot's wife." Lot could have argued with God that he had lived in Sodom
all his life and had many friends there and that Sodom was not such a bad
place to live. Did God actually expect him to leave his home and his friends?
Yes, He did. Did God actually destroy Sodom? Yes, He did. Will God destroy Babylon? Yes, He will. You are His child, and He is calling you out of
Babylon. He expects no less of you or me than He expected of Lot.

He has not yet called you to leave your home like Lot, but He is calling
you to come out of Babylon. Child of God, I urge you to obey your Master,
who says, "He that is unwilling to take up His cross in unworthy of Me."
The cross was a cruel form of torture. Christ chose to die on the cross out

of love for you. He wants you to follow Him out of love for Him. Do you love Him enough to hear His voice and follow Him out of Babylon?

Where does God say the majority of His children are just before He comes to get His people? He says that they are in the churches that make up "spiritual" Babylon. *Does God condemn His children for being in Babylon? No! God loves His children and calls them out. God does not condemn His children, but He does condemn "Babylon." So if you have chosen Christ as your Master, you are probably in one of the churches that constitute Babylon, because that is where God says His people are.*

You are not condemned for belonging to one of these churches that God calls "Babylon," but you will be condemned and receive the seven last plagues if you stay in "Babylon."

All of those who are following their Master, Jesus Christ, will hear His call and come out. Lot was not condemned for living in Sodom, but His wife lost her life when God called them out of Sodom and she turned back toward Sodom. Child of God, your Master Jesus Christ is calling you to follow Him out. Listen to His voice, and you will be safe."

What a Shock!

Many Christian leaders condemn God's warning message, just as the religious leaders condemned Christ, saying, "Have any of the rulers or of the Pharisees believed?" Many Christian leaders have fought, are fighting, and will fight unpopular truths, teaching that God has sealed the books of Revelation and Daniel.

Many teach that no one can understand these prophecies. But by rejecting the unpopular messages from Revelation, they are rejecting God.

8

Who Is Babylon?

Two prophetic books—Daniel in the Old Testament and Revelation in the New Testament—speak of "Babylon." In the book of Daniel, we read of a physical empire under the control of "Babylon." The nation of Babylon had conquered God's chosen people, the Jews, and taken them captive in a very literal way. In Revelation, it is "spiritual Babylon" that has taken God's children captive.

Some so-called "religious experts" try to convince you that the prophecy of Revelation 14 and 18 is a prophecy that will be fulfilled through the actual rebuilding of Babylon. But that will never happen. Saddam Hussein made plans in the past to rebuild Babylon, but the prophecies of the Bible are against his dreams. The prophet Isaiah predicted the overthrow of ancient Babylon (Isaiah 13:19-22), and God said, "She will never be inhabited or lived in through all generations."

This prophecy lets us know that in Revelation 14 and 18, God is not speaking of the physical empire of Babylon. God is warning all mankind, just before Jesus comes the second time, to come out of "spiritual" Babylon. In the book of Daniel, God called His people out of physical Babylon—and in the book of Revelation, He calls His people out of spiritual Babylon.

When God refers to a church that He wishes to correct, we all must realize that God loves each of its members. We as individual members are not bad or good as a result of the particular church to which we belong. We need to keep listening to Jesus and be willing to go in the direction He wants for our lives, regardless of what decision the organization makes. Listen to the voice of Jesus from the Bible, and He will guide you in making the right decisions.

In Revelation 17 God pictures Babylon as a woman. The Bible prophecies use the word *woman* as a symbol for a church. A good woman symbolizes a good church, and a bad woman symbolizes a church that has strayed away from the teachings of Christ. The woman of Revelation 17 is dressed in purple and crimson red color. She is wearing gold jewelry and expensive stones and pearls, and "on her forehead was written the name, 'Babylon the Great, the mother of prostitutes,'" or "Babylon the Great, the mother of the churches that have rejected many unpopular teachings of Christ."

Christ here is concerned with "the errroneous teachings of the Christian church. The fact that God says the churches are falling is not a condemnation of His people, but rather a condemnation of the false teachings of the churches that claim to represent God. God has His special children in every denomination—Catholic, Protestant, or other religions—as well as those in cults or who attend no church at all. Many love God, and God loves them. God loves everyone. Reader, God loves you, whether you are a member of any church or not. You are reading God's last message of concerned love for all His children. He wants to save you. Let God plant the truth—the seed of His Word—in your heart.

"I saw the woman drunk with the blood of the saints, and with the blood of the martyrs of Jesus." God pictures the church as drunken on the blood of those she has killed. Through the dark ages, the church killed over 50 million people who chose to obey God instead of obeying church leaders. God also calls Babylon "that great city, which reigns [rules] over the kings of the earth." Revelation 17:4-6, 18. This international religious power has power over world leaders.

No man has the right to judge another person regarding sincerity, motives, attitudes, or choice of belief. God, however, does warn us to "come out of Babylon." Most people don't understand what that means. Who or what is Babylon? And if God is addressing me, how do I come out of Babylon? It is vitally important that you and I know the answers to these two questions. Once you read this book, your actions will reveal whether you really understand the answers. The fact that you are reading this book is no accident. Reader, God loves you! He has led you to this very book. God wants you to be safe through the coming crisis.

Five Identifying Marks!

1. The purple, the scarlet color, and the gold reveal to us that Babylon is a power that has great wealth and great power.

2. That Babylon is "drunken with the blood of the saints" reveals another identifying mark of Babylon. Babylon is a cruel persecuting power.

3. Babylon has power over "the kings of the earth." This tells us that Babylon is an international church-state combination. The church uses governments to persecute those with whom she disagrees.

4. Babylon is considered "the mother of prostitutes," suggesting that this world power has "given birth" to many other churches that are like "their mother."

5. Immediately before the coming of Christ, many of God's children are in Babylon.

Which Is the ONLY Power That Has All These Characteristics?

The papacy:

a) is a magnificent church that

b) cruelly persecuted and killed millions, often by torture, for not obeying church teachings. The papacy killed more than fifty million people in the dark ages for not accepting her unscriptural beliefs. (See *Fox's Book of Martyrs*—Item No. 14 in the Appendix.)

c) is a religious organization that has power over the kings and governments of the earth.

d) gave birth to many churches that, for a time, believed in "the Bible and the Bible only." Many have since turned back, accepting many unscriptural beliefs and becoming more like their mother. (More information is found in the Appendix.)

e) can also be identified by the fact that the majority of God's people are in Babylon just before Christ returns. God's people are to come out of Babylon. That means that most of God's children today are in Babylon. Where are most of Christ's followers? They are in the various Protestant, as well as Catholic, churches. Could the Protestant churches be part of Babylon also? The sad answer is Yes.

Revelation 14, announcing the fall of Babylon, must apply to religious organizations that were once pure and have since turned away from a pure faith in Jesus Christ. According to the Bible, most of God's people today are still in Babylon.

In what churches are a large number of Christ's followers found? Without a question, they are in the many churches claiming to be Protestant. "You played the prostitute because of your popularity." Ezekiel 16:15. The conflicting beliefs of the Protestant churches are another identifying mark. The word *Babylon* is related to a word meaning "confusion" and signifies confusion.

Paul, the apostle, predicted that the Christian church would reject Bible truth. The church did exactly that. The church rejected some unpopular Bible truths when it rejected and replaced some Bible's teachings with pagan practices. The hope was to make it easier for those who worshiped idols to accept Christianity.

History reveals that in order to grow quickly, the requirement for church membership was lowered. A pagan flood swept into the church. Many in the church outwardly looked like Christians, but inwardly they had never changed. They still believed in the same false gods they had served before, only now they worshiped their idols in secret.

Popular Ministers Do Not Condemn Popular Sins

Our danger today is that we blindly cling to what we learn about God from our parents and our church. Many teachings that we learn, we assume are direct from the Word of God, the Bible. People trust without question what they learn from their parents or their minister about God.

The trouble is that this style of learning has gone on for hundreds of years. During those years, parents passed on unscriptural teachings to their children, from parent to child. Our danger is in believing that because our church or our parents teach us something, it must therefore be from God's Word. Sorry! Just because a person in authority says it is so does not make it so! Our eternal destiny depends on our making the right choices. The only unchanging, absolute guide is God's Word, the Bible.

We often listen to popular ministers who are well paid. Often their high salary stops many ministers from condemning popular sins. Popular ministers can become unpopular if they speak unpopular truth. If they become unpopular, they could lose their income. Some ministers are afraid to speak the truth for this very reason. So fashionable sinners live on with their fashionable sins, concealed under a mask of godliness.

Religion has become popular with most people everywhere. World leaders, politicians, lawyers, doctors, and business people join the church to get the respect and confidence of society and to improve their own financial situation. They often try to cover their own unrighteous lifestyle by claiming to be Christians. Many have been baptized into the church who know nothing of Christ.

Baptism does not make a person a Christian. Popularity does not make a person a Christian. Attending church does not make a person a Christian. Many are baptized into the church and claim to be Christians but are not. They could also stand in a garage and claim to be a car, because cars belong in garages, but that does not make them a car.

Many people are looking for the benefits without the duties of Christianity. Is the church doing the work of the devil? Raising money often involves bingo and lotteries, appealing to greed instead of sacrifice.

False Doctrines Are Intoxicating!

The great sin charged against Babylon is that she "made all nations drink of the wine of the wrath of her fornication." What is the wine of her fornication? It is the false doctrine the church has passed on through tradition.

What are some of those false doctrines?

One of those intoxicating false doctrines is her unlawful connection with the great ones of the earth. Friendship with the world corrupts her faith.

Rome substituted her teachings for the Bible. When it had the power to do so, Rome banned the Bible and required all men to accept her teachings in its place. The churches of our time are doing the same thing when the creeds and teachings of the church become more important than the teachings of the Bible. They teach men to rest their faith upon the opinions and the teachings of their church rather than on the Scripture.

In this way the teachings of the church are putting aside the Bible as really as Rome did, though in a less noticeable way. Before the coming of the Lord, Satan will work "with all power and signs and lying wonders." 2 Thessalonians 2:9, KJV.

9

Prophecies From Daniel

These great prophecies are for the hungry in heart. Their fulfillment gives the honest in heart real evidence that God truly exists and that He knows the future before it happens!

The biblical foundation for God's three messages to modern man is the verse, "Unto two thousand and three hundred days, then shall the sanctuary be cleansed." Daniel 8:14, KJV. *(The year-day prophetic principle. See notes in the Appendix.)*

God promised that He would cleanse His sanctuary in 2300 prophetic days, 2300 actual years, "a day for a year." The cleansing of the sanctuary in heaven, the beginning of our day in court, is the beginning of God's work of judgment. God told Daniel that the work of cleansing His sanctuary in heaven, His work of judgment, would begin in 2300 years.

What God did *not* tell Daniel in chapter 8 was the beginning date for the 2300 years. Daniel wanted to understand this and prayed. "While I was speaking and praying, confessing my sin, Gabriel came to me in swift flight and said to me, 'Daniel, I have come to give you understanding. Seventy weeks are determined upon your people and on your holy city to finish the transgression, and to make reconciliation for iniquity, and to bring in ever-

91

lasting righteousness, and to seal up the vision and prophecy, and to anoint the most Holy. . . .

"Know therefore and understand that from the going forth of the command to restore and to build Jerusalem unto the Messiah [Anointed One] the Prince shall be seven weeks, and sixty two weeks: the street shall be built again, and the wall, even in troublous times. And after sixty two weeks shall Messiah be cut off, but not for himself: . . . And he shall confirm a covenant with many for one week: and in the middle of the week he shall bring an end to sacrifice and offering." Daniel 9:24-27, NKJV.

Notice that God, through Daniel, spoke of **7** weeks and **62** weeks and **1** week.

7 + 62 + 1 = 70 weeks.

Three Prophecies Begin With the Commandment to Restore and Rebuild Jerusalem in 457 B.C.

1.

70 weeks = 490 years—A 490-year prophecy

The 70 week (490-year) prophecy of Daniel 9:24 begins with the commandment to restore and rebuild Jerusalem in 457 B.C.

2.

69 weeks = 483 years—A 483-year prophecy

7 + 62 weeks = 69 weeks—The first 483 years of the 490-year prophecy. The 483-year prophecy of Daniel 9:25 begins with the commandment to restore and rebuild Jerusalem in 457 B.C.

3.

2300 days = 2300 years—A 2300-year prophecy

The 2300-year prophecy of Daniel 8:14 begins with the commandment to restore and rebuild Jerusalem in 457 B.C.

What do all three of these prophecies have in common? They each begin with "the commandment to restore and to build Jerusalem." Daniel 9:25.

The commandment of Artaxerxes for the restoration and building of Jerusalem went into effect in the autumn of 457 B.C.

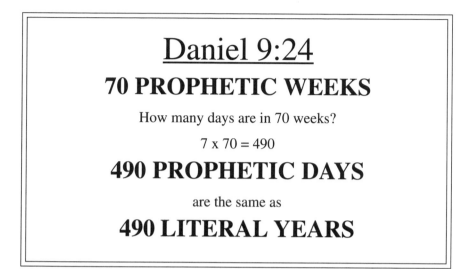

Daniel 9:24

70 PROPHETIC WEEKS

How many days are in 70 weeks?

7 x 70 = 490

490 PROPHETIC DAYS

are the same as

490 LITERAL YEARS

The 490-year Prophecy

"Seventy weeks are determined upon your people and upon your holy city, to finish the transgression, and to make an end of sins." Daniel 9:24, NKJV. The word here translated *determined* literally signifies "cut off," as specially for the Jews. But from what were they cut off? As the 2300 days was the only time mentioned in chapter 8, that must be the period from which the seventy weeks were cut off. In other words, God gave 70 prophetic weeks to His people and to Jerusalem to repent, each day representing a year.

This comes to 490 years. This period is the first part of the 2300-year prophecy. God has given these 490 years to the Jewish people in which to stop their rebelliousness, repent of their sins, and accept His offer of salvation.

Seventy weeks times seven days in a week equals 490 days. Using the year-day prophetic principle, we understand God as giving His people, the Israelites, a special time, 490 years long, to return to Him. The beginning date is found in Daniel 9:25. That date was "from the issuing of the decree to restore and to build Jerusalem," which was 457 B.C.

Seven weeks plus 62 weeks plus 1 week = 70 weeks. The 70 weeks are the first 490 "prophetic days," or literal years, of the 2300 prophetic day/ literal year prophecy. Each time period of this prophecy has meaning. We will look at each part separately.

A

"Seven weeks"

King Artaxerxes commanded the rebuilding of Jerusalem in 457 B.C. Forty nine years later (7 x 7 = 49), by 408 B.C., it was completely rebuilt.

B

*"And **sixty two weeks**"*

7 x 62 = 434 "prophetic days" or 434 "actual years." Continuing from 408 B.C. takes us to A.D. 27. This was the year that the Messiah, "the anointed one," was predicted to appear. Christ was anointed in baptism in 27 A.D. He was anointed "on time."

49 + 434 = 483 — 483 years after 457 B.C. is A.D. 27.

C

*"He shall confirm the covenant with many for **one week**"*

One prophetic week = 7 actual years.

7 weeks + 62 weeks + 1 week = 70 prophetic weeks.

"Until the anointed One comes, there will be seven weeks and sixty-two weeks. It will be rebuilt, and after the sixty-two weeks the Anointed One will be cut off [killed] . . . He will confirm a covenant with many for one week." Daniel 9:27, NKJV. This is the last seven years of the 490-year prophecy—A.D. 27 to A.D. 34.

D

"In the *middle of the week* He will put an end to sacrifice . . ." In the middle of this seven-year period, Christ was to be crucified. This "week" of 7 years was from A.D. 27 to A.D. 34. In the middle of this 7-year period, in A.D. 31, Christ was crucified. Daniel 9:27, NKJV.

Multiply 7 days in a week times the 70 weeks.

7 x 70 = 490 prophetic days or 490 literal years.

Starting with a date of 457 BC,
the 70 prophetic weeks end with A.D. 34.

Since we are using the year-day prophetic principle, God would anoint Christ with His Spirit exactly 483 years (69 weeks) after the commandment to restore and build Jerusalem. Four hundred eighty three years after King Artaxerxes made the decree to rebuild Jerusalem (457 BC) is A.D. 27. This is the year John the Baptist baptized Christ and the Holy Spirit anointed Christ, coming down on Him in the form of a dove.

King Artaxerxes gave the commandment to restore Jerusalem in 457 B.C., and God anointed Christ 483 years later in A.D. 27. That is why Christ said "The time is fulfilled." Mark 1:15, KJV. John the Baptist and the Holy Spirit baptized Jesus on time.

The prophet Daniel predicted:

■ The baptism of Christ in A.D. 27.

■ His death in A.D. 31.

1. John The Baptist baptized Christ on time.

2. The people crucified Him on time.

3. Daniel predicted it all exactly, hundreds of years before.

Sixty-nine weeks, the first 483 of the 2300 years, were to reach to the Messiah, "the Anointed One." Christ's baptism and anointing by the Holy Spirit in A.D. 27 exactly fulfilled this part of the prophecy. In the middle of the seventieth week, men would "cut off" or kill, the Messiah. Half of one week is three and a half days. Three and a half years after His baptism, the Jewish leaders brought Christ to the Romans to be crucified. They crucified Him in the spring of A.D. 31. He died on time!

Isn't this a wonderful prophecy? Either the Bible is 100 percent accurate or it is a cruel hoax, an outright lie. Paul says it like this: "All scripture is given by inspiration of God, and is profitable for doctrine, for reproof, for correction, for instruction in righteousness." 2 Timothy 3:16, KJV.

How did Daniel know, over five hundred years ahead, the exact year in which Christ would be baptized, and that three and one half years later He would be crucified? God gives us convincing evidence for faith. Faith is not blind. Won't you choose Jesus Christ as your Saviour? The way to accept Christ is found in the Introduction of this very book. Why not trust and follow the One who knows the future ahead of time?

E

"Unto two thousand and three hundred days,
then shall the sanctuary be cleansed." Daniel 8:14, KJV.

The seventy weeks, or 490 years, were to pertain especially to the Jews. At the end of this period the nation sealed its rejection of Christ by the persecution of His disciples, and the apostles turned to the Gentiles in A.D. 34. The first 490 years of the 2300 having then ended, 1810 years remained. From A.D. 34, 1810 years extend to A.D. 1844. "Then," said the angel, "will the sanctuary be cleansed."

457 B.C. — 2300 prophetic days later, or 2300 literal years later = A.D. 1844.

"Then shall the sanctuary be cleansed."

"The hour of God's judgment *has come.*"

2300 - 490 (the 70 prophetic weeks) = 1810. 1810 years later "shall the sanctuary be cleansed."

34 + 1810 = 1844. In A.D. 1844 God began His work of judgment.

Back in the early 1800s, people from around the world studied this prophecy. The common belief in those years was that this world was God's sanctuary. From this prophecy, they concluded that God would cleanse the world with fire in 1844. This meant that Christ would be coming in 1844. Thousands around the world came to the same conclusion.

This was in fulfillment of Revelation 10:9-11. "I went to the angel and asked him to give me the little scroll. He said to me, 'Take it and eat it. It will turn your stomach sour, but in your mouth it will be as sweet as honey.'" This actually happened. God knew that His children would conclude that He was coming in 1844. They had "eaten," or studied, the book of Daniel, and it was so wonderful that Jesus was coming so soon. That turned to sadness when He did not come at that time.

It was similar to the sadness the disciples felt when they thought Jesus would become a king in Jerusalem, but instead He was tortured and nailed to a cross. The prophecy in Revelation, chapter 10, continues with the words, "You must prophesy again about many peoples, nations, languages, and kings." Revelation 10:11.

The year 1844 came and went, and Jesus did not come to the earth in flaming fire. God did not cleanse the earth, thought to be God's sanctuary, with fire in 1844 as many had thought He would do. Many of those Bible students rechecked the prophecy. They concluded that they had interpreted the prophetic time correctly but had not understood the true biblical definition of the sanctuary. They searched the Bible and made new discoveries.

God asked Moses to build a structure called the *sanctuary*. Today we have model airplanes, model railroad trains, and model cars. They are a miniature of the real thing. God told Moses that the great original sanctuary is in heaven and that he, Moses, was chosen to build a model of it. He was to build it according to the directions God would give him. It would help people understand God's covenant, the plan of salvation—the purpose of the true sanctuary, God's great original in heaven.

God's covenant with the people of Planet Earth is His agreement on how He would save sinful people and still be a just God. His covenant agreement meant that He would become a human being. Christ chose to become a man as a gift to the people of Earth. He chose to pay the just penalty for sin.

Those who chose could, by Christ's death, find forgiveness of their sins. Through a conscious decision, they could overcome sin through the life and death of Jesus Christ. God explained this salvation agreement though the sanctuary service.

"Then have them make a sanctuary for me, and I will dwell among them." Exodus 25:8. God's plan brings God and man together through the work of the sanctuary. The apostle Paul explains the sanctuary. He says: "The first covenant [agreement] also had rules of divine service, and a worldly sanctuary. The candlestick, and the table with bread were in the first room of the tabernacle, the sanctuary.

"Behind the second curtain was a room called the Most Holy Place, which had the golden altar of incense and the gold-covered ark of the covenant. This ark contained the gold jar of manna, Aaron's staff that had budded, and the stone tablets of the covenant." Hebrews 9:3, 4.

"And above it were the cherubim [angels] of glory overshadowing the mercy seat." Hebrews 9:5, NKJV.

The first apartment contained:

■ The candlestick.

■ The table of holy bread, before the veil.

■ The altar of incense.

Is Noah's Ark Different From the Ark of God's Testament?

Four times, the Bible talks about *arks.*

FIRST, the word *ark* refers to a huge boat known as Noah's Ark.

SECOND, the word *ark* refers to a small basket boat used to hide baby Moses among the reeds in the Nile river.

THIRD, the word *ark* refers to the chest of wood covered with gold that was a container for the two tables of the covenant, the Ten Commandments. The Israelites made the second ark in Moses' day, and it remained in the second apartment of the earthly sanctuary. This ark was eventually hidden in a cave and lost sight of to this day. This is the ark the fictional character "Indiana Jones" supposedly found in Egypt, in the movie "Raiders of the Lost Ark."

FOURTH is the great original ark of the covenant (also called the ark of His testament). This ark is in God's sanctuary in heaven (see Hebrews, chapters 8 and 9. The ark of the covenant is God's throne and contains God's original Ten Commandment law.

Two things God considers most precious are His people and His law. Both were protected by arks. God's plan, as seen in Hebrews chapter 8, is to put the two things that are most precious to God together. His plan is to put His law inside the heart, the mind, of man. God says, "I will put my laws in their minds and write them on their hearts. I will be their God, and they will be my people."

The temple of Solomon replaced the sanctuary built under Moses. The words *temple, sanctuary,* and *tabernacle* are three names for the same thing and refer either to the copy on earth or to the great original in heaven.

According to Hebrews 9, the sanctuary built under Moses is the sanctuary of the first covenant. The great original in heaven is the New Covenant Sanctuary, where Jesus ministers today.

10

The Sanctuary

The apostle Paul says Jesus is High Priest and minister of the sanctuary in heaven. He suggested the existence of a second, or new-covenant sanctuary. "The first covenant had also ordinances of divine service, and a worldly sanctuary." The use of the word *also* suggests that Paul has mentioned this sanctuary before.

Turning back to the beginning of the previous chapter, we read: "Now this is the main point of the things we are saying: We have such a High Priest, who is seated at the right hand of the throne of the Majesty in the heavens; a Minister of the sanctuary, and of the true tabernacle, which the Lord erected, and not man." Hebrews 8:1, 2, NKJV. Man built the copy, the earthly sanctuary, and God built the heavenly sanctuary.

When you see somebody's shadow move, you know that the actual person moved. You can tell what they are doing by what their shadow is doing. Jesus has given us a shadow so that we can know what He is doing in heaven. You may see Christ's shadow in the work that took place in the earthly sanctuary.

The earthly sanctuary was a pattern (or copy) "of things in the heavens." It was "the example and shadow of heavenly things." "Christ has not entered the holy places made with hands, which are the figures of the true;

but He has entered into heaven itself, now to appear in the presence of God for us." Hebrews 9:9, 23; 8:5; 9:24, NKJV.

Tabernacle and Sanctuary: Two Words for the Same Thing

"Make the tabernacle and its instruments according to the pattern I showed you." Again God gave the command, "Make this tabernacle and all its furnishings exactly like the pattern I will show you." Exodus 25:9, 40. The sanctuary in heaven, in which Jesus ministers for us, is the great original, of which the sanctuary built by Moses was a copy.

The two apartments in the sanctuary on earth represent the two holy places in the sanctuary in heaven. John, the writer of Revelation, saw into the first apartment in heaven and saw the "seven lamps before the throne" and a golden censer. Revelation 4:5; 8:3. The golden candlestick and the altar of incense in the sanctuary on earth represent the "seven lamps of fire" and "the golden altar" that John saw in heaven.

"The temple of God was opened in heaven." Revelation 11:19. John, the writer of Revelation, looked into the second apartment of the sanctuary in heaven. He saw "the ark of his covenant" containing the Ten Commandments, fifty years after the death of Christ on the cross. This, then, is proof that the death of Christ on the cross did not "do away" with God's law. It has always been there, and always will be.

Is There Bible Proof of the Existence of a Sanctuary in Heaven?

1. **Moses** made a copy of it. Exodus 35-40.

2. **Paul** tells us about both the original (in heaven) and the copy (on earth) in the book of Hebrews, chapter 9.

3. **John** saw the great original sanctuary, the temple in heaven. He looked inside the sanctuary and saw the ark of His testament (containing the Ten Commandments). Revelation 11:19.

When He died, Jesus went to God's throne as a priest, and not as a king. When His work as priest is over, God the Father will crown Him "King of kings and Lord of lords." Then He will return, not as the suffering Saviour, but as "King of kings and Lord of lords."

He "will sit and rule upon His throne; and He will be a priest upon His throne."

As a priest, Christ is now sitting with the Father in His throne. Revelation 3:21. Soon He will sit upon the throne of His glory;" God the Father will "give Him the throne of His father David," and "His kingdom will never end." Luke 1:32, 33.

11

What Is the Sanctuary?

God had a problem. How could He save man, show mercy, and still be a just God? The answer is in the sanctuary service. "The wages of sin is death" and "all have sinned and come short of the glory of God." Without God's plan of salvation, as brought to view in the sanctuary service, our sins would have doomed us. The sanctuary service teaches us a part of the plan of salvation Satan does not want us to understand. Romans 3:23 and 6:23.

Christ's death on the cross is one part of the sanctuary service. In the sanctuary service Christ is both the lamb and the priest: the *lamb* that died and the *priest* who ministered the blood of the innocent lamb. Christ is both (a) the sacrifice and (b) our Priest. Others often teach us about Christ's sacrifice on the cross, but they seldom teach us of His work today as our High Priest. Both are essential to salvation. When your clothes get dirty, you take them to the laundry. Sin makes us "dirty." The sanctuary is God's laundry for sin.

First, we learn of the earthly sanctuary built by Moses. Second, we learn of the "true tabernacle." The Lord built the sanctuary of the new covenant. "The Lord built it, and not man." Hebrews 8:1, 2. " Unto two thousand and three hundred days; then shall the sanctuary be cleansed." In other words,

"After two thousand and three hundred days God will cleanse the sanctuary." Daniel 8:14. God would cleanse His sanctuary in 2300 prophetic days, or 2300 actual years. (*The year-day prophetic principle; see the Appendix.*)

Paul teaches us that the new-covenant sanctuary in heaven needed to be "purified"or cleansed. It is God who purifies His sanctuary. It is God who cleanses it.

"The law requires that nearly everything be cleansed with blood, and without the shedding of blood there is no forgiveness. It was necessary then, for the copies of the heavenly things to be purified with these sacrifices, but the heavenly things themselves with better sacrifices than these." Hebrews 9:22, 23.

What Is Happening in Heaven?

How can we understand what is happening in the sanctuary in heaven? We cannot see what is happening there. However, we can read about the sanctuary on earth from the biblical records. The sanctuary on earth was an "example and shadow of heavenly things." Hebrews 8:5, KJV. The sanctuary on earth had two separate rooms, representing the two parts, the two divisions, of the plan of salvation.

There were two divisions. One division was represented in what occurred daily in the earthly sanctuary. The second was represented in what occurred once a year. Day by day, the sinner transferred his sins from himself to an innocent sacrifice, by confessing his sins over the head of an innocent lamb, symbolic of Christ. He then killed the innocent lamb. The priest took some of the lamb's blood and sprinkled it in the first room of the sanctuary. This represented the symbolic transfer of the sinner's sins to the first room of the sanctuary. Leviticus 3 and 4.

The Sanctuary (Symbolically) Is God's Laundry

Just as we send dirty clothes to the laundry, we send our dirty sins to the sanctuary every time we confess our sins. We must send our dirty sins to the sanctuary each day. God eventually removes sin from the sanctuary. This is like removing dirty water from the laundry.

"He will make an atonement for the holy place, because of the uncleanness of the children of Israel, and because of their transgressions in all their sins: and so will he do for the tabernacle of meeting which remains among them in the midst of their uncleanness." He will "cleanse it, and consecrate it from the uncleanness of the children of Israel." Leviticus 16: 16, 19, NKJV.

Once a year, on the great Day of Atonement, two goats were chosen. One goat represented Christ, and the other represented Satan. "One lot for the Lord, and the other lot for the scapegoat." Leviticus 16: 8.

The priest killed the goat, representing Jesus, as a sin offering. He sprinkled the blood of this sin offering over the ark, the container for the Ten Commandments. The priest, representing Christ, carried all the sins that had accumulated in the sanctuary, out of the sanctuary. "He is to lay both hands on the head of the live goat and confess over it all . . . their sins and put them on the goat's head." Leviticus 16:21.

This put the sins on the goat, "and he shall send the goat away into the desert in the care of a man appointed for the task. The goat will carry on itself all their sins to a solitary place; and the man shall release it into the desert." Leviticus 16:21, 22. The goat carries the sins into the wilderness and wanders until he dies. These sins of God's people were then considered forever separated from them.

When we confess our sin to Jesus, we send our sin to Jesus, and Jesus sends it to the new-covenant sanctuary in heaven. Before Christ's death on the cross, the earthly sanctuary daily explained the plan of salvation in the death of the lamb. Every time they killed a lamb, they were saying, "I believe God will send His Son to die for me. I believe my sin is so great that there is no other way to find forgiveness. Sinless God will become a man, live a sinless life, and die the death I deserve. My faith in God's plan will permit God to give me the life He deserves. What a trade! He will take my punishment and give me His life!"

The law of gravity causes us to fall if we get off balance. We have discovered another law that allows us to defeat the law of gravity. We have discovered the law of aerodynamics. This law allows us to overcome the law of gravity and fly like the birds in airplanes. The law of sin is that sin kills. Sin would have killed everyone eternally unless God had a plan that would overcome the law that sin kills. "All have sinned" and "the wages of sin is death." We were all doomed. God's plan on how He could save us from death is found in His sanctuary. Romans 3:23, 6:23.

How Were Sinners Saved Before the Cross?

Were people saved before Christ died, as some teach, by keeping God's law? Has that changed and now we are saved by the death of Christ on the cross? No! The plan of salvation has always been the same. Salvation is now and always has been through the death of Christ. The sinner, before Christ died on the cross, was saved as a result of what Christ would do in the future. The sinner foresaw the death of Christ in each lamb that was killed. The innocent lamb died in the sinner's place. This represented the fact that Christ would come and die in the sinner's place. Before Christ died, God's children lived by the promise that He would come and die for them. After Christ died on the cross, we look back at what He did and find salvation in what He did. Now we live by the promise that He did come and die for us. In both cases, we are all saved by the same sacrifice, the sacrifice of Christ.

1. I am sinful and guilty and deserving of death. I have sinned. I have broken God's Ten Commandment law.

2. I confess my sin over the head of a lamb. This transfers my sin to the lamb. I no longer have that sin. Now the lamb has my sin. "The wages of sin is death," so the lamb must die. Day by day a substitute (innocent lamb) died in the sinner's place.

3. After killing the lamb, the sin is symbolically in the animal's blood. The Priest takes blood from the lamb. Now the Priest has my sin.

4. He enters the holy apartment of the sanctuary and sprinkles it before the veil (behind the veil are the Ten Commandments I have disobeyed). Where is my sin? I do not have the sin I confessed. It is now in the sanctuary.

5. Before Christ's death on the cross, this act would symbolically transfer my sins from me to the earthly sanctuary.

6. After Christ's death on the cross, when I confess my sins, they are in fact transferred to His great original sanctuary in heaven.

Day by day, through confession, I send my sin into the sanctuary. Confession of sin to Jesus does not cancel the sin. Confession transfers the sin from me to Christ, who transfers them to the heavenly sanctuary. God does not remove, cancel, or blot out sin until the day of atonement. In the earthly sanctuary the day of atonement came once a year. In the new-covenant sanctuary in heaven, this work began in 1844.

7. On the day of atonement, the high priest would take the blood of an offering, representing Christ's sacrifice, and sprinkle it over the mercy seat. The mercy seat was the top of the ark. Beneath the mercy seat, within the ark, were the Ten Commandments. He would, then, take the sins *from* the sanctuary.

8. The high priest would then confess them over the head of the live goat, representing Satan. The goat was led away. The goat wandered until he died, and the sins were then considered forever gone from God's children.

They did not kill the goat that represented Satan, as a sacrifice. It had nothing to do with the actual plan of salvation. God is just, and He will make Satan ultimately responsible for all the sin he has tempted people to commit. God will blot out Satan's life in the final destruction of sin and sinners.

What can we learn from the earthly sanctuary about what is happening in the heavenly sanctuary where Jesus now is? What can we learn from this example and shadow of heavenly things?

First Division: Sins to the Sanctuary
Second Division: Sins From the Sanctuary

For eighteen centuries God took all sins, confessed through Christ, from the sinner and transferred them to the first apartment (first division of Christ's work) of the sanctuary. Nevertheless, the sins of all people remained upon the record books. Before Christ's work for the salvation of men is completed, there is a work of atonement for the removal of sin from the sanctuary (second division of Christ's work). In 1844 our High Priest entered the most holy, to begin the last division of his solemn work—to cleanse the sanctuary.

1. When we confess our sins, Christ transfers them to the new-covenant sanctuary in heaven.

2. The actual cleansing of the heavenly sanctuary is the removal, or blotting out, of the sins that God has recorded in the books of heaven. Revelation 22:12.

The prophecy "unto 2300 days, then shall the sanctuary be cleansed" was preached worldwide before 1844. At that time in history, people thought the earth was the sanctuary. They thought that the cleansing of the sanctuary would be the cleansing of the world by fire at the second coming of Christ. Jesus, however, did not come to earth, cleansing it with fire, in 1844. Instead, He came to the second part of His sanctuary to begin the second part of His work. He began the work of judgment in the most holy apartment of the heavenly sanctuary, in preparation for His return to Planet Earth.

12

The Key

The subject of the sanctuary was the key that unlocked the mystery for those who expected Jesus to come in 1844. They learned that their compassionate High Priest had entered the most holy apartment of the heavenly sanctuary to cleanse it. He began the work of judgment. He began the work of blotting out the sins or the names of all who claim to follow Him. "The hour of God's judgment is come."

Jesus is now comparing our lives with His law, the Ten Commandments, and then, He will blot out either:

■ Our sins, or,

■ Our names.

The cleansing of the sanctuary in heaven and the judgment is the work of Christ now, in the most holy place of the sanctuary. The judgment is of those who claim to know Christ. In this judgment, God will blot out one of two things from the record books. He will blot out either the (a) sins, or the (b) names of all who have ever claimed to serve Christ.

Think about it for a moment. Have you ever been accused of a crime and had to go to court? The innocent that are accused and found innocent are greatly relieved. They go home with a clean record. The guilty, on the other hand, who are found guilty and sentenced to prison or death usually are sad they got caught and punished. Your case will soon be brought before the God of the universe. Your record will be investigated. It will be determined whether you have let Jesus pay for your sins or whether you have chosen, by neglect or outright rejection, to pay the penalty yourself, which is death.

God will either remove your name from the book of life or will remove your sins from the book of life. It is your choice. You may choose to ask Christ right now to forgive your sins. His promise is, "Though your sins are like scarlet, they shall be as white as snow." "If we confess our sins, He is faithful and just to forgive us our sins and to cleanse us from all unrighteousness." Isaiah 1:18; 1 John 1:9, KJV. Take this step now! It is called the new birth. Continue to follow Him day by day wherever He leads. Take up the cross of Christ, Christian soldier, and follow your Master. The way of the cross leads home.

Both of the Following Verses Refer to the Judgment

"Unto 2300 days then shall the sanctuary be cleansed."
Daniel 8:14, KJV.

"Fear God, and give glory to Him;
for the hour of his judgment is come."
Revelation 14:7, KJV.

In 1844, Jesus came to the Ancient of Days (not to earth) to begin the second division of His plan of salvation. He then began the work of judging His people and of cleansing the new-covenant sanctuary in heaven.

"I saw in the night visions. I looked and saw the Son of man. He came with the clouds of heaven, and came to the Ancient of Days." Daniel 7:13, KJV.

"The Lord, whom you seek, will suddenly come to His temple." Malachi 3:1, NKJV.

No one was looking for Christ to come to "His temple." They were looking for Him to come to Planet Earth. It was this coming that took place in 1844 and not His coming "in flaming fire taking vengeance on them that know not God, and that obey not the gospel." Christ will return to Planet Earth *after* the judgment. The judgment must occur *first*.

Prepare Now!

"Who can endure the day of His coming? Who can stand when He appears?" Malachi 3:2.

People will be living on the earth when Christ finishes His work as our priest in the sanctuary above. They will stand in the sight of a holy God without a priest. Their robes (characters) must be spotless.

Christ's blood must cleanse their characters from sin. Through the grace of God and their own diligent effort, they must be conquerors in the battle with evil. God will remove the sins of confessing believers from the sanctuary. They will overcome sin. The followers of Christ will then be ready for His appearing.

These Four Comings of Christ All Describe the Same Event

1. The *coming* of Christ as our High Priest to the most holy place, for the cleansing of the sanctuary. Daniel 8:14.

2. The *coming* of Christ to the Ancient of Days. Daniel 7:13.

3. The *coming* of the Lord to His temple. Malachi 3:1.

4. The *coming* of the bridegroom to the marriage in the parable of the ten virgins. Matthew 25:1-13.

All four of these refer to the work Christ is doing today:
His work of judgment!

In the summer and autumn of 1844, God used people to announce, "Behold, the Bridegroom comes; they that were ready went in with him to the marriage. And the door was shut." The coming of the bridegroom, here brought to view, takes place before the marriage. The marriage represents Christ's reception of His kingdom, "the bride, the Lamb's wife." "Come here, I will show you the bride, the Lamb's wife." "He carried me away in the spirit, and showed me that great city, the holy Jerusalem, descending out of heaven from God." Matthew 25:10; Revelation 21:9, 10, NKJV.

The "wedding" is the symbol God uses to describe the change in Christ's work from High Priest to King. It is the coronation of Christ as "King of kings and Lord of lords" and of His rule of, and from, the capital city of the universe, New Jerusalem. Jesus is the Groom. New Jerusalem is the bride, and the virgin guests at the marriage supper represent the church.

In Revelation, the people were guests at the marriage supper. Revelation 19:9. If guests, they cannot also be the bride. By faith we are to go with Him to the marriage. Nevertheless, physically, we are to "wait for" Him to "return from the wedding."

"Look. The Bridegroom comes." The Bridegroom came, not to the earth, as the people expected, but to the Ancient of Days in heaven, to the marriage, the reception of His kingdom. "They that were ready went in with Him to the marriage: and the door was shut." Now His people are to "wait for their Lord, when He will return from the wedding." Luke 12:36, KJV.

What is the difference between the wise and foolish virgins?

The wise virgins learn and accept the second part of the plan of salvation, the judgment—and the foolish do not!

God's Sanctuary, the Shelter in the Time of Storm

Wise virgins (wise Christians) are those who enter the second apartment of God's sanctuary, "by faith," to the marriage. "In the time of trouble He will hide me in His tabernacle [sanctuary]." Psalm 27:5, NKJV. Foolish Christians (foolish virgins), without the Holy Spirit, the oil, do not follow Jesus into the most holy apartment. They do not understand His work in the sanctuary.

Those that had oil, symbolic of the Holy Spirit, in their containers with their lamps went into the marriage. God pours out the true Holy Spirit only on those who follow Christ into the most holy apartment of the heavenly sanctuary.

Before the wedding the king, Christ, comes in to see the guests. He looks to see if all are wearing the wedding clothes. Those who are not wearing the character of Christ, the spotless robe of His character washed and made white in the blood of the Lamb, are thrown out. The door of mercy is shut. Matthew 22:11; Revelation 7:14.

Only those who understand both divisions of the plan of salvation and enter (by faith) into the second division of His work in the most holy apartment will be safe. They will be safely shut in, and the world will be shut out. "They that were ready went in with him to the marriage: and the door was shut."

The door used previously to reach God was no longer open. To those would-be guests, the door was shut. Now we should gather about the sanctuary and in the most solemn manner humble our souls before God. We must know what duties God requires of us.

In Noah's day the saved were safely shut into the ark. The world was shut out. Noah and his family were safe inside the ark. Today we can only find safety by following Christ, by faith, in His closing work in the second apartment of the heavenly sanctuary. We must, by faith, be shut into the most holy place of the heavenly sanctuary, as Noah was shut into the ark.

A storm is coming, relentless in its fury. Those who follow Christ, by faith, into the most holy place will be close to Jesus. They are close to Jesus and His throne—the ark of the covenant containing the Ten Commandments. They go through the coming storm, the coming crisis, successfully because, by faith, they are close to Jesus in the most holy place. They have found "the shelter in the time of storm."

Are there any lessons we should learn by comparing the most holy apartment of the heavenly sanctuary with Noah's Ark? The boat known as Noah's Ark was a place of safety in the time of storm. A storm is coming, relentless in its fury. We need a place of safety. The most holy apartment of the heavenly sanctuary is just such a place of safety. It is where God is and from whence His mighty angels come. We enter the most holy part of the heavenly sanctuary by faith. Jesus shuts us in and the world out. We see Jesus and God the Father in the work of comparing our lives with His holy law, and we ask Him to write His law in our hearts. His promise is, "Ask and it will be given you." Matthew 7:7.

God sent a warning message from heaven to the world in Noah's day, and their salvation depended on the manner in which they treated that message. They rejected the warning, and they died in the Flood. Jesus warned the religious people of His day: "Your house is left to you desolate." Matthew 23:38. They "received not the love of the truth that they might be saved." "For this cause God will send them strong delusion, that they should believe a lie: that they all might be damned who believed not the truth, but had pleasure in unrighteousness." 2 Thessalonians 2:10-12, KJV.

Three Biblical Warnings

1. Noah warned the people of his day of a coming flood. Everybody on earth died except for the eight who obeyed God's warning and got aboard the ark. Popularity did not win. Obeying and loving God did. It pays to listen when God gives a warning

2. Jesus warned the people of His day of the imminent destruction of Jerusalem. Jerusalem was destroyed in A.D 70. "In the siege and the slaughter that followed, more than a million of the people perished; the survivors were carried away as captives, sold as slaves, dragged to Rome to grace the conqueror's triumph, thrown to wild beasts in the amphitheaters, or scattered as homeless wanderers throughout the earth." Christians obeyed Christ's warning and fled Jerusalem when they saw the signs He foretold, and not one Christian died in this great battle. It pays to listen when God gives His warning. See Matthew 24:15, 16 and *The Great Controversy,* pages 17 to 38.

Millions Will Soon Die in the Coming Crisis

3. Today we must warn people everywhere of the soon coming plagues of Revelation chapter 16 and Daniel 12:1, so they can find safety. Our only safety is in listening to Jesus Christ and following His instruction.

■ It paid to listen to God's warning in Noah's day. Those who listened and obeyed God, Noah's family, survived the Flood. The majority did not listen. Only eight people listened to and obeyed God's warning. Only eight people got on the ark. If you wanted to be popular in Noah's day, you made jokes about "that silly old lunatic Noah." Noah and his family dared to believe God's warning, even though it was the unpopular thing to do.

■ It paid to listen to, remember, and obey Christ's warning concerning the destruction of Jerusalem. Roman armies destroyed Jerusalem about 39 years after Christ was crucified. Christians remembered Christ's warning to them and though over one million people lost their lives in the destruction of Jerusalem, not one Christian was killed. Matthew 24:15-20.

■ It will pay to listen to God's warning today. Do you think spiritual conditions are better in our world today than they were in Noah's day? There was so much sin that God washed the world clean in Noah's day. The popular majority did not believe and were all killed in the Flood. Jesus says, "As it was in the days of Noah, so it will be at the coming of the Son of Man. For in the days before the flood, people were eating and drinking, marrying and giving in marriage, up to the day Noah entered the ark; and they knew nothing about what would happen until the flood came and took them all away. That is how it will be at the coming of the Son of Man." Matthew 24:37-39. God will use the seven last plagues to cleanse the earth of sin. Don't wait. Get right with God today!

13

The Wise Choice

T hen will the kingdom of heaven be like ten virgins who took their lamps and went out to meet the bridegroom. Five of them were foolish and five were wise.The foolish ones took their lamps but did not take any oil with them. The wise, however, took oil in jars along with their lamps. The bridegroom was a long time in coming and they all became drowsy and fell asleep.

"At midnight the cry rang out: Here's the bridegroom! Come out to meet him! Then all the virgins woke up and trimmed their lamps. The foolish ones said to the wise, Give us some of your oil; our lamps are going out. No, they replied, there may not be enough for both us and you. Instead go to those who sell oil and buy some for yourselves. But while they were on their way to buy the oil, the bridegroom arrived. The virgins who were ready went in with him to the wedding banquet. And the door was shut." Matthew 25:1-10.

In 1844 Jesus went into the marriage, the reception of His kingdom. Only the wise virgins, wise Christians (those with the oil, the Holy Spirit) enter by faith with Him. They are shut in. And all who do not enter by faith are considered foolish Christians.

The wise are, by faith, shut into the most holy place. The foolish Christian "virgins" are still in the first apartment, the first division of Christ's plan of salvation.

Just as a wise Boy Scout would not go hiking at night without batteries for his flashlight, a wise Christian will choose the power of the Holy Spirit. The Holy Spirit is the Christian's power source, just as batteries are the flashlight's power source or oil is the power source for the oil lamps of the parable.

The true power of the Holy Spirit is to be found when we enter by faith into the work Christ is doing right now. He has begun the second part of His plan for the salvation of His children. God has plenty of "oil," plenty of "batteries," plenty of power. If we want that power, we must go to God, by faith, in the most holy apartment of the heavenly sanctuary and ask for it. "Ask, and it will be given you." Matthew 7:7.

To live successfully through the coming crisis, we will need the power of God's Holy Spirit. Prayer is the key in the hand of faith that unlocks heaven's storehouse. Let us enter the most holy apartment of the heavenly sanctuary by faith and get powered up. Let us enter the most holy apartment of the heavenly sanctuary by faith and get the true infilling of the Holy Spirit.

Settle for no cheap imitation! Get the real thing! In these final scenes of earth's history, the real infilling of the Holy Spirit comes only to those who follow Jesus, by faith, understanding His closing work. The infilling of the Holy Spirit is necessary to carry God's warning message to the world. The infilling of the Holy Spirit also gives us the power to obey God's warning message, the power to keep His commandments. "Here are they that keep the commandments of God, and the faith of Jesus." Revelation 14:12, KJV. God says that in the last days there will be a choice to make. One choice is a wise choice, and one choice is a foolish choice. Make the right choice, and choose wisdom. Choose the path of obedience.

14

Eternal Values

Read a copy of God's great original,
the Ten Commandments,
in Exodus, chapter 20.

J ohn writes in the book of Revelation that he saw the ark of God, containing the Ten Commandments. In vision, he saw the Ten Commandments in heaven fifty years after the death and resurrection of Jesus Christ.

"The temple of God was opened in heaven," and John, the writer of Revelation, looked in and saw inside God's temple. He saw "the ark of the covenant" (Revelation 11:19) in the Most Holy Place. The ark in the tabernacle on earth contained the two tables of stone, upon which God wrote the words of His law. The ark was merely a container for the tables of the law.

God, With His Own Hand, Wrote His Law on Two Tables of Stone

The Bible is made up of sixty-six different books written by forty different men filled with God's Holy Spirit. According to the Bible, the only words God actually wrote with His own hand are the Ten Commandments! He wrote them down twice. The original is in heaven, and the copy was given to Moses and all mankind at Mount Sinai. God considered His Ten Commandment law so important that He wrote His commandments in stone, to show that they never change.

Of those Ten Commandments God wrote with His own hand, one begins with the word *remember.* It was God who wrote, "Remember the sabbath day to keep it holy. Six days will you labor, and do all your work: but the seventh day is the sabbath of the Lord your God." God Himself says, "I the Lord do not change." Malachi 3:6. God knew people would change, so He took the trouble to write with His own hand on one of the two tables of stone the words, "Remember the sabbath day to keep it holy." Read what God wrote in Exodus, chapter 20.

God wrote His law on two tables of stone kept in the ark within the sanctuary on earth. God, also with His own hand, wrote His great original law that is kept in the ark in God's sanctuary in heaven.

Within the holy of holies, in the sanctuary in heaven, God sacredly elevates His holy law. The law of God in the sanctuary in heaven is the great original.

The Ten Commandments written by God Himself on the two tables of stone and which Moses recorded in the book of Exodus was an exact copy. "Until heaven and earth disappear, not the smallest letter, not the least stroke of a pen, will by any means disappear from the Law." "Forever, O Lord, Your word is settled in heaven." "All His commandments are sure. They stand fast forever and ever." Exodus 20, Matthew 5:18, Psalms 119:89; 111:7, 8, KJV.

God Knew People Would Forget! So He Said, "Remember."

"Remember the Sabbath day, to keep it holy. Six days you shall labor and do all your work, but the seventh day is the Sabbath of the LORD your God. In it you shall do no work: you, nor your son, nor your daughter, nor your male servant, nor your female servant, nor your cattle, nor your stranger who is within your gates. For in six days the LORD made the heavens and the earth, the sea, and all that is in them, and rested the seventh day. Therefore the LORD blessed the Sabbath day and hallowed it." Exodus 20:8-11, NKJV.

Look up the word *Sabbath* in the dictionary. What do you find? "The seventh day of the week." In 105 languages around the world, the word for Saturday is "Sabbath." Take Spanish, for example. In Spanish, the word for Saturday is *El Sabado*—the Sabbath.

Notice! The fourth commandment says the seventh day is the Sabbath of the Lord, not the first day. It is not the Sabbath of the Jews, but it is the Sabbath of the Lord. Look at your calender and find the seventh day. It is Saturday, not Sunday. Saturday, the seventh day of the week, is "the Sabbath of the Lord." It is *the* Sabbath, not *a* Sabbath. It is the Sabbath of the Lord, not of the Jews, Seventh-Day Baptists, or Seventh-day Adventists.

Many people, when confronted with these truths, have become convicted that they have ignorantly broken God's law by disregarding the Creator's rest day. They see themselves disobedient of God's law, sorrow fills their hearts, and they choose loyalty to God by keeping His Sabbath holy.

The earthly sanctuary is a pattern of the heavenly sanctuary. The law in the ark, the gold-plated chest, in the earthly sanctuary is an exact copy of the one in God's great original ark in heaven. We then know that the fourth commandment is important to obey as well as all the others. Man may try to change God's law on earth, but he will never succeed, because the great original is in the ark of the covenant in heaven. All mankind will be judged by that great original law of God, written by God Himself.

Will You Follow Jesus?

"What He opens, no one can shut, and what he shuts no one can open." "See, I have placed before you an open door that no one can shut." Revelation 3:7, 8. The open door is the door into the most holy apartment of the heavenly sanctuary. In 1844 Jesus shut the door to the first apartment of the sanctuary and opened the door to the second apartment, the second division of His work in salvation. He wants us to follow him there by faith.

15

Worship

A Preparation for the Lord's Second Coming

Read God's Ten Commandment law in the second book of your Bible, Exodus, chapter 20. The commandments are also quoted in the Appendix. The Ten Commandments will judge us. Nothing will be secret. God will even judge our secrets by the Ten Commandments. God says, "The hour of his judgment is come." Revelation 14:7, KJV. The message prepares God's children to stand in the judgment. The message commands them to "fear God, and give glory to Him, and worship Him that made heaven, and earth, and the sea, and the fountains of waters." "Here are they that keep the commandments of God, and the faith of Jesus." Revelation 14:12, KJV.

To be prepared for the judgment, it is necessary that men should keep the law of God. "As many as have sinned in the law will be judged by the law, . . . in the day when God will judge the secrets of men by Jesus Christ." "The doers of the law will be justified." Romans 2:12-16, KJV. "Without faith it is impossible to please Him." And, "whatever is not of faith is sin." Hebrews 11:6, KJV; Romans 14:23, KJV.

We are to "fear God, and give glory to Him." "Fear God, and keep *his* commandments: for this is the whole duty of man." Ecclesiastes 12:13, KJV. "This is the love of God, that we keep His commandments." "One who turns away his ear from hearing the law, even his prayer is an abomination." 1 John 5:3, KJV; Proverbs 28:9, NKJV.

Revelation 14 reveals people that, as the result of the threefold message, are keeping the commandments of God. "The seventh day is the Sabbath of the Lord your God: . . for in six days the Lord made heaven and earth, the sea, and all that in them is, and rested the seventh day: therefore the Lord blessed the Sabbath day, and hallowed it [made it holy]." "Keep my Sabbaths holy, that they may be a sign between us. Then you will know that I am the Lord your God." "It is a sign between Me and the children of Israel forever; for in six days the Lord made heaven and earth, and on the seventh day He rested, and was refreshed." Exodus 20:10, 11, NKJV; Ezekiel 20:20; Exodus 31:17, NKJV.

The Sabbath will always be God's sign, His seal, that sets His worshipers apart from those who worship the "beast." It reminds us constantly of the true reason we worship God. He is the Creator, and we are His creatures.

Whom Will You Worship?

Who do you worship? Most people believe in God. When we talk about "worshiping the beast," many don't realize that those who will end up worshiping the beast won't even be aware of it. They will think they are worshiping God. God's Word says that before Christ comes again, everyone, everywhere, will either worship the beast or the Creator. The fact that the Bible uses the word *worship* lets us know that God is talking about religious deception. The word *beast* is a biblical word that means "a power" and has been used to represent various nations and powers.

The word *beast* sounds like something big and ugly. Anyone who hears about the beast will be prepared to avoid anything in the future that is big and ugly. The beast is not atheism. It is not the outside forces of communism and atheism that we have to fear, so much as it is deception within the church. It was not atheism that went after Christ to put Him on the cross. It was church leaders who laid the plans to capture Christ and persuade Pilate to crucify Him.

The beast is not atheism. It is not a communist or a Moslem power. Those who "worship the beast" will be supposedly worshiping God and Christ. There has always been a right way to worship God the Father and Christ and a wrong way to worship them. That is pointed out in the parable of the ten virgins of Matthew 25. They were all "virgins" (Christians), but five were wise, and five were foolish. They all had lamps, representing the

Bible, but five were saved, and five were lost. Those who look for a Moslem beast will be deceived. Those who look for a communist beast will be deceived. Those who look for an atheist beast will be deceived.

If the beast of Revelation 13:1-10 were ugly, it would not be a deception. We usually avoid the ugly, mean-looking dogs with sharp teeth that growl at us. The strange thing is that worshiping the beast will be the most popular form of Christianity and worship before Jesus Christ returns. The Bible tells us that most people will not even realize that they are worshiping the beast—a religious power. Another strange thing is that most people have absolutely no idea what or who the real beast is.

God's Word says that you will either "worship Him who made the heavens, the earth, the sea and the springs of water," or you will "worship the beast and his image." Those who "worship the beast and his image" will think they are doing right. They do not realize that in God's eyes, they "are wretched, pitiful, poor, blind and naked." They will think they are honoring God and will not be aware that they are in need of repentance. Revelation 14:7; 14:11; 3:17.

The three characteristics of those who worship the Creator are that:

1. They "obey God's commandments."

2. They "remain faithful to Jesus."

3. They have "the seal of the living God" on their foreheads.

In other words, they have let God write His law in their minds. Check the following Bible verses in your very own Bible: Revelation 14:9, 10, 12; 7:2, 3; Hebrews 8:10.

Those who "worship the beast and his image, and receive his mark in his forehead, or in his hand, the same will drink of the wine of the wrath of God." The mark in the hand relates to actions, and the mark in the forehead relates to thoughts. Revelation 14:7, 9, 10, KJV.

Since the seal of God has to do with God writing His law in our minds, the mark of the beast has to do with the acceptance of rebellion to God's law in the minds and in the actions of those who will ultimately be lost. The mark and the seal can be seen by God and angels, but it is not a physical mark or a physical seal that can be seen by men. Who is the beast? And what is its mark? We'll look at the "mark of the beast" later. Let's find out who the beast is first.

Both the books of Daniel and Revelation use beasts or different type of animals to describe various world powers. We do that with the American eagle, the Russian bear, the Democratic donkey, and the Republican elephant. God showed to Daniel in visions which future nations would rule the world from Daniel's time to the second coming of Christ.

God showed Daniel four animals—beasts—that represented four world empires. God told Daniel: "The four great beasts are four kingdoms." Daniel 7:17. God foretold that Babylon, represented by a lion, would be conquered by Medo-Persia, represented by a bear, and that Greece, represented by a leopard, would be the next world ruler. This would be followed by a dragon-like animal representing pagan Rome, which appeared as a beast with ten horns. In Daniel 7:24, God says, "The ten horns are ten kings," or kingdoms.

The ten horns represented the breakup of the empire into ten divisions. The Roman Empire was invaded in A.D. 376 by Visigoths, followed later by other tribes that make up the European nations of today. There were, in random order:

1. Visigoths — Spain

2. Burgundians — Switzerland

3. Lombards — Italy

4. Anglo-Saxons — England

5. Franks — France

6. Alemanni — Germany

7. Suevi — Portugal

8. Heruli — destroyed

9. Vandals — destroyed

10. Ostrogoths — destroyed

The Bible says that the papacy would overcome three of those powers. "There before me was another horn, a little one which came up among them; and three of the first horns were uprooted before it. The ten horns are ten kings who will come from this kingdom. After them another king will arise, different from the earlier ones; he will subdue three kings." Daniel 7:8, 24. The Catholic emperors Zeno and Justinian eliminated the Heruli in 493, the Vandals in 534, and broke the power of the Ostrogoths in 538.

John continues Daniel's prophecy with a vision of pagan Rome, represented by the dragon. "A great and wondrous sign appeared in heaven: a woman clothed with the sun, with the moon under her feet and a crown of twelve stars on her head, She was pregnant and cried out in pain as she was about to give birth . . . an enormous red dragon . . . stood in front of the woman who was about to give birth, so that he might devour her child the moment it was born. She gave birth to a son, a male child who will rule all the nations with an iron scepter." Revelation 12:1-5.

Pagan Rome

The dragon of Revelation 12 sought to kill Christ at His birth. The dragon is Satan, and the nation Satan used to seek to kill Christ at His birth, Rome, pagan Rome. The dragon primarily represents Satan; it is in a secondary sense a symbol of pagan Rome. Revelation 12:9.

Papal Rome

"I saw a beast coming out of the sea. He had ten horns." He "resembled a leopard but had feet like those of a bear and a mouth like that of a lion." Revelation 13:12. In Daniel 7 the three empires that existed before Rome were pictured as a lion, a bear, and a leopard. So the power that followed pagan Rome, the papacy, was to have similar characteristics to all the empires that came before it. In Revelation 17:15, an angel explained that waters represent "peoples, multitudes, nations, and languages." Let's see how the Bible identifies the beast.

The Beast of Revelation 13:1-10

As we have already seen, the word *beast* in the Bible merely means "powers or nations or kingdoms." It is not a good word or a bad word. The goodness or badness is dependent on the character of the beast—the power. God has many of His own children who believe in the system spoken of in Revelation 13:1-10. Many of them will be saved and spend eternity in heaven and the earth made new.

No man has the right to judge another person regarding sincerity, motives, attitudes, or choice of belief. Even when we believe that another person's beliefs are incorrect, we are to treat that person with love. Forcing another to believe the same way we believe is the spirit of anitichrist. God wants us to treat each other with love, whatever our skin color or faith. Once we find out who the beast is, God expects us to treat those who are deceived by the beast with the same love we treat others. We are even called upon to pray for those who mistreat us. There is no hatred or unkindness intended or implied in identifying the beast power. God warns us against receiving "the mark of the beast." It is necessary, then, to seek an understanding of who this beast power is.

The Bible says:

1. God predicted that the beast of Revelation 13:1-10 would arise from a heavily populated part of the earth.

The beast power is seen "coming out of the sea." Since waters represent "peoples, multitudes, nations, and languages," this leopard beast power rises in a heavily populated area. Europe was heavily populated, in contrast to areas like North America in the early centuries. Papal Rome rose in Europe. Revelation 13:1; 17:15.

2. God predicted that the beast would be the power that would dominate the earth immediately after pagan Rome dominated the earth.

"The fourth beast," said the angel, "is a fourth kingdom that will appear on the earth." The fourth empire was pagan Rome. Whatever power followed would be known as the "new" beast—the beast, or power, spoken of in Revelation 13:1-10. Papal Rome was the dominant power after pagan Rome. Only the papacy fulfills this prophecy.

3. God predicted that the beast of Revelation 13:1-10 would receive power from pagan Rome and would be headquartered in the city of Rome.

The "fourth beast"—"the dragon," or pagan Rome—was to give "his power, and his seat, and great authority" to the beast of Revelation 13:1-10. "The dragon gave the beast his power and his throne and great authority." Revelation 13:1, 2. Emperor Constantine moved the "seat" of his empire in A.D. 330 and founded Constantinople (now Istanbul) as the empire's new capital. This left a power vacuum that the bishop or "pope" of Rome filled. The old "seat" of his empire, Rome, became the "seat" of papal Rome. Other emperors continued to give the Bishop of Rome more power.

God, in Daniel 7, predicted the world empires beginning with Babylon, Medo-Persia, Greece, and pagan Rome. "The fourth beast," pagan Rome, gave the next "beast" his "power and his seat and great authority." Emperor Constantine moved the headquarters of his empire to Constantinople (now Istanbul). Emperor Constantine gave the Bishop of Rome "his seat," or "his throne," just as Bible prophecy predicted. The seat or throne of the Roman empire was Rome. Only the papacy fulfills this prophecy.

4. God predicted that the beast, known in Daniel as "another horn," would overthrow three of the ten divisions of Europe at the end of the rule of pagan Rome.

"Another horn, a little one which came up among them; and three of the first horns were uprooted before it." "The ten horns are ten kings who will come from this kingdom. After them another king will arise, different from the earlier ones; he will subdue three kings. This horn had eyes like the eyes of a man and a mouth that spoke boastfully." Daniel 7:8, 24. Thus was predicted the papal overthrow of the Heruli, the Vandals, and the Ostrogoths.

The Catholic emperors Zeno and Justinian eliminated the Heruli in A.D. 493, the Vandals in 534—and broke the power of the Ostrogoths in 538, thus giving the papacy the ability to rule unopposed. The papacy fulfilled this prophecy.

5. God predicted that the beast of Revelation 13:1-10 would speak "proud words and blasphemies."

"And the beast was given a mouth to utter proud words and blasphemies. . . . he opened his mouth to blaspheme God." Revelation 13:5, 6.

What is the Bible definition of blasphemy? In the tenth chapter of the book of John, Jesus says, "I and the Father are one." John 10:30. Notice that the Jews picked up stones to stone Him. But Jesus said to them, "I have shown you many great miracles from the Father. For which of these do you stone me?" "We are not stoning you for any of these," replied the Jews, "but for blasphemy, because you, a mere man, claim to be God." John 10:31-33.

Christ would in fact have been guilty of blasphemy if He had been only a mere man. But He was, and is, God in human flesh. Any man who claims to be God is guilty of blasphemy. I would be guilty of blasphemy if I told you that I am God. I am but a mere man. Yet there are numerous instances in which the papacy claims to be God. Look for references in the Appendix.

Another time when Jesus was accused of blasphemy was when He spoke to the paralyzed man just before healing him physically. Read it in Mark 2:3-7. Jesus said to the paralyzed man, "Son, your sins are forgiven." Some were thinking, "Why does this fellow talk like that? He's blaspheming! Who can forgive sins but God alone?" They were right that only God can forgive sins. For man to claim to forgive sins would be blasphemy. It would be an attempt to exalt man's power above God's power. Why was it not blasphemy for Jesus to forgive that man's sins? Because Jesus is God in human flesh.

So any man who claims to forgive sins is guilty of blasphemy. I cannot forgive sins—only God can. The papacy claims both of these powers. They claim the power to forgive sin and that they are God on earth. See the Appendix. When they do either of these, they are guilty of blasphemy. The papacy fulfills this prophecy.

6. God predicted that the beast of Revelation 13:1-10 would be a persecuting power.

"He was given power to make war against the saints and to conquer them. And he was given authority over every tribe, people, language, and nation." Revelation 13:6, 7.

Over more than 1,000 years of papal supremacy, millions lost their lives for believing differently than the papacy. Over 50 million were killed by the papal persecutions. They were found guilty of reading the Bible or of worshiping differently than the established church. Jesus never put any person in a torture chamber for not worshiping Him, but the papacy ordered it. The papacy made "war against the saints." Daniel 7:21, NKJV. See *Fox's Book of Martyrs* or *The Great Controversy* for a historical account of this bloody history. The papacy fulfilled this prophecy.

Anyone who claims to represent the Master must live like the Master and be willing to die for another. Jesus set the example. The papacy has never uplifted the cross of self denial but has rather chosen the crown. Jesus teaches that the cross must come before the crown.

7. God predicted that the beast of Revelation 13:1-10 would have authority over "every tribe, people, language and nation." Revelation 13:6, 7, NKJV.

At the moment, it is reported that the papacy has over one billion people on Planet Earth, all around the world, who claim to follow the papacy. The papacy fulfills this prophecy.

8. God predicted that the beast of Revelation 13:1-10 would be taken prisoner after ruling exactly 1,260 years.

"Power was given unto him to continue forty and two months." "I saw one of his heads as it was wounded to death." "He who leads into captivity will go into captivity: he who kills with the sword must be killed with the sword." Revelation 13:10, NKJV.

$$30 \times 42 = 1260$$
42 Months x 30 Days in a Month =
1260 Prophetic Days
or 1260 Literal Years

The "time and times and the dividing of time," the forty-two months, and the 1260 days, all refer to a period of 1260 years of papal rule. The 1260 years are understood using the year-day prophetic time principle. See the Appendix, Daniel 7:25, and Revelation 13:3, 5 and 12:6.

The papacy became supreme in A.D. 538. That supremacy ended in 1798, exactly 1260 years later, just as prophecy predicted. Then, Napoleon's army, under General Alexander Berthier, took the pope captive. On February 15, 1798, he arrested Pope Pius VI in the Sistine Chapel and proclaimed that the rule and authority of the popes had ended. The papacy power received its captivity or "deadly wound," just as the Bible predicted. "He who leads into captivity will go into captivity." Revelation 13:6. The papacy fulfilled this prophecy.

9. God predicted that the beast that went into captivity and received what seemed to be "a deadly wound" or fatal wound would recover and that the whole world would "worship the beast."

"One of the heads of the beast seemed to have had a fatal wound, but the fatal wound had been healed. The whole world was astonished and followed the beast. . . . and they worshiped the beast." Revelation 13:3, 4.

Here we have God predicting that the beast would be a church-state combination. The word *worship* always denotes religion or "church," and the word *beast* in Bible prophecy always denotes a kingdom or power. God predicted that the beast of Revelation 13:1-10 would be different than the other beasts or world powers. It would be a church-state combination. God predicted that this end-time world power would receive a "deadly wound," that it would go into captivity after ruling unopposed for 1260 years (A.D. 538 to 1798), and that it would then recover and take center stage again. Look around the world today. The papacy joined hands with the other great end-time power—the other power of Revelation 13—and disrupted communism. "The whole world was astonished and followed the beast." Revelation 13:3.

10. God predicted that this power would try "to change the times and the laws." Daniel 7:25.

Compare the Catechism's ten commandments with the Bible's Ten Commandments. The Catechism changes two of God's biblical commandments. First of all, the Catechism has removed one of them. The second commandment that forbids idolatry and bowing down to images or worshiping them was removed. The second biblical commandment reads: "You shall not make for yourself an idol in the form of anything in heaven above or on the earth beneath or in the waters below. You shall not bow down to them or worship them." Exodus 20:4. That leaves only nine commandments in the Catechism. To cover up this fact, the tenth commandment was divided into two parts, making one part the ninth commandment and the other part the tenth commandment.

God said, "Remember the Sabbath day by keeping it holy. Six days you shall labor and do all your work, but the seventh day is the Sabbath to the Lord your God. On it you shall not do any work, neither you, nor your son or daughter, nor your manservant or maidservant, not your animals, nor the alien within your gates. For in six days the Lord made the heavens and the earth, the sea, and all that is in them, but he rested on the seventh day. Therefore the Lord blessed the Sabbath day and made it holy." Exodus 20:8-12.

The papacy changed the only commandment that deals with time—the Sabbath commandment. "He will speak against the Most High and oppress his saints and try to change the set times and the laws." Daniel 7:25.

In the *Catholic Catechism of Christian Religion*, in answer to a question as to the day to be observed in obedience to the fourth commandment, this is what is written: "During the old law Saturday was the day sanctified; but the church, instructed by Jesus Christ, and directed by the Spirit of God, has substituted Sunday for Saturday; so now we sanctify the first, not the seventh day." In *An Abridgment of the Christian Doctrine,* page 58, papal writers say: "The very act of changing the Sabbath into Sunday, which Protestants allow of; . . . because by keeping Sunday, they acknowledge the church's power to ordain feasts, and to command them under sin." God knew this would happen, which is why He began the Sabbath commandment with the word *remember.* The papacy fulfills this prophecy.

The Bible clearly identifies the "beast" power of Revelation 13:1-10 and the "horn" power of Daniel 7 as the very same power—the papacy. God loves you, reader, and if you have been deceived by the beast of Revelation 13:1-10, take courage. God is guiding and letting you learn these great truths so that you can make the very best choices and be safe through the coming crisis!

Through the centuries, various Roman Catholic spokesmen have felt that the pope—either the current one or a future one, or the papacy as a whole (the entire line of popes)—was the antichrist. For example, during a time of deep spiritual laxness in Rome, Arnulf, the bishop of Orleans, deplored the Roman popes as "monsters of guilt" and declared in a council called by the king of France in 991 that the pontiff, clad in purple and gold, was "Antichrist, sitting in the temple of God, and showing himself as God"— a reference to 2 Thessalonians 2:4.

Eberhard II, archbishop of Salzburg (1200-1246) stated approvingly at a synod of bishops held at Regensburg in 1240 (some say 1241) that the people of his day were "accustomed" to calling the pope antichrist.

When the Western church was divided for about forty years between two rival popes, one in Rome and the other in Avignon, France, each pope called the other pope antichrist—and John Wycliffe is reputed to have regarded them as both being right: "two halves of Antichrist, making up the perfect Man of Sin between them."

Martin Luther, as an Augustinian monk in the University of Wittenberg, came reluctantly to believe that "the papacy is in truth. . . . very Antichrist, though he was willing to exclude certain individual popes." *God Cares,* vol. 1, p. 123. Also see the Appendix.

16

The United States of America in Revelation

"I beheld another beast coming up out of the earth; and he had two horns like a lamb, but he spoke like a dragon." Revelation 13:11.

Daniel records beasts or "kingdoms" arising from "the great sea." Seas, in prophecy, represent "peoples, and multitudes, and nations, and tongues." So "coming up out of the earth" would suggest a country coming up out of a comparatively unoccupied territory. Daniel 7:2; Revelation 17:15.

The animal with two horns symbolizes the United States, innocent like a lamb. Identifying marks are that this nation would rise to power in a comparatively unoccupied territory around A.D. 1798 at the end of the 1260-year prophecy. What nation of the New World was in 1798 rising into power? The United States of America was seen, "coming up out of the earth"—the nation must rise in territory that had previously been largely unoccupied.

"He had two horns like a lamb." He "spoke as a dragon. He exercised all the authority of the first beast on his behalf, and made the earth and its

135

inhabitants worship the first beast, whose fatal wound had been healed. He ordered them to set up an image in honor of the beast who was wounded by the sword and yet lived."Revelation 13:11-14. This pictures what we are seeing today. The papacy received its deadly wound in 1798 after ruling 1260 years. In 1798 the papacy was dissolved by the French General Berthier, under Napoleon. Its deadly wound is now healed.

He spoke "as a dragon," having "all the power of the first beast." He "causes the earth and them that live on the earth to worship the first beast." "He says to them that dwell on the earth that they should make an image to the beast." As of the writing of this book, this part of the prophecy is yet to be fulfilled completely. Nations "speak" through their legal systems— through the making of laws.

The United States of America has been known as the home of the brave and the land of the free. The United States of America has been known as a country offering both religious freedom and civil freedom. The time will come when the United States will speak like a dragon, forcing everyone to either honor Sunday, the commandment of the papacy, or face a variety of punishments including prison, fines, and/or death. This seems impossible today, but it is not only possible—it will happen!

17

The Image of the Beast

W hat is the "image of the beast?" The two-horned beast, the United States of America, makes an image to the beast. Whenever the church has obtained secular power, she has used it to punish differences of opinion from her doctrines. The apostasy of the church led the early church to seek the aid of the civil government. The apostle Paul said there would "come a falling away, . . . and that man of sin be revealed." 2 Thessalonians 2:3. So apostasy in the church is what Paul predicted would occur. Timothy wrote that they would have "a form of godliness, but deny God's power." 2 Thessalonians 2:3, KJV; 2 Timothy 3:5.

"In the last days perilous times will come. For men will be lovers of themselves, lovers of money, boastful, proud, abusive, disobedient to their parents, ungrateful, unholy, without love, unforgiving, slanderous, without self-control, brutal, not lovers of the good, treacherous, rash, conceited, lovers of pleasure rather than lovers of God—having a form of godliness but denying its power. Have nothing to do with them." 2 Timothy 3:1-5.

"The Spirit says that in the latter times some will abandon the faith and follow deceiving spirits and things taught by demons." 1 Timothy 4:1. The devil will work his deception "with all power and signs and lying wonders, and with all deceiveableness of unrighteousness." Notice that the apostle Paul says that in the last days the devil will work with *"all power and signs."* He also says, "They will have a form of godliness." So expect the devil to work within the church with those who "have a form of Godliness" and work in the name of Christ performing miracles. Real miracles come both from God and from the devil. The Bible says so. 2 Thessalonians 2:9, NKJV; 2 Timothy 3:5.

Have you ever seen a counterfeit seven-dollar bill or a counterfeit nine-dollar bill? No? Why not? Because a counterfeit always resembles the real thing in order to be accepted. Jesus warned us that our great danger would be from "false Christs and false prophets" who would "perform great signs and miracles to deceive even the elect." Matthew 24:24.

I must warn you right now that there are thousands of different books on the market today teaching false prophecies in the name of Jesus Christ. Some of these book have been written by seemingly "nice people" who may have been deceived. Let me ask you—how many false prophets do you think lived in the days of Noah? If you happened to enter a religious bookstore in one of the towns near Noah's home, how many of those books do you think predicted the coming worldwide flood correctly? Not one. A worldwide flood was not a popular topic mentioned by any of the religious leaders of Noah's day.

Noah and the Ark

The false prophets predicted prosperity and peace and condemned Noah as a crazy old lunatic. Noah preached for 120 years as he and his family built the ark. Noah told all his friends and neighbors that a worldwide flood was coming and that their only safety would be in getting aboard the ark. A few days before the flood came, God's invisible angels led the animals aboard the ark. People gathered around the ark to watch this mysterious event. Noah came to the door and made a final appeal for the people to come aboard. He said, "God will wash this world clean of sin and sinners. Your only hope is to come aboard this ark as you saw the animals coming aboard."

They weren't sure what to do, but no one wanted to look like a coward in front of their friends, so no one got on board except Noah, his wife, and his three boys and their wives. Out of the entire world, only eight people believed God enough to actually step inside the ark.

God shut the huge door on the ark with His own invisible hand, and then it was too late. Nothing happened all that day or all the next. It was seven days before the first raindrops fell, and then the sky opened up and water just seemed to pour down without let-up day after day. People moved to higher ground.

Some tied themselves to the outside of the ark. Others pleaded, "Noah, we believe you now! Please open the door!" But Noah could not open the door. The door was so huge only God could open it. They all drowned because they would not believe. You, reader, have a choice—you can believe and prepare for the coming crisis, or you can be like the people in Noah's day. The choice is yours. If you make the right choice, it will be no more popular than the choice of Noah. But it will bring you ultimate happiness.

Let's look at a different time period. Let's walk into a religious book-store around the time Christ was born in Bethlehem. How many of those religious books accurately predicted the coming of the Messiah? How many showed evidence of understanding the great prophecies? Many very educated people did not know that the Messiah had come "to take their sins away."

The popular religious opinion of the day and the popular religious teachings promoted by word of mouth or written book was that the Messiah would come to lead their armies to victory. Jesus Christ chose twelve men. He spent three and one half years educating them and teaching them that His purpose was to die on the cross. Jesus said that He "must go to Jerusalem and suffer many things at the hands of the elders, chief priests and teachers of the law, and must be killed and on the third day be raised to life." Peter took him aside and began to rebuke him. "Never, Lord," he said. "This shall never happen to you." Jesus turned and said to Peter, "Get behind me, Satan! You are a stumbling block to me; you do not have in mind the things of God but the things of men."

Peter was never "the first pope." Peter was not infallible, and Jesus rebuked Peter with the words, "get behind me, Satan." Surely Peter would have known that Jesus had come to die on the cross, because Jesus had told him so. But no. Peter chose to believe what the popular religious teachers were teaching. He chose to believe that there would be no cross. He wanted a crown, not a cross. Human nature looks for the crown and rejects the cross. It is a hard thing to realize, but the popular religious opinion concerning prophecy has always been wrong. A good counterfeit, but wrong nevertheless. Mark 8:33.

Prophecies of Christ's First Coming

The blindness of the people who lived during Christ's appearance on earth as the Messiah should not surprise us. It is not a question of race—it is a question of human nature. God says that modern man is no less blind to spiritual truth than were the people who lived at that time. God says to modern man, "You say, I am rich; I have acquired wealth and do not need a thing. But you do not realize that you are wretched, pitiful, poor, blind and naked. I counsel you to buy from me gold refined in the fire, so you can become rich; and white clothes to wear so you can cover your shameful nakedness; and salve to put on your eyes, so you can see." Revelation 3:17, 18.

The religious writers and teachers avoided prophecies like Isaiah, chapter fifty-three. Isaiah predicted that the Messiah would be "a man of sorrows," "pierced for our sins," and that He would carry "the sins of everyone." And Isaiah even wrote that a rich man would provide him a grave: "he was assigned a grave . . . with the rich in his death." You recall how rich Joseph of Arimathea helped take Christ off the cross and then put Him in Joseph's own tomb.

Why the ignorance concerning this prophecy? The actual words Christ spoke on the cross were predicted by David in the book of Psalms. "My God, my God, why have you forsaken me?" Psalm 22:1. *(Compare Psalm 22:1 with Matthew 27:46.)* David, in the book of Psalms, predicted the very words Christ would speak on the cross hundreds of years later. Also, the very mocking words of the religious leaders were predicted in the same chapter. "He trusts in the Lord; let the Lord rescue him." *(Compare Psalm 22:8 and Matthew 27:43.)*

The prediction was that they would "divide my garments among them and cast lots for my clothing." *(Compare Psalm 22:18 with Matthew 27:35.)* Psalm 22:16 predicted that "they have pierced my hands and my feet." His birthplace, Bethlehem, was predicted by the prophet Micah. The exact year He would be anointed in baptism, A.D. 27, was predicted by the prophet Daniel hundreds of years earlier. And the actual year He would be crucified, A.D. 31, was also predicted by Daniel hundreds of years earlier. Micah 5:2.

Why were the people blind to these prophecies? Because they were taught to leave their religious lives in the care of "religious experts." They did not do enough independent Bible study. Jesus taught that the people "worship me in vain; their teachings are but rules taught by men." Matthew 15:9. "You have let go of the commands of God and are holding on to the traditions of men." Mark 7:7 History repeats itself. The issues today are the same. We "have let go of the commands of God and are holding on to the traditions of men."

It is really sad that this generation has no greater knowledge of coming events than did the people who lived in the days of Noah or the people who lived at the time of Christ's first coming. "False prophets" churn out books filled with false prophecy that overwhelm the prophetic areas of most bookstores. In Matthew 25 Jesus separates His church into "the wise" and "the foolish."

The devil was able to deceive Peter and all the disciples into believing the religious writers and speakers of their day even though Christ Himself taught them for three and one half years about the cross. Are we greater than Peter, who wrote part of the Bible? What is the possibility that this modern generation really understands the prophecies? If you or I had been taught by Jesus Christ for three and one half years, we would have believed Christ. Isn't that right? I doubt it! When Christ died on the cross, we would no doubt have been as hopeless as the disciples. The disciples went into hiding behind locked doors, fearing that they would be crucified next.

Revelation. Notice the name. The name is not "Hidden." The name is "Revelation." That means that God has something He wants to reveal to us. Like gold, it requires some effort to search Revelation. Take the time. Make the effort. You must dig deep to find gold, because it does not lie on the surface. Dig deep into Revelation.

John writes about the coming of Christ in Revelation 14:14: "I looked, and there before me was a white cloud, and seated on the cloud was one 'like a son of man' with a crown of gold on his head and a sharp sickle in his hand." Notice that in Revelation 14:6-12, just before John writes about the return of Christ as described in verse 14, he gives us three messages from God that prepare the world for this second coming of Christ.

Why the ignorance of the religious world concerning these three messages? When is the last time you read about these three messages? When is the last time you heard a sermon on these three messages? The usual answer is, Never. Most people have never heard of the "three angels' messages." John writes, "I saw another angel". . . "a second angel followed" . . . "a third angel followed."

Occasionally you may hear someone mention or read what someone has written about the *mark of the beast*. When they do mention it, they are usually very inaccurate about it. If they do not share all of the three angel's messages, they are "false prophets." The message concerning "the mark of the Beast" is part of the third angel's message and never stands alone. These three angels' messages always are to be taught together. Together they are God's warning message to the people of Planet Earth. We are not to guess at who the beast is or what his mark is. We are to know and understand these messages as a unified message. We can know—and we must know and understand. God says, "Blessed is the one who reads and hears and takes to heart what is written, because the time is near." Revelation 1:3.

The Worst Curse in the Bible!

The worst curse in the entire Bible is pronounced on those who "worship the beast and his image, or for anyone who receives the mark of his name." They will "drink of the wine of God's fury which has been poured full strength into the cup of his wrath." Shake off your sleepiness and search these truths out. Your eternal happiness and destiny depend on your knowing what will happen and how to prepare for it. Your very safety and that of your loved ones depends on being prepared!

Many who have claimed Christianity "received not the love of the truth, that they might be saved." Have you received a love of the truth? Do you love God and His truth, even though truth is unpopular with many Christians? Those who do not love the truth accept a "powerful delusion, so that they will believe the lie." 2 Thessalonians 2:9-11.

Notice that 2 Thessalonians 2:3, 4 predicted that there would be a major "falling away" in the church and that a man would assume a dominant leadership role, to the point of claiming to be God on earth. *(For the fulfillment of these verses through the papacy, see the Appendix.)* The words *falling away* also lead down through the stream of time to our day. God's final call is: "Babylon is fallen, is fallen. Come out of her, My people." (See the NIV and KJV.)

The church has been falling for a long time and will reach its ultimate fall in the law against Sabbathkeepers worldwide and the punishment of those who honor God, not allowing them to "buy or sell." The effort will be made to starve them into submission—an effort which will backfire and result in worldwide plagues. God promises His children that their "bread and their water will be sure," and He also promises protection from the plagues that are killing millions.

Those who try to starve God's children will themselves face starvation and the most destructive plagues that have ever been known in the history of mankind. The persecutors will "drink of the wine of God's fury which has been poured full strength into the cup of his wrath."

An Image = a Copy

You see your image when you look in the mirror. The churches of the United States will make an image—a mirror-like copy—of the beast. Leading churches of the United States will unite upon the doctrines they commonly believe. They will get local, state, and national government to enforce their decrees and to maintain their organizations. Then Protestant America will have formed an image of the papacy. Protestant America will punish those who do not agree with their unscriptural belief in Sunday sacredness. Punishment will include such methods as boycott, fines, and prison. (See Revelation 13:14-16.)

The Mark of the Beast

He "also forced everyone, small and great, rich and poor, free and slave, to receive a mark on his right hand or on his forehead, so that no one could buy or sell unless he had the mark, which is the name of the beast or the number of his name." Revelation 13:16, 17.

"If any man worship the beast and his image, and receive his mark in his forehead, or in his hand, the same will drink of the wine of the wrath of God." Revelation 14:9, 10. Since the worst curse in the entire Bible comes on those who receive "the mark of the beast," wouldn't everyone in the world want to understand who the beast is and how to avoid receiving its mark?

To avoid receiving the *mark of the beast* and the seven last plagues, we must keep all of God's commandments.

After the warning against the worship of the beast and his image, the prophecy says: "Here are they that keep the commandments of God, and the faith of Jesus." Revelation 14:12, KJV. Those who keep God's commandments are placed in contrast with those that worship the beast and his image and receive his mark.

This means that the difference between the worshiper of God and the worshipers of the beast is between keeping God's law or not keeping it. The special characteristic of the beast, and therefore of his image, is the breaking of God's commandments. "He will think to change times and the law." Daniel 7:25, R.V. The only law that deals with time is the Sabbath commandment. Only by changing God's law could the papacy raise itself above God.

The Catechism or the Bible

The papacy dropped the second commandment, forbidding image worship, from the law. They changed the fourth commandment. God said in the fourth commandment, "The seventh day is the Sabbath of the Lord your God." The papacy claims in their catechism, "Saturday was the day sanctified; but the church has substituted Sunday for Saturday; so now we sanctify the first, not the seventh day." God predicted this change in His Holy Word, the Bible. God had Daniel write that "he will think to change the times and the law." Daniel 7:25.

"The Son of man is Lord also of the Sabbath." "The seventh day is the Sabbath of the Lord." God calls it "My holy day." Mark 2:28; Isaiah 58:13, KJV. "Do not think that I have come to abolish the Law or the Prophets; I have not come to abolish them but to fulfill them. I tell you the truth, until heaven and earth disappear, not the smallest letter, nor the least stroke of a pen, will by any means disappear from the law until everything is accomplished. Anyone who breaks one of the least of these commandments and teaches others to do the same will be called least in the kingdom of heaven, but whoever practices and teaches these commands will be called great in the kingdom of heaven." Matthew 5:17-19.

The papacy did "break one of these least commandments," and they do "teach men so." The papacy did this, not with just one, but with two commandments. It removed the second commandment regarding image worship. It then divided the tenth to give the appearance of still having ten commandments.

The papacy also changed the fourth commandment from the day God made holy, the seventh day, to the first day of the week. According to this verse, how does God look at the papacy? God recognizes the papacy as "least" in the kingdom of heaven. "Least" does not mean that in God's rating system, He has a place for the papacy—a very low place. It means He has *no* place for the papacy.

Papal leaders teach that Protestants, by observing Sunday, recognize her power. *The Convert's Catechism of the Catholic Doctrine*, by Peter Geiermann, p. 50, says: "Saturday is the Sabbath day. We observe Sunday instead of Saturday because the Catholic Church transferred the solemnity from Saturday to Sunday." Yet God's law is holy, and God says, "I the Lord do not change." The change of the Sabbath is a sign, or mark, of the authority of the Roman church—"the mark of the beast." Malachi 3:6.

Protestant churches claim the authority of Bible, and the Bible only, is the religion of Protestants. The papacy can see that they are deceiving themselves. The enforcement of Sunday keeping by Protestant churches is an enforcement or worship of the papacy—of the beast.

The Issue: Either . . .

Honor the Papacy by Keeping Its Commandments

or

Honor God by Keeping God's Commandments

You cannot do both!

Whoever will disobey the command of God, to obey a teaching that has no higher authority than that of the pope, will then honor the papacy above God. Such will accept the sign of allegiance to the papacy—"the mark of the beast." The issue will be plainly set before the people. All will be forced to choose between the commandments of God and the commandments of men. It is at this time that those who continue breaking the fourth commandment will receive "the mark of the beast."

Can I depend on miracles to tell me what God wants me to do?

Many will say "God is performing wonderful miracles for us, proving that Sunday is sacred." Can we depend on miracles? Isn't it a miracle when a snake speaks to people, calling them by name and carrying on a conversation with them? That happened to our great grandmother Eve in the garden. Remember that Eve is related to every one of us. Lucifer, alias the devil, used a miracle to deceive her then, and he uses "Christian miracles" to deceive us today. We must depend on God's Word, regardless of what miracles are performed.

"The Spirit says that in the later times some will abandon the faith, and follow deceiving spirits and things taught by demons."1 Timothy 4:1. The devil will work his deception "with all power and signs and lying wonders, and with all deceiveableness of unrighteousness." It does not say, "the devil will work with power." It says he will "work with *all* power."

Oh how much those words "all power" include. Not only will he work with *all* power, but he will include "signs and lying wonders, and all decieveableness." When someone deceives you, they are lying to you and getting you to believe they are telling the truth. 2 Thessalonians 2:9, KJV.

Identical twins can often times deceive those around them into be-lieving that one of them is really the other. In these last days the devil will deceive the world into believing that popular Christianity is the religion of the Bible.

Identical twins can decieve friends or sometimes even close rela-tives into believing they are the other twin because they look so much like each other. To deceive the Christian church, the devil must not come as the devil but rather "as an angel of light." There must be enough good mixed in with the error to make it hard to tell the false from the true.

There Will Only Be Two Choices

This crisis will divide Christianity into two classes—not three.

1. Those who keep all the commandments (including the fourth com-mandment.

2. Those who do not.

In the coming crisis, all who claim to be Christians will make a choice.

Will I obey God—or will I obey a man?

Doing both will be impossible.

18

The Real Issue

The problem is that obeying man will be popular.

Obeying God will be unpopular.

Real crosses and real electric chairs have never been popular.

Jesus says, "Take up your cross and follow Me." Roman soldiers nailed the hands and feet of Jesus Christ to the cross. He felt more pain than we can imagine, for our benefit. He did not do the popular thing. Dying in an electric chair is not popular today. When have you seen crowds of people pushing to be the first one to die in the electric chair? Death from the torture of the cross would today be even less popular then electrocution in the electric chair.

Having someone drive nails through your hands and feet into a wooden cross was not popular. Neither was feeling the torture of tearing flesh from the jarring drop of the cross as it thudded into the hole prepared for it. After the drop, the nail wounds gaped from the weight hanging from the nails.

Blood flowed freely, dripping from the hands and feet and even from the backs of those whom the soldiers whipped before they crucified them. Crosses were tools of torture. Jesus is calling you to a life of discipline and a willingness to be unpopular and unashamed.

Jesus is calling for Christian soldiers. Onward, Christian soldiers! Onward to service, onward to choosing the life of the cross and knowing that Christ is beside you and that He surrounds you with angels. You will go through trials, but He will go through with you. Let other soldiers fight with their guns and their fear and their hatred. God is calling for volunteers. God is calling you! Yes, you! He is speaking to your heart, assuring you that you can find total and complete forgiveness for your sins and true meaning in service.

You must be willing to surrender all, even if necessary your life, for Him. He gave His life for you and wants to be first in your life. He loves you in spite of all the bad things you may have said or done. He will forgive all. In return, He wants your love. He wants your life. He wants to fill your life with purpose and meaning and power.

When Jesus walked among His disciples, He saw Peter and John and James washing their nets at the lake of Galilee. They were fishermen. Jesus called them to leave all that behind. He said, "Come and follow Me, and I'll make you fishers of men." That call included women and children. Now, instead of catching fish in a net, they were to invite sinners to know Jesus as their Savior from sin.

Jesus will forgive you for your disobedience, unkindness, and sin of all kinds—even crimes that society will never forgive. But He wants to do even more for you. He wants to give you His Holy Spirit to give you the power to be fishers of men, women, and children. God wants to give you the privilege of working with Him for the salvation of your family, your friends, your neighbors, and anyone with whom you come in contact. God wants you to be His partner. What a privilege—working with the Creator of all!

Take God's Word and give it away. Talk to others about what you are discovering. Many will not listen. The majority did not accept Christ. Otherwise they would not have nailed Him to a cross. But some here and some there accepted Him. God has put the power in His Word. The only reason this book is powerful is that it is filled with God's word. It was by His word that He created this world. He spoke, and the creative energy of His word brought the world into existence.

The Word—Small, but Powerful!

The secret of life that many have never discovered is that the Word of God looks plain and ordinary. Many think of it as an ordinary book. But it is full of power just waiting to be released. Read the Word, believe the Word, share the Word, and your life will have a power and purpose that you never dreamed possible. Share the Word with another, and it is like a farmer planting a very small seed in the ground. It looks ordinary and tiny, but within a watermelon seed planted in the ground are many huge watermelons waiting to be grown and harvested.

Plant God's Word by sharing it with others, and you will see some of those people again in heaven and in the earth made new. They will throw their arms around you and say, "Oh, thank you! Thank you! If it weren't for you, I wouldn't be here!" "The harvest is the end of the world, and the angels are the reapers." Plant God's Word by sharing it with your friends, neighbors, relatives, and anyone you come in contact with, and you will have a big harvest. Matthew 13:39.

You will never know when you have planted a seed of God's Word in someone's heart that will take root in their mind and grow and guide them into choosing Jesus Christ and the way of the cross. You will be surprised someday at how many are saved as a result of your life. The one you helped will help yet another, and that person will help another choose Jesus, and the harvest will multiply.

You might begin by using this very book you are reading. Either buy extra copies for your friends, or give them the Internet URL— *www.prophecymadeeasy.com*—to look up and read on their computers.

God will use you mightily in the closing conflict, Christian soldier. Take up your cross and follow Jesus. The reward is eternal life and the knowledge that your life purpose has been realized. God has placed a God-shaped hole in every heart—a void that men and women and children try to fill. Many try to fill it with liquor, cigarettes, drugs, sex, violence, pleasure, or money. But none of those things will ever fill that hole. Ask Jesus Christ to fill that hole for you.

You and I are related in two ways. We share common distant grandparents—Adam and Eve. We also share a new-birth commitment and relationship with Jesus Christ, providing you have asked Christ into your heart and are seeking to continue that relationship with Christ.

I'm Praying for You!

Dear friend of mine, let's make a pact to pray for each other. I probably haven't met you yet, but I will if we both stay close to Christ. I will pray for you, the reader, and ask that you pray for me. We will meet in New Jerusalem, the beautiful city of the future. There will be no more death, no more pain, no more tears, no more loneliness, and no more struggles.

It will be exciting! I'm already looking forward to meeting you in God's beautiful city. Read more about it in chapters 29 and 30 of this book and the last two chapters of your Bible—Revelation 21 and 22. You will have a beautiful house in the earth made new. Jesus Himself said, "Blessed are the meek, for they shall inherit the earth." You may not qualify as "meek" now, but don't let that stop you. The word *meek* does not mean what many think it does. It does not describe a fearful, milk-toast of a person. It is a word that suggests strength under difficult situations. Jesus comes into the heart, and you no longer have to prove how tough you are. You have a new strength—a quiet strength.

Jesus is telling you to "take up your cross and follow" Him. "If anyone would come after me, he must deny himself and take up his cross daily and follow me. For whoever wants to save his life will lose it, but whoever loses his life for me will save it. What good is it for a man to gain the whole world, and yet lose or forfeit his very self? If anyone is ashamed of me and my words, the Son of Man will be ashamed of him when he comes in his glory and in the glory of the Father and of the holy angels." Luke 9:23-26. Jesus wants you to follow Him even when it is the unpopular thing to do. No one naturally wants to be unpopular. Will you be ashamed of Christ when you must make an unpopular decision in order to continue following Him?

Those who obey God keep the commandments of God and the faith of Jesus.

But those who do not obey God worship the beast and his image.

They receive his mark and must endure the seven last plagues.

"All, both small and great, rich and poor, free and slave" (Revelation 13:16), receive "the mark of the beast." The only exception is a small group of people who know part two of God's plan and put God first. They are those who have "gotten the victory over the beast, and over his image, and over his mark, and over the number of his name, [and] stand on the sea of glass, having the harps of God." Revelation 15:2, 3.

You must choose between popular sin and unpopular truth.

What Is the Mark of the Beast?

"Seal the law among My disciples." Isaiah 8:16. The seal of God's law is found in the fourth commandment. This only, of all the ten, includes both the name and the title of the Lawgiver. It says that He is the Creator of the heavens and the earth. When the papal power changed the Sabbath, it took God's seal from His law. Revelation 7:1-3, Daniel 7:25.

In the days just preceding the second coming of Christ, every person on Planet Earth will either have the seal of God and keep the Sabbath day holy, or they will have the mark of the beast. Leaders of the Roman Catholic Church acknowledge that the change of the Sabbath was made by their church and say that Protestants, by observing Sunday, are recognizing her power. In the *Catholic Catechism of Christian Religion*, in answer to a question as to the day to be observed in obedience to the fourth commandment, this is what is written: "During the old law Saturday was the day sanctified; but the church, instructed by Jesus Christ, and directed by the Spirit of God, has substituted Sunday for Saturday; so now we sanctify the first, not the seventh day." In *An Abridgment of the Christian Doctrine,* page 58, papal writers say that "the very act of changing the Sabbath into Sunday, which Protestants allow of; . . . because by keeping Sunday, they acknowledge the church's power to ordain feasts, and to command them under sin."

Thus we can see that the change of the Sabbath is a sign or mark of the authority of the Roman Church— "the mark of the beast." Revelation, chapter 14 tells us that just before Christ returns, three messages will be carried worldwide to prepare the world for the second coming of Christ. The first message is: "Fear God, and give glory to him; for the hour of his judgment is come." The second message (seen in both Revelation 14 and Revelation 18) is: "Babylon is fallen, is fallen . . . Come out of her, my people, that you receive not of her plagues." The third message is: "If any man worship the beast and his image, and receive his mark in his forehead, or in his hand, the same shall drink of the wine of the wrath of God, which is poured out without mixture [without mercy]." Revelation 14:7, 9, 10; 18:2, 4, KJV.

Does anyone have the mark of the beast now? No. Not until the time when all men will be forced to choose whether or not to receive it. The mark of the beast is the mark of the beast power's authority. When that authority is enforced with Sunday laws with worldwide application, then those who choose to obey that authority above the authority of God will be choosing the mark of the beast. All people everywhere will either have the mark of the beast or the seal of God, which is found in God's holy Sabbath observance. Those with God's seal will enter the New Jerusalem, and those with the mark will ultimately be no more.

God told Noah He would destroy the world with a flood. Noah warned the world, but only eight people believed and got into the ark of safety. In other words, God says to modern man, "Sin has become so great that I will destroy the world again. I will not destroy it with water. I will destroy it with the seven plagues that I warn you about in the sixteenth chapter of

Revelation. You can choose to believe it or disbelieve it. But if you believe and come into my ark of safety, I will take care of you, and I will save you. And if you choose to disbelieve, you will be choosing death. Please choose life!" We can, by faith, enter God's ark of safety. "In the time of trouble He shall hide me in His tabernacle [the sanctuary]." Psalm 27:5, KJV. Enter God's sanctuary in heaven, by faith, and see Christ in His work of judgment and let Him write His holy law in your heart.

"To the law and to the testimony, if they speak not according to this word, it is because there is no light in them." Isaiah 8:20, KJV.

"Cry aloud, spare not, lift up your voice like a trumpet, and show my people their sin." Isaiah 58:1, 2, NKJV.

"You will raise up the foundations of many generations; and you will be called, the repairer of the breach." Isaiah 58:12-14, NKJV.

19

Dam Busters

On the night of May 16, 1943, the British Air Force sent a group of "dam buster" planes to attack the Mohne Dam in The Ruhr Valley, Germany's industrial heartland. Their plan was to put a hole in the dam so that the sudden release of water would then kill many people downstream.

The planes came in at 60 feet above the ground and dropped their bombs. The bombs did not completely destroy the dam. But they did exactly what they wanted them to do. They put a big enough hole in the dam so that billions of gallons of water rushed through the opening and swept down the Ruhr Valley. Thirteen hundred people were killed as a result of a relatively small hole in a very large dam.

Satan is the great original "dam buster." He knew that the whole dam, God's Ten Commandment dam, would not need to be destroyed. He decided to just make a big hole in God's law, and the result would be sure death for millions of God's children.

"You shall raise up the foundations of many generations; and you shall be called, The *repairer of the breach,* the restorer of streets to dwell in. If you turn away from doing your pleasure on My holy day; and call the *Sabbath* a delight, the holy of the Lord, honorable; and shall honor Him, not doing

153

your own ways, nor finding your own pleasure, nor speaking your own words: then you shall delight yourself in the Lord." Isaiah 58:12-14, NKJV.

Notice that God used the prophet Isaiah not only to predict that a breach would occur in God's law but to tell us even which commandment would be breached—the Sabbath commandment. You are reading this book because God cares about you and wants you to know what is really happening. God plans to use you to help repair the hole in His law.

The papacy made the breach, or "hole," in the law of God when they changed the Sabbath from the seventh day of the week to the first day of the week. God will repair the breach, the hole, made in His law.

The Definition of Breach

A "breach" is a gap or opening made by breaking or battering, as in a wall or fortification, the space between the parts of a solid body rent by violence, a break, a rupture.

The Ten Commandments Are a Wall—
a Barrier Against Sin . . .

. . . when taken into the heart through the power of Jesus.

There are many different types of walls in the world. One type of wall is called a dam. It holds back rivers, thus forming lakes. You now know what happened when the British dam busters blew a hole in the Mohne Dam. Thirteen hundred people lost their lives. Did it matter that nine-tenths of the dam was still standing? No, it only took a hole in the dam to release billions of gallons of water and kill hundreds.

Notice that many years after the death and resurrection of Christ, James wrote that all ten of God's commandments were still of vital importance. James 2:10 in God's Word says, "Whoever keeps the whole law and yet stumbles at just one point is guilty of breaking all of it." God is saying, "I am particular, and eight or nine out of ten is not good enough." God's law, His dam against sin, must include all ten commandments. Try and explain to the relatives of the thirteen hundred dead people that the dam was still a good dam because nine-tenths of the dam was still standing.

When the papacy attempted to change the fourth commandment, it made a breach, a gap, in God's protective Ten Commandment wall. Daniel predicted that this would happen. Read Daniel 7:25, NKJV. Prophecy states very clearly that this power "shall speak pompous words against the Most High, shall persecute the saints of the Most High. And shall intend to change times and law." The only law that has to do with time is the one that begins with the words "Remember the Sabbath day by keeping it holy." God said that this power, identified as the papacy, would change God's holy day—and the papacy claims that very change. See *The Convert's Catechism of Catholic Doctrine*, p. 50: "Saturday is the Sabbath day. . . . the Church substituted Sunday for Saturday." God said that man was to keep the seventh day holy, and man said, "I will change God's law to keep the first day of the week, Sunday." God has called us to repair the breach that the papacy made in God's holy law, and to "call the Sabbath a delight." We are to restore the fourth commandment to its rightful place.

As the result of the threefold message, God says: "Here are they that keep the commandments of God, and the faith of Jesus." Revelation 14:12, KJV. Obedience to the fourth commandment requires a sacrifice that most people are not willing to make. Many reason from the worldly person's viewpoint. What was good enough for my father is good enough for me. God is calling for those who will hear and obey His voice and do his will. God calls for those who, if need be, will speak unpopular, disagreeable truths, not fearing to condemn popular sins.

Since the popular religious world cannot defeat those who speak unpopular Bible truths with Scripture, they choose another way. Attacking character and motives with vicious lies is the preferred weapon of choice. "Everyone who does evil hates the light, and will not come into the light for fear that his deeds will be exposed." John 3:20.

The popular religious world always attacks unpopular truth in this way. They have always attacked the character and motives of all the great men. They attacked Elijah, Jeremiah, and the apostle Paul in this way. They called Elijah "a cause of trouble in Israel," Jeremiah a traitor, and Paul a polluter of the temple.

From that day to this, many have denounced those who would be loyal to truth, as seditious. God wants us to be willing to condemn fashionable sins. "Lift up your voice like a trumpet, and show my people their transgression, and the house of Jacob their sins."

You Must Share What You Are Learning With Others!

"Son of man, I have made you a watchman for the house of Israel."

"When I say unto the wicked, O wicked man, you will surely die; and you do not speak to warn the wicked from his way, that wicked man shall die in his iniquity; but his blood will I require at your hand. Nevertheless, if you warn the wicked to turn from his way, and he does not turn from his way, he shall die in his iniquity; but you have delivered your soul." Ezekiel 33:7-9, NKJV.

The great obstacle both to the acceptance and to the speaking of the truth is the fact that it involves inconvenience and criticism.

Inconvenience and criticism!

The twelve disciples followed Christ for three and one half years. Christ told them over and over that He had come to die on a cross for them. They accepted Christ as their "king." They were looking for the honor of ruling under Christ "the King." They did not listen very well when Christ spoke of dying on a cross. The most common interpretations of the prophecies concerning Christ—the ones that they had been taught by the religious "experts"—were inaccurate.

People looked at the prophecies of Christ's second coming, such as Psalm 50:3, 4 and accepted those because they seemed to mean honor and riches. Their religious leaders had not taught them the prophecies of His first coming in such places as Isaiah 53 and Psalm 22:1, 7, 8, 16-19 and Daniel 9:25-26. Most people were then—and are now—used to leaving the subject of religion up to the "experts." They accepted then, as we do now, what the "religious experts" have to say.

The disciples were unprepared for Christ to die on the cross. When Christ died on the cross, their hopes and dreams were crushed. They did not remember that Christ had told them this was going to happen. All they could remember were the false prophecies that their former religious leaders had taught them. When Christ did not assume the throne as king but instead was stripped naked and nailed to two pieces of wood which hung between heaven and earth, their hopes were shattered.

They were looking for a Messiah who would break them free of Rome, which had conquered their nation. They were looking for worldly honor and power. If Christ had come the way they had been taught by their religious leaders, the majority would have accepted Him. They did not want a Saviour from sin. They wanted someone to lead their armies to glory. They wanted the riches that come to the conquerer.

We are in the same danger as the Jews were at the time of Christ's first coming. Most popular books on prophecy are blinding the majority of people into sleeping on, unprepared for the overwhelming surprise. A crisis is coming—a storm relentless in its fury. Only those who are willing to follow Christ to "the cross," to live a life of self denial, a life of inconvenience and persecution, will obtain the crown of eternal life. The cross must come before the crown!

A very popular false prophecy is that of the "second chance" theory. Many are taught that Jesus will rapture His people secretly away and that after His children are taken to heaven, evangelism will continue on Planet Earth for another seven years. That's not how it happened in Noah's day. There was no second chance then, and there will be no second chance when Christ comes the second time.

Christ Himself says: "As it was in the days of Noah, so it will be at the coming of the Son of Man." Christ compares His second coming to a lightning storm. Have you ever seen a "secret" lightning storm? He says: "Every eye will see him," and that we will hear Him "shout" and will hear "the trumpet of the Lord." It will be grand and majestic, but it will not be a secret. Matthew 24:37, 27; Revelation 1:7; 1 Thessalonians 4:16, NKJV.

Christ did not say, "Take up your Mercedes and follow me." He said, "Whoever will come after me, let him deny himself, and take up his cross, and follow me." The cross was an instrument of cruel torture. Are you willing to follow Christ when it is not convenient? Are you willing to follow Him when you are criticized and hated? Following Him through the coming crisis will require that willingness. Those who follow Him through the coming crisis will know what it means when Christ says, "If anyone would come after me, he must deny himself and take up his cross and follow me." They also will know His love and protection when He fights for His people with the weapons of nature in the seven last plagues. Mark 8:34 and Revelation 16.

Do Not Wait for Truth to Become Popular. Deliberately Accept the Cross!

"Our light and momentary troubles are achieving for us an eternal glory that far outweighs them all." Moses "regarded disgrace for the sake of Christ as of greater value than the treasure of Egypt, because he was looking ahead to his reward." 2 Corinthians 4:17; Hebrews 11:26. Choose "disgrace for the sake of Christ." God will richly reward you! Some say the plan of salvation has changed from the days of Moses to our day. But Paul says Moses was a follower of Christ! Moses believed in Christ's coming to die for him. Moses looked forward to salvation through the death of Jesus, and we look back to the death of Christ. Either way, it requires faith in Christ!

Choose the Right Because it *Is* Right!

Choose the right because it is right! Leave the consequences with God. "Hear me, you who know what is right, you people who have my law in your hearts: Do not fear the reproach of men or be terrified by their insults. For the moth will eat them up like a garment: the worm will devour them like wool. But my righteousness will last forever, my salvation through all generations." Isaiah 51:7, 8.

Before Christ comes again, all who are faithful will endure the "cross" of persecution. The vast majority of books on Bible prophecy are filled with false prophetic information that is blinding millions. The very blindness of this end time generation was foretold by Jesus in the last book of the Bible—in Revelation 3:17. Jesus warns the Christian world that the judgment is going on right now, and they don't even know it. They don't feel a need and do not even realize that Christ is outside knocking on the door of their heart. "You say I am rich; I have acquired wealth and do not need a thing. But you do not realize that you are wretched, pitiful, poor, blind and naked. I counsel you to buy from me gold refined in the fire, so you can become rich; and white clothes to wear, so you can cover your shameful nakedness; and salve to put on your eyes, so you can see. Here I am! I stand at the door and knock. If anyone hears my voice and opens the door, I will come in and eat with him, and he with me." Revelation 3:17-21.

This is similar to the message of Revelation 14 and 18, where Christ is on the outside of the religious experience, and the people and the churches don't even realize it. Christ is withdrawing from the churches composing Babylon, and that is why he is calling *His* children: "Come out of her, my people." Jesus is knocking on the door of your heart today, calling you to a full understanding of the gospel.

You may have understood a part of the gospel in the past. Just as there are two rooms in the sanctuary, there are two parts of the gospel. He wants you not only to accept Him as your Saviour from past sin, but He also wants to be your Priest and blot the records of your sin from the book of life. The work God is doing right now is called the investigative judgment. He will erase either your sins or your name from the book of life.

Jesus will soon complete the investigative judgment, and then He will say, "Let him who does wrong continue to do wrong; let him who is vile continue to be vile; let him who does right continue to do right; and let him who is holy continue to be holy. Behold, I am coming soon! My reward is with me, and I will give to everyone according to what he has done." Revelation 22:11, 12.

At a trial, when does the judge sentence the accused? Does he sentence him before investigating the charges and conducting a trial—or after the trial is over and the accused is either found innocent or guilty? Of course, you say, it is after the trial. It is after the accused is found innocent that he is set free—or if he is found guilty, that he is sentenced to prison or death.

Notice that when Jesus comes again, He brings his reward with Him. He says, "I am coming soon! My reward is with me, and I will give to everyone according to what he has done." The sentence has already been decided; the judgment is over. This thought may be new to you, but it is still the truth. Jesus says, "You shall know the truth, and it shall make you free." Follow these great truths of Revelation 14, and you will be free. You will be prepared for our Lord's second coming!

20

Is it a Painful Burden?

M any religious teachers teach that Christ, by His death, abolished the law. They represent it as a painful yoke, and say that the gospel frees us from obedience to God's law.

If You Do Not Love the Law, You Do Not Love the Gospel

Both the law and the gospel are mirrors reflecting the true character of God. Modern theology separates what God has put together.

What do The Bible Writers Say?

1. **David:** "I will always obey your law, for ever and ever. I delight in your commands because I love them." Psalm 119:44, 47, NKJV.

"O how I love Your law! I meditate on it all day long." Psalm 119:97.

"Blessed is the man who does not walk in the counsel of the wicked or stand in the way of sinners or sit in the seat of mockers. But his delight is in the law of the Lord, and on his law he meditates day and night. He is like a tree planted by streams of water which yield its fruit in season and whose leaf does not wither. Whatever he does prospers." Psalm 1:1-3.

2. **James,** who wrote after the death of Christ, calls the Ten Commandments "the royal law" and "the perfect law of liberty." James 2:8; 1:25, KJV. The law of God, which Satan has called "a yoke of bondage" and "the chains of slavery," will be honored as the law of liberty.

3. **John the Revelator,** half a century after the crucifixion, announces a blessing upon them "that do His commandments, that they may have the right to eat of the tree of life, and may enter through the gates into the city." Revelation 22:14, KJV.

John says that those who claim to know Christ and do not keep God's commandments are liars: "He who says, I know Him, and does not keep His commandments, is a liar. But whoever keeps His word, truly the love of God is perfected in him." 1 John 2:4, 5.

4. **Jesus** did not come to change the smallest part of God's law. Did Jesus say, "When I die on the cross, I will destroy the Ten Commandments. I'll nail them to the cross"? No! *Absolutely not!*

The claim that Christ by His death abolished His Father's law is without foundation. He said: "Think not that I am come to destroy the law"; "until heaven and earth disappear, not the smallest letter, nor the least stroke of a pen, will by any means disappear from the Law." Matthew 5; 17, 18. About Himself, He says, "I delight to do Your will, O my God: yes, Your law is within My heart." Psalm 40:8.

Jesus Himself obeyed His Father's law and expects us to obey God's law as well. Jesus says, "I have kept My Father's commandments." "I do always those things that please Him." John 15:10; 8:29, KJV.

5. **Paul** calls God's law "holy, just and good." Does that sound like a law done away with? "The law is holy, and the commandment holy, and just, and good." Romans 7:12, KJV.

The apostle Paul says that God's law is holy, just, and good. Would God destroy something that is holy, just and good? No, absolutely not! He would not and did not. "Love is the fulfilling of the law." Romans 13:10, KJV. "Your law is truth"; "all Your commandments are righteousness." Psalm 119:142, 172, NKJV.

Did Christ Nail the Ten Commandments to the Cross?

Some people use a quote from Paul in Colossians 2:14-17 to try and convince others that the Ten Commandments were done away with, or "nailed to the cross." The Ten Commandments were on two tables of stone. Have you ever tried nailing stone?

The sabbaths that were done away with at the cross were the ceremonial sabbaths like Passover—yearly sabbaths. All of these verses refer to the ceremonial law, which was done away with at the cross, and not to the Ten Commandments. Colossians 2:17 tells us that the sabbaths that were done away with are those that are "a shadow of the things that were to come"— religious festivals that involved eating and drinking.

The first yearly sabbath was the feast of "Passover," which looked back to the Israelites' escape from Egypt and forward to the death of Christ on the cross. The Israelites were saved from the plague of death that came to the Egyptians. The Israelites each killed a lamb and painted their door frames with the blood of a lamb, which was a foreshadowing of the death of Christ. The apostle Paul said it like this: "Christ, our passover lamb, has been sacrificed." 1 Corinthians 5:7.

Christ died on the cross at the very day and moment of the year that the passover lamb was going to be killed. At that very moment, Christ died. The earth shook, and the lamb escaped, and the curtain in the temple was torn from top to bottom by the unseen hands of an angel, showing that "the shadow of things" was done away with, now that the true "lamb of God"— the Messiah—had died for the sins of all mankind. In other words, the cross cast its shadow back to the sacrifice of the lamb and to the protection that the lamb's blood provided in the first Passover service in Egypt.

No longer did this yearly Sabbath hold the promise of the coming sacrificial Messiah who would shed His blood for the sins of the world. The true "lamb of God" died on the cross. The sacrifice of lambs was a central part of the work of the temple. The curtain in the temple was torn from top to bottom by the unseen hands of an angel—an angel shouting, as it were, to the world that the work of the earthly temple—the sacrifice of lambs—was now meaningless, since the true Lamb of God had shed His blood.

The Sabbath commandment was part of the great moral law. The moral law is a perpetual and universal law. One law was temporary, written on paper. The other was permanent, written on stone. The temporary law was written by Moses, and the permanent law was written by God.

Sin means disobeying God's law. "Everyone who sins breaks the law; in fact, sin is lawlessness." "Sin is the transgression of the law." (KJV.) God's law is the only way we have of defining sin. Those who attempt to change God's law are sinners. The papacy tried to change God's law. Scripture identifies the papacy as "that man of sin." "He will oppose and will exalt himself over everything that is called God or is worshiped, so that he sets himself up in God's temple, proclaiming himself to be God." 1 John 3:4,

KJV; 2 Thessalonians 2:3, 4. You remember that it was this very issue of self-exaltation that introduced sin, pain, suffering and death into a pain-free, death-free universe. Lucifer had said, "I will exalt my throne above the stars of God." He was saying that he would exalt his throne above God's throne. "I will sit also upon God's mountain. I will make myself like the Most High." Isaiah 14:13, 14.

What Do the Bible Writers Say?

Instead of doing away with God's law, faith confirms and establishes it!

PAUL: "Do we then break the law through faith? God forbid: we establish the law." "How shall we, that are dead to sin, live any longer in it?" "By the law is the knowledge of sin." Romans 3:31, RSV; Romans 6:2, NKJV; Romans 3:20, NKJV.

JOHN: "This is the love of God, that we keep His commandments: and His commandments are not grievous [painful]." 1 John 5:3.

DAVID: "O how I love your law! It is my meditation all day long." Psalm 119:97. "The law of the Lord is perfect, converting the soul." Psalm 19:7.

Any change in God's perfect law would make it imperfect! If God's law is "holy, and just, and good," character formed by obedience to that law will also be holy.

What Did Jesus Do?

JESUS said, "I have kept My Father's commandments." "I do always those things that please Him." John 15:10; 8:29.

JESUS did not come to change the smallest part of God's law. He obeyed the Ten Commandments.

"Do not think I have come to abolish the Law or the Prophets; I have not come to abolish them but to fulfill them. I tell you the truth, until heaven and earth disappear, not the smallest letter, not the least stroke of a pen, will by any means disappear from the Law." Matthew 5:17, 18. "I delight to do Your will, O my God: yes, Your law is within My heart." Psalm 40:8. "I have kept My Father's commandments." "I do always those things that please Him." John 15:10; 8:29.

Holy People Never Claim to Be Holy or Sinless

Sanctification has a spirit of humility. Our eyes need to be opened so we can see our own unworthiness in contrast with the purity and exalted perfection of the Infinite One.

DANIEL: Known by God as greatly beloved, he saw his own weakness and sinfulness. "I was speaking and praying, confessing my sin and the sin of my people Israel. I had no strength left, my face turned deathly pale and I was helpless." I "was speaking, and praying, and confessing my sin and the sin of my people." "I stood up trembling." Daniel 10:11: Daniel 9: 15,20; 10:8, 11.

JOB: "I abhor myself, and repent in dust and ashes." Job 42:6.

ISAIAH: "Woe is me! I cried. I am ruined! For I am a man of unclean lips." Isaiah 6:3, 5.

PAUL: "I am less than the least of all God's people." 2 Corinthians 12:2-4, Ephesians 3:8.

JOHN: "When I saw Him, I fell at His feet as though dead." Revelation 1:17.

Those who have an understanding of Jesus Christ's sacrifice on the cross have no praise for themselves, no proud claim of freedom from sin. Our only hope is in the perfection and love of our crucified and risen Saviour.

Sanctification requires effort, humility, acceptance of God's law, self-denial and a divorce from the follies of the world. The sanctification now becoming popular in the religious world carries, with it, a spirit of self-important arrogance and ridicule for the law of God. Its defenders teach that sanctification is an instantaneous work: "Only believe." The receiver is not supposed to have to make any further effort.

21

An Easy Life

We naturally want everything in life to be easy. Our natural hearts want an easy religion with no battles, no self-denial, and no separation from the foolishness of the world. No wonder that the doctrine of faith, and faith only, is such a popular doctrine. But what does the Bible say?

James says, "Speak and act as those who are going to be judged by the law that gives freedom. What good is it, my brothers, if a man claims to have faith but has no deeds? Can such faith save him? . . .

"You foolish man, do you want evidence that faith without deeds is useless? Was not our ancestor Abraham considered righteous for what he did when he offered his son Isaac on the altar? You see that his faith and his actions were working together, and his faith was made complete by what he did. You see that a person is justified by what he does and not by faith alone." James 2:12-24.

What Does the Bible Call Ministers and Christians Who Do Not Keep God's Commandments?

Liars.

John says that those who claim to know Christ and do not keep God's commandments are liars. "He who says, I know him, and does not keep his commandments, is a liar, and the truth is not in him." 1 John 2:4, NKJV. Those who believe God's law is unimportant and teach this to others don't know God.

In Matthew chapter 7, Jesus says that many who evangelize and "drive out demons" and do many wonderful miracles in the name of Jesus are not doing God's will and will never enter the kingdom of heaven. They may have claimed to be holy. They may have been popular. They may have preached and performed apparent miracles in the name of Jesus. But if they taught that God's law was done away with, they are responsible for opening the floodgates of disobedience and filling the world with sin and suffering, while at the same time professing to serve God.

False Christian Leaders in Sheep's Clothing

Near the beginning of Christ's ministry, He told those around Him many things that they had never heard from their religious leaders. He said, "Do not think that I came to abolish the Law. . . . Whoever therefore breaks one of the least of these commandments . . . shall be called least in the kingdom of heaven, but whoever does and teaches them, he shall be called great in the kingdom of heaven." He said we break the commandment that says "You shall not murder" when we get angry with another and call him a fool. He said we break the commandment that says "You shall not commit adultery" when we look at a woman lustfully. Matthew 5:17, 19-28, NKJV.

In the book of Matthew, Christ warned that the false prophets and false Christians will look like outstanding Christians. They may fast and pray and give to the needy and prophesy and call Jesus Lord and drive out demons and perform miracles. But if they don't do the "will of God," Christ says they are "false prophets." He says that they are ferocious wolves in sheep's clothing.

A person who fasts and prays and helps others, who prophesies and casts out demons and performs miracles, is thought of by many as a great Christian leader. But Christ says none of those things count if the person is violating God's will—God's law. Matthew 7:21-28.

"Many will say to me on that day, Lord, Lord, did we not prophesy in your name, drive out demons, and perform many miracles? Then I will tell them plainly, 'I never knew you. Away from me, you evildoers! Not everyone who says to me, Lord, Lord, will enter the kingdom of heaven, but only he who does the will of my Father who is in heaven.'"

Christ says, "Not everyone who says to me, Lord, Lord, will enter the kingdom of heaven, but only he who does the will of my Father who is in heaven." Matthew 7:21-23.

The claim to be without sin is evidence that he who makes this claim is far from holy. People who have no true understanding of the measureless purity and holiness of Jesus and the deadliness of sin consider themselves holy. The one who sees himself as most righteous reveals the great distance between himself and Christ. He reveals a true ignorance of God's character and His requirements.

Sanctification includes the entire person—spirit, soul, and body. May your "whole spirit and soul and body be preserved blameless unto the coming of our Lord Jesus Christ." 1 Thessalonians 5:23, KJV. "I beseech you therefore, brethren, by the mercies of God, that you present your bodies a living sacrifice, holy, acceptable to God." Romans 12:1, NKJV.

God has commanded that the offering be "without defect." So Christians are encouraged to present their bodies "a living sacrifice, holy, and pleasing to God." Give Him the best service of your life!

"Abstain from [avoid] sinful desires, which war against your soul." 1 Peter 2:11.

"Let us purify ourselves from everything that contaminates body and spirit, perfecting holiness out of reverence for God." 2 Corinthians 7:1.

With the fruits of the Spirit—"love, joy, peace, kindness, goodness, faithfulness, gentleness"—Paul includes "self-control." Galatians 5:22, 23.

Many are perverting their godlike manhood by gluttony, by drinking alcoholic beverages, and by indulging in forbidden pleasure. The church itself often appeals to the desire for gain or love of pleasure to replenish her treasury. What about smoking? Slaves of tobacco will not enter God's kingdom. "Nothing impure will ever enter." Revelation 21:27.

Don't "you know that your body is the temple of the Holy Spirit who is in you? You are not your own. You were bought at a price: therefore glorify God in your body, and in your spirit, which are God's." 1 Corinthians 6:19, 20, NKJV. He whose body is the temple of the Holy Spirit will not allow a deadly habit to be in control. Christians should set an example of temperance, self-denial, and self-sacrifice.

Avoid "The lust of the flesh, and the lust of the eyes, and the pride of life." Come out from among them, and be separate, says the Lord. Do not touch what is unclean. And I will receive you, and will be a Father to you, and you shall be My sons and daughters, says the Lord Almighty." 2 Corinthians 6:17, 18, NKJV.

"If you then, being evil, know how to give good gifts to your children: how much more shall your heavenly Father give the Holy Spirit to them that ask Him?" Luke 11:13. "You may ask me for anything in My name, and I will do it." "Ask, and you will receive, and your joy will be complete." John 14:14; 16:24.

Humility should be a part of our life. We do not need to live our lives with constant sadness and feelings of worthlessness. It is the privilege of everyone to live in a way that God will approve and bless. It is not the will of our heavenly Father that we should always feel condemned and in darkness. "Therefore, there is now no condemnation for those who are in Christ Jesus, because through Christ Jesus the law of the Spirit of life set me free from the law of sin and death." Romans 8:1.

God Wants Us to Find Joy in the Christian Life!

"The joy of the Lord is your strength." Nehemiah 8:10. "Rejoice in the Lord always. I will say it again: Rejoice." "Be joyful always; pray continually; give thanks in all circumstances, for this is God's will for you in Christ Jesus." Philippians 4:4; 1 Thessalonians 5:16-18.

"Blessed is the man who walks not in the counsel of the wicked or stands in the way of sinners or sits in the seat of mockers. But his delight is in the law of the Lord, and on his law he meditates day and night. He is like a tree planted by streams of water, which yields its fruit in season and whose leaf does not wither. Whatever he does prospers." Psalm 1:1-3.

22

Candid Camera!

Thrones were set in place and the Ancient of Days took his seat. His clothing was as white as snow; the hair of his head was white like wool. His throne was flaming with fire. A river of fire was flowing, coming out from before him. Thousands upon thousands attended him, ten thousand times ten thousand stood before him. The court was seated, and the books were opened." Daniel 7:9, 10. The Son of man came "with the clouds of heaven. He approached the Ancient of Days. He was given authority, glory and a kingdom, that all people, nations, and languages, should serve Him: His dominion is an everlasting dominion, which will not pass away." Daniel 7:13, 14, KJV.

This pictures the Son of man coming to the Ancient of Days in heaven to receive a kingdom, given Him at the close of His work as a mediator. The judgment of those who claim to know Christ and the judgment of the wicked are two separate events, at two separate times. God will only judge those who claim to know Christ now. "It is time for judgment to begin with the family of God; and if it begins with us, what will the outcome be for those who do not obey the gospel?" 1 Peter 4:17.

The Book of Life

God has "video tapes" (books) of every word and deed of our lives. God

171

is now judging those who died claiming Christ as their Saviour. Soon God will judge the living who claim Christ as their Saviour. The Judgment is going on now. God will compare the video tapes of our lives with His holy Ten Commandment law. "The judgment was set, and the books were opened." John, the writer of Revelation, describing the same scene, adds: "Another book was opened, which is the book of life: and the dead were judged according to what they had done as recorded in the books." "Rejoice that your names are written in heaven." Daniel 7:10, KJV; Revelation 20:12; Luke 10:20.

The Book of Remembrance

Those who serve Christ have their "names . . . in the book of life." Philippians 4:3. Those who enter the city of God are those whose names "are written in the lamb's book of life." Revelation 21:27. Angels of God write the good deeds of those "that feared the Lord, and that thought on His name" "in a book of remembrance." Malachi 3:16. "Remember me, O my God, . . . and do not wipe out what I have so faithfully done for the house of my God." Nehemiah 13:14. "You know my wanderings: put my tears into Your bottle: are they not in your book?" Psalm 56:8, NKJV.

God brings everything we do into this time of judgment—even the things we think nobody knows. "For God will bring every deed into judgment, including every hidden thing, whether it is good, or evil." "For by your words you will be acquitted, and by your words you will be condemned." Ecclesiastes 12:14; Matthew 12:36, 37. God "will bring to light what is hidden in darkness, and will expose the motives of men's hearts." 1 Corinthians 4:5. "See, it stands written before me . . . both your sins, and the sins of your fathers, says the Lord." Isaiah 65:6, 7.

Have you been living a holy life lately? Have your deeds been holy? Have you been speaking holy words and thinking holy thoughts? If not, there is hope for you. The good news is that Jesus "is able to save completely those who come to God through Him, because He always lives to intercede for them." Hebrews 7:25.

Christ Blots Out Your Sins or Your Name

In the Judgment, before Christ comes the second time to Planet Earth, God will erase, or blot out, the sins of those who have allowed Christ to put His law in their hearts. And He will erase, or blot out, the names of those who have not asked for forgiveness and have not turned from their sins. God accepts names and rejects names. God will either blot out your name, or your sins, from the Book of Life and the Book of God's Remembrance.

"Whoever has sinned against me, I will blot out of my book." Exodus 32:33. "If a righteous man turns away from righteousness, and commits sin and does the same detestable things the wicked man does, will he live? None of the righteous things he has done will be remembered. But if a wicked man turns away from the wickedness he has committed and does what is just and right, he will save his life." Ezekiel 18:24.

Those whose lives have been brought into harmony with God's law will have their sins blotted out. In the Judgment before the second coming of Christ, God will blot out either our sins or our names. "I, even I, am He that blots out your transgressions for My own sake, and will not remember your sins." Isaiah 43:25.

The promise is to the person who overcomes sin. "He who overcomes will be dressed in white. I will never blot out his name from the book of life, but will acknowledge his name before my Father and his angels." Are you ashamed of Christ? Are you ashamed to speak His name and tell others of your Saviour and Lord, Jesus Christ? "Whoever acknowledges me before men, I will also acknowledge him before my Father in heaven. But whoever disowns me before men, I will disown him before my Father in heaven." Revelation 3:5; Matthew 10:32, 33.

The truth of the Judgment may surprise you, reader, but don't be discouraged. There is great hope for you! God says, "I will forgive their wickedness, and I will remember their sins no more." "In those days at that time, declares the Lord, search will be made for Israel's guilt but there will be none, and for the sins of Judah, but none will be found." Isn't that wonderful news? Jesus Christ will erase yours sins from His record books and even from His mind. When He looks at you throughout eternity, He won't even remember your sins. Jeremiah 31:34; 50:20.

God will blot out sins before the second coming of the Lord. The Judgment—the work of investigation and blotting out of sins—began in 1844. God will judge the living and the dead "according to what they had done as recorded in the books." Revelation 20:12.

Life Record

God has an accurate record of your life. A person may have sinned in broad daylight or in the darkness of the darkest night. God and the angels of God see each action and hear each word as clearly at night as during the day. Angels of God see each sin and record it in living video. People may hide their sins or lie about them and cover them up. Dad and mom and your husband or wife may not know. Your children and your friends may not know. You might be the only one on earth, humanly speaking, who knows. But the angels of heaven clearly see it. You can't even hide one thought from God. He knows your inner life. You can never erase words that you have spoken or deeds you have done.

Candid Camera

Smile, you are on candid camera. Every word you speak and every thing you do is accurately video taped in the heavenly record books. If we could see what is really happening in the invisible world around us, we would see an angel recording everything we say and do. Those video books will be carefully examined in the judgment. If we could see into the invisible world of the angels all around us, many of our unkind words would not be spoken. Many of our unkind thoughts would never be acted on. Instead, we would be pleading with Jesus to help us think good thoughts and perform good actions. Why not help someone today? The angels also record the kind deeds performed in honor of Jesus. Our lives will be investigated not only for the bad thoughts, words, and actions, but also for our good thoughts, words, and actions. God will judge us by what we do to help others and by what we could have done to help another person in need.

In the judgment, God will inspect the use we have made of every ability He has given us. How have we used our time, our abilities, our voice, our money, and our influence? What have we done for the poor, the disadvantaged, the orphan, or the widow? See the story Jesus tells about the sheep and the goats in the twenty-fifth chapter of Matthew.

Time is like money. We have twenty-four hours in a day. How are you spending it? Are you spending it on pleasure, dressing in flashy clothing, and on building a financial empire? Our future and the future of those we associate with is dependent on taking the time to search God's Word earnestly and prayerfully.

A crisis is soon to break upon our world! We must understand for ourselves the position and work of our great High Priest. Otherwise, we will utterly fail in meeting this crisis successfully. Each must meet the great Judge face to face. It is extremely important that everyone often meditates on the solemn scene when the Judgment begins and God opens the video book of your life.

The Rest of the Story!

God's plan has two divisions. Most have only heard of the first division.

Most have heard of Christ's death on the cross nearly 2,000 years ago, but very few understand the rest of the story. What is Christ doing today in the heavenly sanctuary?

1. What He Has Done

2. What He Is Doing

Christ's present work in the sanctuary is as necessary to the plan of salvation as was His death upon the cross. We must, by faith, follow Him in His work in the most holy apartment of the heavenly sanctuary. This is "where Jesus went before us." Hebrews 6:20. He wants us to follow Him there by faith. "He who covers his sins will not prosper: but whoever confesses and forsakes them will have mercy." Proverbs 28:13, NKJV. "My grace is sufficient for you." 2 Corinthians 12:9. "Take My yoke upon you, and learn of Me; for I am gentle and humble in heart: and you will find rest for your souls. For My yoke is easy, and My burden is light." Matthew 11:29, 30. Let none, then, regard their weaknesses as hopeless. God will give faith and grace to overcome them.

Surprise! The Judgment Has Come as "A Thief in the Night" Experience

It is necessary that Christians solemnly prepare to meet Jesus. Get serious with God! Invest your time in searching the Holy Bible as though your very life depended on it. It does!. We are not saved by the knowledge of the "religious experts" we trust. We must be saved individually. You must know God now, personally, if you want God to know you as His child when He returns in glory. The hour of God's judgment has come like a thief in the night, and most of those who claim to follow Christ do not even know it!

The Judgment soon—none know how soon—will begin with those who are now living and claim to be Christians. Your case will come before the King of the universe. Your King, Jesus Christ, wants you to be ready! "Be on guard! Be alert! You do not know when that time will come." Mark 13:33. "Wake up! . . . repent. But if you do not wake up, I will come like a thief, and you will not know at what time I will come to you." Revelation 3:3.

God will have decided whether you are saved or lost, before our Lord appears the second time in the clouds of heaven. When Jesus finishes His work of judgment, He will say, "Let him who does wrong continue to do wrong; let him who is vile continue to be vile; let him who does right continue to do right; and let him who is holy continue to be holy. Behold, I am coming soon! My reward is with me, and I will give to everyone according to what he has done."

Judges always give out the sentence—the reward—after the judgment. When Jesus comes, He will say, "My reward is with me"—again showing that the decision part of the judgment is over. The rewarding, or sentencing part of the judgment is the part of the judgment that takes place when He comes. Revelation 22:11, 12.

Planet Earth is on probation. God will soon judge the living. Won't you accept His mercy now? Soon the Judgment will be over. When the Judgment is over, probation will also be over. Soon it will be too late! Silently, unnoticed as the midnight thief, will come the last call of mercy. Mercy's offer to guilty sinners will be withdrawn. Then "a time of trouble such as never was" will burst on Planet Earth as an overwhelming surprise! Daniel 12:1, KJV. Angels will protect those who have chosen to follow Christ in His work and let Him write His law in their minds.

When "He comes suddenly, do not let him find you sleeping." Mark 13:36. Prepare so that you will not be "weighed in the balances, and found wanting." Daniel 5:27, NKJV.

23

What Really Happens When I Die?

Lucifer began his rebellion in heaven. And his rebellion is now isolated to Planet Earth. Today he wants everyone on Planet Earth to unite with him in his warfare against God—against His law and His government. He tricked our first parents into joining his rebellion. He performed his first miracle. He made it appear that a snake was talking to Eve. The devil spoke to Eve and said, "Did God really say, 'You must not eat from any tree in the garden?'" "The woman said to the serpent, 'We may eat fruit from the trees in the garden, but God did say, 'You must not eat fruit from the tree that is in the middle of the garden, and you must not touch it, or you will die.' 'You will not surely die,' the serpent said to the woman. 'For God knows that when you eat of it your eyes will be opened, and you will be like God, knowing good and evil.'" Genesis 3:1-5.

She chose to believe Lucifer and to disbelieve God. This lie from the devil—"You shall not die"—is repeated from the pulpit today as though these were the words of Jesus and not of the devil. This is the lie behind the immortality of the soul. We are not immortal—only God is immortal and never-dying. "The King of kings and Lord of lords, who alone is immortal." 1 Timothy 6:15, 16.

The miracle of the talking snake was the first miracle of deception used by the Devil. Today Satan stands behind many of the miracles performed in the name of the Lord in an attempt to trick us into joining his rebellion. Jesus says "Many will say to me on that day, 'Lord Lord, did we not prophesy in your name, and in your name drive out demons and perform many miracles? Then I will tell them plainly, I never knew you. Away from me, you evildoers!" Matthew 7:21-23.

Death

One of Babylon's intoxicating false doctrines is the first lie: "You will not surely die"—immortality of the soul. The words of Lucifer, using the puppet serpent, to Eve in Eden—"You will not surely die"—became the first sermon ever preached upon the immortality of the soul. Yet Christian ministers are echoing Satan's own seducing lie. Most people everywhere accept this lie as quickly as our first parents accepted it, but what does God's Word say? "The soul who sins, is the one who will die." Ezekiel 18:20. "As surely as I live, declares the . . . Lord, I take no pleasure in the death of the wicked, but rather that they turn from their ways and live. Turn! Turn from your evil ways! Why will you die?" Ezekiel 33:11.

Hell

The theory of eternal torment is one of the false doctrines that is part of the wine of the abomination of Babylon. Revelation 14:8; 17:2.

Purgatory

Ministers have even twisted the Scriptures concerning David and his son Amnon. They put drunken Amnon in purgatory to prepare him for the eternal friendship of sinless angels. They take the verse from Samuel that says "King David longed to go to Absalom, for he had been comforted concerning Amnon because he was dead." Those who pervert scripture tell us that our salvation does not depend upon anything we do in this life. They say it does not depend on receiving a new heart and life change from Christ, or on what we believe. 2 Samuel 13:39, NKJV.

Misinformed ministers preach that when drunken Amnon died, angels immediately took him away, purified him, and prepared him for the companionship of the sinless angels! This is a pleasing hoax, one of Satan's own doctrines. God's Word says that "no drunkard will inherit the kingdom of God." "To him who is thirsty I will give to drink without cost from the spring of the water of life." 1 Corinthians 6:10, KJV; Revelation 21:6.

Watch a person who is really thirsty for water. What are they thinking about? What about their actions? A really thirsty person's priority is to get a drink of water. What is your priority? Are you thirsty for God's Word? Have you made it your priority? Revelation 21:6. "He who overcomes will inherit all things. I will be his God, and he will be My son."

Here, also, God specifies conditions. Those who inherit all things must resist and overcome sin. Revelation 21:7. "Tell the righteous it will be well with them." "Woe to the wicked! Disaster is upon them! They will be paid back for what their hands have done." Isaiah 3:10, 11. "Although a wicked man commits a hundred crimes and still lives a long time, I know that it will go better with God-fearing men, who are reverent before God. Yet because the wicked do not fear God, it will not go well with them." "Though a sinner does evil a hundred times," says the wise man, "and still lives a long time," yet "it will go better" with those who love God. Ecclesiastes 8:12, 13. God will "give to each person according to what he has done." Romans 2:6.

"No immoral, impure or greedy person—such a man is an idolater—has any inheritance in the kingdom of Christ and of God." "Make every effort to live in peace with all men and to be holy; without holiness no one will see the Lord." "Blessed are those who do His commandments, that they may have the right to the tree of life, and may enter through the gates into the city. But outside are the dogs and sorcerers and sexually immoral and murderers and idolaters, and whoever loves and practices a lie." Ephesians 5:5; Hebrews 12:14; Revelation 22:14, 15, NKJV.

God has given to men a knowledge of His character and of His method of dealing with sin. "The Lord came down in the cloud. . . . And he passed in front of Moses, proclaiming, 'The Lord, the Lord, the compassionate and gracious God, slow to anger, abounding in love and faithfulness, maintaining love to thousands, and forgiving wickedness, rebellion, and sin. Yet he does not leave the guilty unpunished." God will destroy all the wicked. "The Lord watches over all who love him, but all the wicked he will destroy." "All sinners will be destroyed." Exodus 34:6, 7; Psalms 145:20, 37, 38. Many sinners hate God because they know that He hates their sins. Will He then chain these rebels to His side? Will He force them to do His will? They have not trained the mind to love purity. A life of rebellion against God has unfitted them for heaven.

The wicked decide their own destiny by their own choice. Their exclusion from heaven is voluntary. "The wickedness of man was great in the earth" and "every imagination of the thoughts of his heart was only evil continually." "The earth also was corrupt before God, and the earth was filled with violence." Genesis 6:5, 11, KJV. In mercy to the world,

God blotted out the wicked people in Noah's time. "The wages of sin is death; but the gift of God is eternal life through Jesus Christ our Lord." Romans 6:23, KJV. While life is the inheritance of the righteous, death is the doom of the wicked. Moses declared to Israel: "I give you the choice today of life and good, or death and evil." "There will be a resurrection of both the righteous and the wicked." "For as in Adam all die, even so in Christ will all be made alive." Deuteronomy 30:15, KJV; Acts 24:15, 1 Corinthians 15:22.

Are you aware that there are two resurrections? The first is the resurrection of life, and the second resurrection—the one after the thousand-year reign with Christ—is the resurrection of the wicked. They will die the second death—eternal death. "All who are in their graves will hear his voice and come out—those who have done good will rise to live, and those who have done evil will rise to be condemned." John 5:28, 29. They, whom God has accounted "worthy" of the resurrection of life, are "blessed and holy." "The second death has no power over them, but they will be priests of God and of Christ and will reign with him for a thousand years." Revelation 20:6. "Yet a little while, and the wicked will not be: yes, you will diligently consider his place, and it will not be." Psalm 37:10. "They will be as though they had never been." Obadiah 16.

Can the Dead Think? No—They Cannot!

When his breath departs, he returns to his earth—"In that very day his thoughts perish." Psalm 146:4, KJV. "For the living know that they will die, but the dead know nothing: they have no further reward, and even the memory of them is forgotten. Their love, their hate, and their jealousy have long since vanished; never again will they have a part in anything that happens under the sun." "Whatever your hand finds to do, do it with all your might, for in the grave, where you are going, there is neither working nor planning nor knowledge, nor wisdom." "There is no work . . . or knowledge or wisdom in the grave, where you are going." Ecclesiastes 9:5, 6, 10; Ecclesiastes 9:10, NKJV. "The grave cannot praise you. Death cannot sing your praise. . . . The living, the living—they praise you, as I am doing today." Isaiah 38:18, 19.

Popular theology represents the righteous dead as in heaven, yet . . .

How Much Can a Dead Man Remember?

Nothing! "In death there is no remembrance of You. In the grave who shall give You thanks?" Psalms 6:5, NKJV.

How Much Can a Dead Man Say?

Nothing! "The dead do not praise the Lord, nor any who go down into silence." Psalms 115:17, NKJV.

Where Did King David Go When He Died?

King David did not go to heaven when he died. He went to the grave to wait for Jesus to come again the second time. "David died and was buried, and his tomb is here to this day. . . . David himself has not gone up into the heavens." "David did not ascend to heaven." Acts 2:29, 34, WE; Acts 2:29, 34, NKJV. David is in the grave. He did not go to heaven when he died! He will be in the grave until the resurrection.

Death Is Compared to Sleeping

"If the dead are not raised, then Christ has not been raised either. And if Christ has not been raised, your faith is futile; you are still in your sins. Then those also who have fallen asleep in Christ are lost." 1 Corinthians 15:16-18.

Do We Go to Jesus When We Die?

When about to leave His disciples, Jesus did not tell them, "You will soon come to me" No! He said, "I go to prepare a place for you," "If I go and prepare a place for you, I will come back and take you to be with me that you also may be where I am." John 14:2, 3. He did not say, "You will come." He said, "I will come back" again. What would be the purpose of His coming for us if we had already gone to heaven and were with Him? Many teach that those who die go to Jesus in heaven. But Jesus says No! He says, "It is not you who come to Me at death—it is I who come for you all."

Jesus is coming again. We do not meet the Lord in death. We wait in the graves until the resurrection, and then we awaken. Angels then take us to "meet the Lord in the air." "The Lord Himself will come down from heaven, with a loud command, with the voice of the archangel and with the trumpet call of God, and the dead in Christ wil rise first. After that, we who are still alive and are left will be caught up together with them in the clouds to meet the Lord in the air. And so we will be with the Lord forever." And he adds: "Encourage each other with these words." I Thessalonians 4:16-18. Both those who are dead and those who are alive wait together on earth until Jesus comes. The dead are not in heaven alive and waiting for us. They are sleeping in their graves until Jesus comes.

Notice the progression of events:

1. First, the Lord comes to earth. He remains "in the air" above the earth.

2. Next, He shouts and wakes up the righteous dead.

3. Next, the righteous dead rise with Christ.

4. Then the righteous living meet the Lord "in the air."

5. Then they complete the journey to heaven together.

Will the righteous receive the approval, "Well done, good and faithful servant: . . . Come and share your master's happiness" when they have been living with the Lord for hundreds of years? Are the wicked called away from the fires of hell to receive the sentence from the Judge of all the earth: "Depart from Me, you who are cursed, into the eternal fire prepared for the devil and his angels"? Matthew 25:21, 41.

The Protestant churches of our day borrowed false doctrines from Rome, and Rome borrowed them from paganism, and paganism got them from Satan. The immortality of the soul was one of those false doctrines that Rome borrowed from paganism. The dead will sleep the sleep of death until "the trumpet will sound, and the dead will be raised . . . .and we shall be changed." "This body which dies must become a body which will never die. When this body which dies becomes one which will never die, what the holy writings say comes true. It says, 'Death is overcome by victory. Death, you have lost the battle. Death, your power to hurt us is gone.' Death is swallowed up in victory." "O death, where is your sting? O grave, where is your victory?" 1 Corinthians 15:52-55, WE, KJV, KNJV.

Can Our Dead Relatives Speak to Us?

The belief that the soul is immortal—that it never dies—was borrowed from paganism. The church compromised with paganism and replaced the truth that the "the dead know not anything" with this pagan belief. This, in turn, prepared the way for another one of the devil's deceptions—the belief that spirits of the dead return to guide the living, which is modern spiritualism.

Satan has power to make it appear that a person's dead friends and relatives have returned from the dead to visit and guide them. These dead loved ones and friends are, in reality, evil angels disguised as dead friends and loved ones watching over their families and friends. They teach the listener that God's law has been done away with and that there is no difference between those who honor God and those who dishonor Him According to these so-called friends and relatives returning from the dead, everyone has eternal life.

The Bible warns us of "the working of Satan with all power and signs and lying wonders" and with all his powers of deception, Satan will deceive people just as he did Adam and Eve, by doing miracles that appear to be from God. "He performs great signs so that he even makes fire come down from heaven on the earth in the sight of men. And he deceives those who dwell on the earth by those signs which he was granted to do." 2 Thessalonians 2:9, 10, KJV; Revelation 13:13, 14, NKJV.

Satan uses spiritualism to tell us, "You will be as gods, knowing good and evil." Genesis 3:5. Spiritualism teaches that a person is constantly improving from the day he is born, getting closer and closer to God each day. Jesus Christ is essentially not needed, because spiritualism teaches that we are *all* Christ–that "the throne is within you" and that "any just and perfect being is Christ."

Spiritualism is a Modern Form of Witchcraft!

Spiritualism is a modern and more subtle form of witchcraft! You have undoubtedly seen spiritualists on television talk shows. Modern spiritualists of today claim to talk with the dead. The spirits of devils impersonating cherished relatives will appear to many. But the Bible calls these so-called "returning loved ones"—these visitors from other worlds—"the spirits of devils." The Bible says the work of dealing with these spirits is forbidden by the Lord under the penalty of death. This is a modern form of witchcraft. Compare Numbers 25:1-3; Psalm 106:28; 1 Corinthians 10:20; Revelation 16:14; Leviticus 19:31; 20:27.

Satan says to the world: "No matter how evil you are, no matter whether you believe or disbelieve God and the Bible or serve the devil, live the way you want, because everyone will have eternal life." But that is not what the Bible says. The Bible says, "Woe to those who call evil good and good evil, who put darkness for light and light for darkness." Isaiah 5:20.

Spiritualists have no interest in Jesus. They have power that the devil gives them, and they are always promoting their own miracles, with the claim that they perform far greater miracles than Christ. Those who promote themselves and their miracles and who speak of how great they are clearly are not following the self-denying Master, Jesus Christ.

Satan has many disguises. Satan's Christian disguise is that of love and miracles. Satan speaks through some in the Christian ministry, presenting the purely emotional aspect of God's love. Satan and those with his "Christian disguise" separate God's love from God's law. However, God's law is a vital part of God's love. If you have been deceived on this point, God will forgive you as soon as you ask Him and use you mightily as you learn the "rest of the story."

God gives us all the freedom of choice. If people want to believe that the law is not part of love, God allows them to believe it. "They received not the love of the truth that they might be saved," therefore, "God will send them strong delusion, that they should believe a lie." 2 Thessalonians 2:10, 11, KJV.

Satan has long been preparing for his final effort to deceive the world. His preparation to deceive the world began with his first miracle and his first lie to Eve in Eden, when he said, "You will surely not die. . . . when you eat of it your eyes will be opened, and you will be like God, knowing good and evil." Genesis 3:4, 5. Satan works miracles to deceive people. "I saw three evil spirits that looked like frogs; they are spirits of demons performing miraculous signs, and they go out to the kings of the whole world to gather them for the battle on the great day of God Almighty." Revelation 16:13, 14.

The devil is smart and charming and uses real religious miracles and a type of lawless love to deceive religious people.

24

Who's in Charge?

When Christ left Planet Earth, He left His vicar, His substitute, to help and guide His children. The night before He died on the cross, Jesus said, "I tell you the truth: It is for your good that I am going away. Unless I go away, the Counselor will not come to you; but if I go I will send him to you. . . . But when he, the Spirit of truth, comes, he will guide you into all truth." Christ was speaking of the Holy Spirit. The Holy Spirit is the only representative, or Vicar, Christ has left behind to lead His people.

What about the papacy? Hasn't the papacy always claimed to be the vicar (substitute) of Christ? Well, let's analyze that thought. Throughout history, how does the character of many of the popes compare with that of our Saviour? Was Christ ever known to put men in prison or on the rack because they did not worship Him as the King of heaven? By the way, the rack used pulleys and ropes to stretch its victims legs and arms out of joint. The rack was just one of many torture devices used to enforce what the papacy thought was "true worship."

Take a trip through Europe, and you will see the old places where torture was administered. Or go see the Menno Hoff museum in Shipshewana, Indiana, near South Bend, Indiana. Was Christ's voice heard condemning to death those who did not accept Him? Jesus said, "The Son of man is not come to destroy men's lives, but to save them." Luke 9:55, KJV.

On one side we have Christ telling us who His representative or vicar is, and on the other side we have people telling us who Christ's representative, or vicar is. What do you think? Should we trust Christ to tell us the truth—or should we trust man to tell us the truth? Christ says that the only vicar, or representative of His over the church, is the Holy Spirit. Have the popes tried to take the place of the Holy Spirit?

There is a huge difference between the spirit shown by Christ and that of His self-proclaimed substitute. The papacy is the same brutally cruel power that crushed out human liberty. The papacy is the apostasy of the latter times. For a thousand years the papacy brutally tortured and killed over 50 million Christians who did not submit to her unbiblical beliefs. One death could possibly have been a mistake, but 50 million deaths is no mistake. 2 Thessalonians 2:3, 4.

The papacy, as recorded in the book *The Great Controversy,* used forgeries and fraudulent "miracles" to support Sunday sacredness. In one instance the papacy used a document that it said God Himself had written. The document outlawed work from three o'clock Saturday afternoon until sunrise Monday. The papacy said that many miracles proved God wrote the document. It also said that God paralyzed people who were found working on Sunday.

A mill operator who attempted to grind his corn saw, instead of flour, a stream of blood come out. The document also claimed the mill wheel stood still, although water cascaded over the wheel. A woman who placed dough in the oven found it raw when taken out, though the oven was very hot. Another had dough prepared for baking at three o'clock Saturday afternoon, but determined to set it aside until Monday. She found the next day that angels had made it into loaves and baked it. A man who baked bread after three o'clock Saturday found, when he broke it the next morning, that blood came out.

By such superstitious hoaxes the supporters of Sunday tried to establish its sacredness. (See Roger de Hoveden, *Annals*, vol. 2.) Revelation 13 declares that the power represented by the beast with lamb-like horns will cause "the earth and them (which dwell therein) that live on the earth" to worship the papacy. The beast of Revelation 13 "like a leopard" symbolizes the papacy. The beast with two horns is also to say "to them that dwell on the earth that they should make an image to the beast." "He also forced everyone, small and great, rich and poor, free and slave, to receive a mark on his right hand or on his forehead, so that no one could buy or sell unless he had the mark." Revelation 13:12, 14, NKJV; 13:16, 17.

The United States is the power represented by the beast with lamb-like horns. The United States will fulfill this prophecy when it enforces Sunday observance, which Rome claims as the special recognition of her supremacy—a recovery of her power.

"One of the heads of the beast seemed to have had a fatal wound." The fatal wound points to the downfall of the papacy in 1798. After this, says the prophet, "the fatal wound . . . healed. The whole world was astonished and followed the beast." Revelation 13:3. Paul states plainly that the "man of sin" will continue until the second coming. 2 Thessalonians 2:3-8. To the very close of time he will carry forward the work of deception. The apostle John, in Revelation, says, also referring to the papacy: "All" people "of the earth will worship the beast—all whose names have not been written in the book of life." Revelation 13:8. It is the boast of Rome that she never changes. Rome is building up huge towering structures. The church of Rome will repeat the persecution and torture of the past in the secret rooms within these buildings.

25

The Last Great Battle

Certain areas in today's bookstores are full of books on the future and on Armageddon. I'm sure there were plenty of religious books in Noah's day and in the days when Christ walked the earth as a carpenter, but none of them predicted the flood correctly or predicted the coming of Christ correctly. The Bible predicted the birth and life of Christ. The religious writers and speakers, however, were blind to the Bible predictions of the birth and life of Christ. They were more interested in reading and writing and hearing what other "religious experts" had to say.

Today you will find exciting books of predictions dealing with military battles, the reconstruction of the temple, and the battle of Armageddon. Most of these books, as far as reliability goes, are "wretched, pitiful, poor, blind, and naked." Revelation 3:17. The worst thing about it, according to this verse, is that "they don't realize it." The battle of Armageddon is not a physical battle of one human army against another army. It is the battle that unites all of the people of Planet Earth against those "who keep the commandments of God and the faith of Jesus." Since God's children are helpless, God rescues them with a more spectacular rescue than has ever been seen on any television thriller. Revelation 14:12.

The last great battle is between the laws of men and the laws of God, between the religion of the Bible and the religion of man-made fiction and tradition. Poison is more dangerous when there is enough poison to kill a person, but it is blended with enough of a good substance to disguise the poison. That is why the religion of fiction and tradition is so dangerous today. It is blended with enough Bible verses to combine into a very deadly disguise. It becomes harder to discern the spiritual poison with a few Bible verses included.

An awful weight of responsibility is on the ministers of the world. False teachers in the ministry are responsible for most of the moral collapse of modern society. The teaching that Christ has set us free to disobey God's law has unleashed a flood of immorality throughout the world. Christ did not come to free us from His very own law, but instead, He came to free us from sin, which is disobedience to His great moral law.

"When Ahab saw Elijah, he said to him, 'Is that you, you troubler of Israel?' 'I have not made trouble for Israel,' Elijah replied, 'but you and your father's family have. You have abandoned the Lord's commandments and have followed Baal.'" 1 Kings 18:17, 18.

Isn't it interesting that the very ones responsible for the moral collapse of society are those who blame it on God's true servants who are true to God and keep His commandments?

The lie and the miracle that Satan used to deceive Eve laid the foundation for the entire future of Satan's work of deception. Satan has repeatedly used his miracle-working power with success throughout history. He will demonstrate as never before his miracle-working power through spiritualism. Dead friends and relatives will appear to come back from the dead to talk with us.

These "spirits of the dead" are actually evil angels in disguise. Our supposedly visiting dead loved ones will tell us to obey the laws of the land and that God has changed His Ten Commandments. "God's day of worship has changed," they will say, "from the seventh day of the week, Saturday, to the first day of the week, Sunday."

Armageddon:
The War Against Those Who Keep God's Commandments

"The dragon was enraged at the woman and went off to make war against . . . those who obey God's commandments and hold to the testimony of Jesus." Revelation 12:17. If you are interested in the last "war," this is it. The war is not against powers in the Middle East. Yes, they may fight, but that is not the war the Bible is talking about. God has a greater interest in His people world-wide than in a little piece of real estate in the Middle East.

God put the two things most precious to Him in "arks"—man, and His law. Read the story of Noah and the Ark. Read the story of baby Moses and the ark of bulrushes. And read the story about God's law in the "ark of the covenant." This last ark is the one refered to in the movie "Raiders of the Lost Ark." It has always been God's plan to put His law in the mind of man. His plan was that the two things He considered most precious—man and His law—should be together. "I will put my laws in their minds and write them on their hearts. I will be their God, and they will be my people" Hebrews 8:10.

You want to understand the battle of Armageddon? Then take your eyes off real estate and put it on God's Word. God tells us that the real battle will be world-wide over the hearts and minds of all mankind. Satan, the devil, hates God and attacks the two things God loves most—His people and His law. "The dragon was enraged at the woman and went off to make war against those who obey God's commandments and hold to the testimony of Jesus." Revelation 12:17.

This is the battle of Armageddon. This is the "final war." The devil deceives the whole world into believing that they are actually doing God's will in their attack on God's commandment-keeping people. This is a regular David and Goliath story. Most people believed Goliath would win because of his tremendous size, his armor, and his weapons. We all know that David won. David had invisible allies, the angels of God. In the closing moments of earth's present history, God's commandment-keeping children look defenseless, but they have invisible allies. God and His angels will fight for them, and God will win!

A woman, in Bible prophecy, represents a church. Read Ephesians 5:25. So when it says, "The dragon was enraged at the woman," it means that the devil is angry with God's true church at the end of time. Two identifying marks of God's true people whom the devil is angry with are that they "obey God's commandments and hold to the testimony of Jesus."

Armageddon is world-wide, and you will be very much involved. Either war will be made against you because you "obey God's commandments and hold to the testimony of Jesus," or you will be involved in making war against those who "obey God's commandments and hold to the testimony of Jesus." Those who make war against their neighbors who serve Jesus are fighting a losing battle. Jesus will rise up with His army of angels and use the seven last plagues of Revelation 16 to defeat the persecutors of His people.

What Will You Follow?
A Popular Minister? Or an Unpopular Truth?

"To the law and to the testimony: if they do not speak according to this word, it is because there is no light in them." Isaiah 8:20, KJV.

None but those who have filled their minds with these great truths of the Bible will stand through the last great conflict. God has given us warnings so important that He represents them as shouted by holy angels flying through the sky. Revelation 14:6-12.

God requires that each person use his reasoning abilities to try to understand and obey His warning message. The frightening punishment God will pour out on the beast and his image should lead all to an earnest study of the prophecies. Learn what the mark of the beast is, and learn how you can avoid receiving it! Revelation 14:9-11.

Most people are looking for comfort and don't want to listen to truth, so they accept lies instead. The apostle Paul declared, looking to the last days, "The time will come when they will not put up with sound doctrine." 2 Timothy 4:3. God has filled the Bible with warnings to the people not to follow blind leaders. The majority of the people of Noah's day were following blind leaders, which is why no one got on the ark with Noah and his family. That is why they all died. They may not have rejected truth. Maybe they believed Noah, but they neglected to get into the ark while there was still time. Don't neglect to act on truth. The result of neglecting to choose truth is to choose death.

Neglecting the Truth Is Rejecting the Truth

Our greatest danger is not crime, injury, death, or even that we openly reject the truth. Our greatest danger is that we just neglect it. To neglect truth is to reject truth! Neglecting to seek earnestly to learn God's plan for our lives is the same as rejecting God. "How shall we escape if we neglect so great a salvation?" Hebrews 2:3, NKJV. "There is a way that seems right to a man, but the end of it is death." Proverbs 16:25. It is not enough to have good intentions—it is not enough to do what a man thinks is right or what the minster or "the religious experts" tell him is right.

What about you? Will you make a decision today to follow the truths found in your Bible as presented here in *Prophecy Made Easy?* If you neglect to openly choose to follow Christ, you are rejecting Him, and ultimately this leads to a rejection of His mercy and the crown of life. I urge you to follow Christ to the cross in a life of self denial. Following Christ will mean that many others who call themselves Christians will think you are making a mistake. Take up your cross, Christian soldier. If you reject the cross or neglect the cross, you have rejected the crown of life that Jesus wants to place upon your head one day.

False teachers teach that the Bible has a secret spiritual meaning and not an obvious meaning. With a pretense of great wisdom, they teach that the Scriptures have a mystical, secret, spiritual meaning that is hard to understand. These men are false teachers. Jesus met many false teachers and said, "You do not know the Scriptures, or the power of God." Mark 12:24.

Bible teachers should explain the language of the Bible according to its obvious meaning, unless the Bible uses a symbol. Christ has given the promise: "If any man will do His will, he will know of the doctrine." John 7:17.

Uncomfortable Truths!

The popular ministry close their eyes to uncomfortable truths that they do not want to follow. Our prayer should be, "Open my eyes, that I may see wonderful things in Your law." Psalm 119:18.

Temptations often appear irresistible because, through neglect of prayer and the study of the Bible, the tempted one cannot readily remember God's promises and meet Satan with the Scripture weapons. Again, let me emphasize—our greatest danger is far worse than the worst danger you can imagine! Our worst danger is not crime, bankruptcy, injury, persecution, or even death. Our greatest danger is not rejecting God or the Word of God or even the commandments of God. Our greatest danger is in neglecting God, His Word and His commandments. Most people will be eternally lost, not because they openly rejected Christ, but because they did not take enough time to build a relationship with Jesus Christ. They were too busy. They had too many exciting things to do or to see and just did not have time to daily pray and daily study the Word of God.

Christ will send His substitute, His vicar, to you whenever you call. He will send you His Holy Spirit to live within your mind and guide you in all things. What an honor! You see, the Holy Spirit has the same kindness and strength and character as Christ. In this way, Christ will walk with you each and every day. Invite the Holy Spirit into your heart each morning and all through the day. Set aside the theater, the violent TV movies, and spend time learning the lessons you must learn in your relationship with Christ.

Make a conscious choice to spend time with the Christ you love. Ask

Him to fill you with His love and put your love into action. One of the finest acts of love will be in caring enough for your neighbors and friends to give them a copy of this very book you are reading. This book is a seed. It is growing in your heart. You are learning things you never dreamed that it was possible to know. That is, if you are anything like me, you are. I never dreamed it was possible to know the future. I not only found out what will happen in the future, I found the God of the future, Jesus Christ, my Friend and Saviour and my Creator. John, chapter 1, and Colossians, chapter 1, teach us that, yes, Christ is also our Creator. Remember in the book of Genesis that God said, "Let US make man in OUR image."

As you spend time with Jesus, angels will guide your mind and teach you the very truths you hunger to learn from your Bible. I believe angels and the Holy Spirit have guided you to read *Prophecy Made Easy* and are teaching you and guiding you right at this very moment. The devil hates *Prophecy Made Easy* and will try to get you to find something else to do or read, because he hates to have his cover blown. And this book clearly "blows his cover." Store God's Word in your mind. The Word you put in your mind has power! The greatest power on earth is the power to conquer sin. "I have hidden Your word in my heart," said David, "that I might not sin against You." Holy angels will be with you all through the day. They "are all around" those who are willing to learn the more powerful ways of God. In your time of greatest danger, they will bring to your memory the very truths that you need. Genesis 1:26, Psalm 119:11; 34:7.

26

The Final Choice

After this I saw another angel coming down from heaven. He had great authority, and the earth was illuminated by his splendor. With a mighty voice he shouted: Fallen! Fallen is Babylon the Great! She has become a home for demons and a haunt for every evil spirit, a haunt for every unclean and detestable bird. For all the nations have drunk the maddening wine of her adulteries." "The kings of the earth committed adultery with her and the merchants of the earth grew rich from her excessive luxuries. Then I heard another voice from heaven say: Come out of her, my people, so that you will not share in her sins, so that you will not receive any of her plagues; for her sins are piled up to heaven and God has remembered her crimes." Revelation 18:1-5.

A few days before Christ was crucified, He cried out, "O Jerusalem, Jerusalem, you who kill the prophets and stone those sent to you, how often I have longed to gather your children together as a hen gathers her chicks under her wings, but you were not willing. Look, your house is left to you desolate." History is repeating itself. A desolation is occurring in the modern churches of our day. If God were inside the churches of modern "Babylon" and He wanted His people out of those churches, He would say, *"Go* out." But God is in the process of leaving those churches, and that is why He says, "Come out."

Will You Obey Jesus? Will You Come Out?

Dear reader, if you are in one of the churches that are part of "Babylon," will you not obey God and "come out" of Babylon? Those who remain in Babylon will receive the wrath of God and the plagues of God. God loves you and wants you to be safe. Soon there will be no safety in the churches that make up Babylon—Protestant or Catholic. Because of their sins, they will receive the seven last plagues.

Man will say, "Conform—or die"

"All, both small and great, rich and poor, free and bond," will be forced to conform to the standards of the church by honoring the false Sabbath. Revelation 13:16. The world will be united in boycotting, fining, punishing, and finally deciding to kill all who refuse to honor the false Sabbath.

God says, "Those who do conform will receive the seven last plagues!"

"Anyone who worships the beast and his image, and receives his mark on the forehead, or on the hand, will drink the wine of God's fury." Revelation 14:9, 10.

The Sabbath will be the great test of loyalty, for it is the point of truth especially disliked and debated. When the final test will come to all people everywhere, the line of contrast will be drawn between those who serve God and those who do not serve Him. Religious discrimination will gain control in the United States. Church and state will join hands in persecuting those who keep the commandments of God.

People everywhere will hear in amazement that Babylon is the church, fallen because of her errors and sins. God calls His people out of her because of her neglect and rejection of the truth sent to her from heaven.

Everyone who will not listen to Christ's last call of mercy will be extremely angry with those who obey God and keep His commandments. They will boycott God's children, fining, imprisoning, bribing, and disinheriting them. They will drive them from home, exile them, and treat them as slaves. Then we will truly understand the words of the apostle Paul. "Everyone who wants to live a godly life in Christ Jesus will be persecuted." 2 Timothy 3:12.

The defenders of truth refuse to honor the Sunday-Sabbath. Though threatened with destruction, they will say, "We dare not change God's Word. We cannot say part of God's law is important but the other part is not important." There are still a few godly people who have governmental power at this time, and they are able to prevent an entire collapse of society until this last warning message is carried to all the world. It is not by chance that you are reading these words. God plans to fill you with His Holy Spirit and use you to welcome others into the family of God.

The Outpouring of the Holy Spirit

Have you ever planted a garden? It takes plenty of water to make it grow and prepare it for harvesting. The same principle applies in planting the gospel "seed"—God's Word. Remember, God compares His Word to "seed" planted in the minds of men, women, and children. The outpouring of God's Holy Spirit compares to the watering of the seed and the plants. Matthew 13:39, KJV.

God gave the "former rain," the outpouring of His Holy Spirit at the opening of the gospel, to cause His precious seed, His truth, to grow. God will give the "latter rain" at its close for the ripening of the harvest. "The harvest is the end of the world, and the reapers are angels." Matthew 13:39.

"If we follow on to know the Lord, He shall come unto us as the rain, as the latter and former rain unto the earth." Hosea 6:3, KJV.

"Be glad then, you children of Zion, and rejoice in the Lord your God: for He has given you the former rain moderately, and He will cause the rain, the former rain, and the latter rain to come down for you." Joel 2:23, NKJV. "In the last days, God says, I will pour out my Spirit on all people." "And everyone who calls on the name of the Lord will be saved." Acts 2:17, 21.

Your prayer might be: "Dear Father in heaven, You promised to give me Your Holy Spirit, the Spirit of truth. You said it is as simple as asking, so I am asking for the power of Your Holy Spirit in my life right now. Thank You for this wonderful gift. In the name of Jesus Christ, Amen."

Jesus will answer your prayer. He says: "Ask and it will be given to you; seek and you will find; knock and the door will be opened to you. For everyone who asks receives; he who seeks finds; and to him who knocks, the door will be opened. Which of you fathers, if your son asks for a fish, will give him a snake instead? Or if he asks for an egg, will give him a scorpion? If you then, though you are evil, know how to give good gifts to your children, how much more will your Father in heaven give the Holy spirit to those who ask him!" Luke 11: 9-14.

In the closing of the gospel, God plans to demonstrate His great power.

You will see many signs of God's power; If you are wondering what you might see, read the fifth book of the New Testament, the book of Acts. The apostle said: "Repent, then, and turn to God, so that your sins may be wiped out, that times of refreshing may come from the Lord, and that he may send the Christ, who has been appointed for you—even Jesus." Acts 3:19, 20.

God will use you, reader. He wants to use you to rapidly hurry from place to place sharing God's last call. It will be similar to the time when Noah made his last appeal to the people to enter the ark. Thousands of people around the earth will give this last warning message. Miracles will be done, the sick will be healed, and signs and wonders will follow the believers. Satan will be busy also. He will also work miracles, even bringing down fire from heaven in the sight of men. Revelation 13:13. Everyone must make a choice. On which side will you stand?

27

Trouble

At that time Michael will stand up, the great Prince who stands for the children of your people: and there will be a time of trouble, such as never was since there was a nation even to that same time: and at that time Your people—everyone whose name is found written in the book—will be delivered." Daniel 12:1, KJV.

All who have proved themselves loyal to God have received "the seal of the living God." Then Jesus ends His work of forgiving sins and cleansing sinners in the sanctuary above. He lifts His hands and with a loud voice says, "It is done."

All the angels take off their crowns as He announces the end of the gospel call and of the Judgment of those who claimed to know Christ: "Let him who does wrong continue to do wrong; let him who is vile continue to be vile; let him who does right continue to do right; and let him who is holy continue to be holy. Behold, I am coming soon! My reward is with me, and I will give to everyone according to what he has done." Revelation 22:11.

Satan has entire control of the finally disobedient. No longer protected by God's angels, they have no protection from the devil and his angels. The whole world will be filled with utter destruction more terrible than has ever happened before on the earth.

Leaders will claim that God has allowed this to happen because of those who have not honored Sunday. They will declare that those who keep the seventh-day Sabbath are dishonoring God and are responsible for the destruction and death that has overwhelmed the world. They also say, "God will save our nation and our world if we kill the Sabbath keepers." This was the same argument made against Christ nearly two thousand years ago.

"It is better for you," said the scheming Caiaphas, "that one man die for the people than that the whole nation perish." John 11:50. This reason will appear powerful. Governments will finally issue a law against those who obey the seventh-day Sabbath—the Sabbath of the fourth commandment. The law will sentence them to die at the hands of the people on a particular day of a particular month. The powers of the papacy and the powers of apostate Protestantism will be united world-wide in their plans to kill all of the Sabbath-keeping Christians.

Commandment Keepers Are Afraid

This very law will result in a very fearful time for God's commandment-keeping children. They will be filled with the fear and sorrow pictured by the prophet Jeremiah, as the time of Jacob's trouble. "Cries of fear are heard—terror, not peace. Ask and see: Can a man bear children? Then why do I see every strong man with his hands on his stomach like a woman in labor, every face turned deathly pale? How awful that day will be! None will be like it." "Alas! For that day is great, so that none is like it; and it is the time of Jacob's trouble, but he shall be saved out of it." Jeremiah 30:5-7; 30:7, NKJV.

Jacob was full of agony the night when he wrestled in prayer, pleading over and over again for safety from Esau's army. Similar events will happen again. These events are pictured by the prophet Jeremiah as "the time of Jacob's trouble." Who is it that experiences this trouble? Who is the "Jacob" at this time? You are "Jacob" if you are going to be true to God. It is thousands of times better to experience "Jacob's time of trouble" with God on your side than to experience the seven last plagues without the protection of God. In the book of Genesis, we find the story of Esau and Jacob. Satan convinced Esau to lead his army against Jacob. In the same way, he will excite the angry people of the world to kill God's obedient children in the time of trouble. Those who serve God and keep His commandments will pass through extreme testing. Genesis 32:24-30.

God promises that He "will keep you from the hour of temptation, which will come upon all the world. Let him take hold of My strength that he may make peace with me. He will make peace with Me." Their confidence does not fail because God does not instantly answer their prayers.

Though suffering the most penetrating fear, terror, and distress, they keep right on praying. They pray to God as did Jacob, who held on to Christ with all of his faith and all of his strength and said, "I will not let You go, unless You bless me." Isaiah 27:5; Revelation 3:10; Genesis 32:26.

Delaying to Prepare for the Coming Conflict Is Preparing to Fail!

Those who wait to prepare until the time of trouble will have waited too long. If you have a hole in your roof, when do you fix it? Do you wait until the middle of a lightning storm when the water is pouring into your house to fix it? "Oh," someone says, "why should I fix it when the weather is good? I don't need it until the weather turns bad." You get the point. When the storm comes, it is too late to prepare for the storm. A storm is coming. It will be relentless! Often our imagination tells us that bad things are going to happen. Often our imagination plays tricks with us, and what we imagined is not nearly as bad as we thought it was going to be. I tell you with deep regret that this time it will be worse than you or I can imagine.

God loves you and wants you to be ready. It will not be possible unless you make some sacrifices now. Sacrifice worldly TV shows and sitcoms so you have the time to fill your minds with the words of the Lord. I have found a couple of TV stations on satellite that will help you prepare for the coming crisis. One of them is 3ABN out of West Frankfort, Illinois. They have a fine combination of 24-hour programing. It is even possible to view 3ABN by computer at *www.3abn.org.* You will find it also in the links section of the website for this book: *www.prophecymadeeasy.com.* Another is KFBN, SAFE TV out of Springdale, Arkansas. Also take the time to learn the great Bible truths in this book, *Prophecy Made Easy,* as well as *The Great Controversy* and the Bible books of Daniel and Revelation.

You must consider this preparation time your number one priority so that you will have a "shelter in the time of storm." The case of all who fail to prepare is hopeless. However, the time of trial, for those who have prepared, will result in a blessing to them.

This time of trial will burn away all that is needless. The entire universe will see Christ's character perfectly revealed in those whom God saves from the last generation. Their difficulties are great. Being placed in this fiery furnace is necessary for them. This ordeal will destroy their worldliness, and their lives will perfectly reflect Christ's character of love. God will have successfully put the two things He loves most together: His people, and His law. And then will be fulfilled the words, "I will put my laws in their minds and write them on their hearts. I will be their God, and they will be my people." Hebrews 8:10.

The terrible pressure of depression does not stop them from praying for the blessing of God, earnestly and in faith, as did Jacob. Seek to develop that faith now so you can say with Jacob, "I saw God face to face, and yet my life was spared." God will then account you as princes, having power to succeed with God and with men. Genesis 32:30.

The "time of trouble, such as never was," is soon to burst upon us, and we will need this Jacob-like faith that many are too neglectful to obtain. "Big trouble will come to the earth and sea! The devil has come down to you. He is very angry. He knows that he has only a short time!" Revelation 12:12.

"As surely as I live, declares the Sovereign LORD, even if Noah, Daniel, and Jacob were in" the world, "they could save neither son nor daughter. They would save only themselves by their righteousness." Ezekiel 14:20.

UFOs

Soon people will see fearful sights of a supernatural character in the sky—a demonstration of the power of miracle-working demons.

Satan Disguised As Christ!

Satan wears no red pajamas and has no horns and no pitchfork. He has much of the power and wisdom he had in heaven. He will appear in different parts of the world with great brightness, declaring that he is Christ. He will have such a dazzling brightness, glory, compassion, and miracle working power that people will shout, "Christ has come! Christ has come!" He will tell the world that he has changed the Sabbath to Sunday and command all to honor the day he has blessed.

Satan will disguise himself as Christ, with dazzling brightness. People will be attracted to Him like metal to a magnet. No one has ever seen such amazing brightness, power, and magnificence! Everyone knows this individual is a supernatural being. But what the majority of people will not know is that this is Satan himself, disguised as Christ.

The reason counterfeiters are so successful is that they make the counterfeit look like the real thing. Perhaps you have seen television shows where you are supposed to figure out who is the man and who is the woman—and they all look like women. I have been fooled. I often didn't know who was the woman and who was the man. Everyone can be fooled part of the time. Satan will be an almost perfect counterfeit of Jesus Christ. He'll have the brilliance, the beauty, and the miracle-working power. Satan is slick! He knows all the techniques of disguise. He will also quote a few Bible verses with the sound of love in his voice.

There is no way you can tell if this is the real Christ or Satan disguised as Christ except by two things. First, by His teachings. Satan claims to have changed the Sabbath to Sunday. Disguised as Jesus Christ, he will deceive many who will believe that this is "the great power of God." Revelation 1:13-15, Acts 8:10. Second, by his manner of appearing. Christ does not set foot on Planet Earth when He comes the second time. The brilliance, beauty, and majesty that surrounds Him has never been seen before.

However, Satan, disguised as Christ, will not mislead the people of God, for two reasons:

1. The teachings of this false Christ are not according to the Bible teachings. He blesses the worshipers of the beast and his image—the very class upon whom the Bible declares that God will pour out His merciless wrath.

2. God does not permit Satan to counterfeit the way Christ comes. The Saviour has warned His people so they would not be fooled on this point and has clearly told the way He will return the second time. When Christ comes the second time, He will not take even one step on Planet Earth. He will remain in the sky, and the angels will take us to meet Him. Then we will return to heaven with Him. Anyone who walks on Planet Earth claiming to be Christ is a fraud, or the devil himself, regardless of how nice he looks or how many miracles he performs.

"False christs and false prophets will appear and perform great signs and miracles to deceive even the elect. . . . So if anyone tells you, There he is, out in the desert, do not go out; or, here he is, in the inner rooms, do not believe it. For as lightning that comes from the east is visible even in the west, so will be the coming of the son of Man." "They will see the Son of man coming on the clouds of the sky, with power and great glory. And he will send his angels with a loud trumpet call, and they will gather his elect from the four winds, from one end of the heavens to the other." This coming, there is no possibility of counterfeiting. It will be universally known—witnessed by the whole world. Matthew 24:24, 27, 30; see also Revelation 1:7; 1 Thessalonians 4:16, 17.

204 PROPHECY MADE EASY

The Death Sentence

Governments will issue an order against those who keep God's commandments, withdrawing governmental protection and giving those who want, permission to kill the commandment keepers. This will cause God's people to leave the cities and villages quickly and live together in the forests and mountains. They will live together in groups, in the most isolated and remote places. Many will find shelter in the mountains. God's children have often found a protective retreat in "the fortress of rocks." Isaiah 33:16.

Those in power will throw many—of all nations and classes, high and low, rich and poor, black and white—into the most unfair and cruel slavery. They will chain many of God's children, shut them in by prison bars, and give them the death sentence. Many will be left to supposedly die of starvation in dark and filthy dungeons and prison cells. The situation will appear hopeless. Nobody seems to care about their pain, and nobody will be there to help them. But God cares, and angels will come to them in prison.

Will the Lord Forget You?
Did He Forget Faithful Noah?

"Zion said, The Lord has forsaken me, the Lord has forgotten me. Can a mother forget the baby at her breast and have no compassion on the child she has borne? Though she may forget, I will not forget you! See, I have engraved you on the palms of my hands." Isaiah 49:14-16. God says, "Whoever touches you touches the apple of his eye." Zechariah 2:8.

"The LORD will rise up as he did at Mount Perazim, he will rouse himself as in the Valley of Gibeon—to do his work, his strange work, and perform his task, his alien task." Isaiah 28:21. To our merciful God, the act of punishment is a strange act. "Say to them, 'As surely as I live, declares the Sovereign LORD, I take no pleasure in the death of the wicked, but rather that they turn from their ways and live. Turn! Turn from your evil ways! Why will you die?'" Ezekiel 33:11. "The Lord is slow to anger, and great in power. The Lord will not leave the guilty unpunished." Nahum 1:3.

And he passed in front of Moses, proclaiming, "The LORD, the LORD, the compassionate and gracious God, slow to anger, abounding in love and faithfulness, maintaining love to thousands, and forgiving wickedness, rebellion and sin. Yet he does not leave the guilty unpunished." Exodus 34:6, 7.

The U.S.A. and the whole world will be involved in receiving the plagues of God's wrath. Christ will end His work of intercession in the sanctuary. He will then pour out His merciless anger against those who worship the beast and his image and receive his mark. Revelation 14:9, 10.

Plagues

"You are just in these judgments for they have shed the blood of your saints and prophets, and you have given them blood to drink as they deserve." Revelation 16:2-6.

Dead Bodies Everywhere

The sun becomes much hotter, "scorching men with great heat." Water is scarce, and fires are raging. The sun has power "to scorch men with fire, and men were scorched with great heat." Revelation 16:8, 9, NKJV.

"The fields are ruined, the ground is dried up; the grain is destroyed, the new wine is dried up, the oil fails. Despair, you farmers, wail, you vine growers; grieve for the wheat and the barley, because the harvest of the field is destroyed. The vine is dried up and the fig tree is withered; the pomegranate, the palm and the apple tree—all the trees of the field—are dried up. Surely the joy of mankind is withered away.

"The seeds are shriveled beneath the clods. The storehouses are in ruins, the granaries have been broken down, for the grain has dried up. How the cattle moan! The herds mill about because they have no pasture; even the flocks of sheep are suffering. To you, O LORD, I call, for fire has devoured the open pastures and flames have burned up all the trees of the field. Even the wild animals pant for you; the streams of water have dried up and fire has devoured the open pastures.

"The fierce heat of the sun has ruined the fields, drying up the ground and destroying the crops. The harvest of the field is gone. The vines have dried up." Happiness has taken a vacation. No one is happy anywhere. "The seed is rotten. The harvests are destroyed. The animals groan! The herds of cattle are dying, because they have no pasture. . . . The rivers of water are dried up, and the fire has destroyed the pastures of the wilderness." Joel 1:10-12, 17-20. "The songs of the temple shall become wailings in that day," says the Lord GOD. "The dead bodies shall be many; in every place they shall be cast out in silence." Amos 8:3, RSV.

These plagues are not worldwide, or all the people of Planet Earth would be dead. Yet it will be the most awful destruction that people have ever known, anytime in history. God has blended all the judgments upon men, before the close of probation, with mercy. The pleading blood of Christ has shielded the sinner from receiving the full measure of his guilt. However, in the final judgment, God pours out His wrath unmixed with mercy.

Food and Water for Commandment Keepers

In that day, many of the wicked will hunger and thirst for the shelter of God's mercy that they have so long rejected. "The days are coming," declares the Sovereign LORD, "when I will send a famine through the land—not a famine of food or a thirst for water, but a famine of hearing the words of the LORD. Men will stagger from sea to sea and wander from north to east, searching for the word of the LORD, but they will not find it." Amos 8:11, 12.

At this time, the wicked will be dying from hunger and disease. Angels, however, will provide food for the righteous. To the person who "walks righteously" is the promise: "Bread will be given him; his water will be sure." "The poor and needy search for water, but there is none; their tongues are parched with thirst. But I the Lord will answer them; I, the God of Israel, will not forsake them." Isaiah 33:16, NKJV; 41:17.

"Though the fig tree does not bud and there are no grapes on the vines, though the olive crop fails and the fields produce no food, though there are no sheep in the pen and no cattle in the stalls, yet I will rejoice in the Lord, I will be joyful in God my Savior." Habakkuk 3:17, 18.

"The Lord is your keeper: the Lord is your shade upon your right hand. The sun will not smite you by day, nor the moon by night. The Lord will preserve you from all evil: He will preserve your soul." Psalm 121:5-7.

"He will deliver you from the trap of the fowler, and from the deadly plague. He will cover you with His feathers, and under His wings will you trust: His truth will be your shield and armor." Psalm 91:3, 4.

Terror Fills the Nights!

"You will not fear the terror of night, nor the arrow that flies by day, nor the pestilence that stalks in the darkness, nor the plague that destroys at midday. A thousand may fall at your side, ten thousand at your right hand, but it will not come near you. You will only observe with your eyes and see the punishment of the wicked. If you make the Most High your dwelling—even the LORD, who is my refuge— then no harm will befall you, no disaster will come near your tent." Psalm 91:5-10.

Like Jacob, all are wrestling with God. Their faces express their internal struggle. Every face is pale. Yet they do not stop praying earnestly. "And shall God not avenge His own elect who cry out day and night to Him, though He bears long with them? I tell you that He will avenge them speedily." Luke 18:7, 8, NKJV. The end will come more quickly than men expect. Remember the childhood games. "Ready or not, here I come!" Are you ready? Ready or not, Jesus is coming soon. Ready or not, "the hour of His judgment has come" now! Revelation 14:6-12. Ready or not, the storm is very near. Make sure you put Christ's words into practice, and you will "not fall." Matthew 7:21:27.

Angels Are Sent in Answer to Prayer!

Angels have appeared in two forms—either with their natural, dazzling "lightning" brightness, or disguised as ordinary men.

Angels have appeared wearing clothes that were as brilliant as lightning. They have also come to church and to other assemblies of people disguised as men.

"The angel of the Lord encamps around those who fear Him, and He delivers them." Psalm 34:7.

"The redeemed of the Lord will return, and come with singing unto Zion."

"The ransomed of the LORD will return. They will enter Zion with singing; everlasting joy will crown their heads. Gladness and joy will overtake them, and sorrow and sighing will flee away." "I, even I, am he who comforts you. Who are you that you fear mortal men, the sons of men, who are but grass, that you forget the LORD your Maker, who stretched out the heavens and laid the foundations of the earth." Isaiah 51:11-13.

"In the time of trouble He shall hide me in . . . the secret place of His tabernacle." Psalm 27:5. "Go, My people, enter your rooms, and shut the doors behind you; hide yourselves for a little while until his wrath has passed by. See, the Lord is coming out of his dwelling to punish the people of the earth for their sins." Isaiah 26:20, 21. God will use angels and the forces of nature in the seven last plagues to make your rescue the most spectacular rescue that can be imagined. Make sure that you are drawing close to God, and do all you can now to share this great message with others. The trials ahead will require patience and knowing God. Be patient—your rescue will be spectacular!

28

Deliverance!

ll of God's commandment-keeping children will eventually be in either prison cells or hidden away in wild forests and mountainous areas. From these locations, God's people still earnestly pray for His protection. All around the world, gangs of armed, demon-possessed men search for and prepare to kill every commandment-keeping Christian. It is now, in this hour of greatest danger, that God Himself takes complete charge of the rescue of His children. "The Lord will cause men to hear his majestic voice and will make them see his arm coming down with raging anger and consuming fire, with cloudburst, thunderstorm and hail." Isaiah 30:30.

All around the world, gangs of armed men are closing in on their targets. But before they can pull the triggers on their guns, God covers the entire earth in a dense blackness, darker than the darkest midnight, without moon or stars. Then it seems as though a searchlight of magnificent colors appears. It is the brilliant searchlight of God's rainbow, but unlike any rainbow ever seen before, so bright and powerful it is.

God speaks. "Look up, my children, look up." We see the symbol of God's power and protection, and it brings joy to our hearts. But wait, we not only see the rainbow, we see the heavy clouds open, and to our astonishment we see Jesus sitting on His throne, talking with His Father and saying, "Father, I want these, my children who have come out of great tribulation, to be given crowns as kings and queens with me. I want them to share our throne and sit with us." We all join together in a great shout of victory. Revelation 3:21.

The Earthquake!
Mountains and Islands Disappear!

All nature responds in celebration to this announcement from the Creator. It appears to be midnight, but the clouds roll back, and the sun breaks through in all its splendor. Rivers and creeks stop flowing. Then God speaks again and shouts, "It is done!" His voice causes the earth to shake; the mountains shake so severely that jagged rocks seem to be torn out and hurled through the air. Colossal tidal waves spread across the oceans. Hurricane-force winds destroy everything in their path. The earth itself is moving. The surface of the earth rolls up and down and cracks apart. Enormous mountain systems sink. The tidal waves swallow up and destroy everything in their path, including all the islands and seaports.

God then destroys everything left standing with enormous hailstones— huge chunks of ice. The elegant palaces and homes of the rich are destroyed. The prison walls that hold His children prisoners are demolished. God's children are FREE at last! FREE at last! Excitement is in the very air! Graves and caskets are opened, and God's children who have been sleeping the sleep of death are awakened by their guardian angels. They shout "FREE! FREE AT LAST! Free from the sleep of death! Free from the prison cell of death."

The amazing things we have seen bring an entire transformation over all God's commandment-keeping children. We can see it in each other's faces. Our faces, so colorless, tense, and tired, are now shining with joyful smiles. You can hear that joy in our voices as we sing together the words of the Psalms: "God is our refuge and strength, a very present help in trouble. Therefore we will not fear, though the earth give way, and the mountains fall into the heart of the sea; though the waters roar and foan and the mountains quake." Psalm 46:1-3.

The Hand in the Sky!

Bright beautiful light shines down from the open gates of God's Holy City, New Jerusalem. As we look up at the beauty of it all, we see a hand holding two tables of stone folded together. "The heavens will announce

His righteousness: for God is judge Himself." Psalm 50:6. This is the moment when the lost finally understand. For those who failed to prepare it will be too late. The time to prepare is now. The way to prepare for this great joyful event is to search God's Word with openness and a hunger to understand and obey.

God speaks. He tells us how long it will be until we are all with Jesus again. In astonishment, we notice that our faces are actually glowing with bright light. And then we remember the words of the prophet Daniel. He predicted that "those who are wise will shine like . . . the stars for ever and ever." And Jesus promised, "Then the righteous will sine like the sun in the kingdom of their Father." At Sinai mountain, Moses experienced this exciting power. When he came down from Sinai mountain with the Ten Commandments, his face was as bright as the sun. Our faces are so very bright that the demon-possessed people who were searching for us can't bear even to look at our faces. God again speaks to us, and we all unite in a great shout of victory. Daniel 12:3; Matthew 13:43.

He Comes Wrapped in Flaming Fire!

Up to this point, we have heard the voice of Jesus, and we saw Him talking to the Father, but now we know He is coming at last. Looking up, we see the small black cloud in the east. I hold my hand up to the sky, and in the distance the black cloud seems to be about half the size of my hand. The cloud continues to get brighter and bigger as it comes closer and closer. We know Christ will soon be with us forever. We stare at that cloud. The closer it comes, the brighter it gets, until it becomes a great white cloud with the appearance of fire underneath and the most brilliant rainbow ever seen above it.

In astonishment, we continue staring at the cloud. Jesus is coming again just as He has promised in all the great prophecies of His Word. Now we can actually see Jesus coming down through the sky to take us home. "On his robe and on his thigh he has this name written, KING OF KINGS, AND LORD OF LORDS." Revelation 19:16. "At the sight of Christ all faces are turned into paleness." The terror of eternal despair falls upon the rejecters of God's mercy. "The heart melts, and the knees shake; much pain is in every side, And all their faces are drained of color." Jeremiah 30:6, Darby; Nahum 2:10, NKJV.

Hundreds of millions of angels fill the sky. We read that just one angel conquered an army and killed 185,000 armed soldiers in one night. The power and majesty and bright, beautiful color of it all are so overwhelming! Jesus and the angels are coming, wrapped in flaming fire. Everyone sees

Jesus and the words, "KING OF KINGS AND LORD OF LORDS" written on His clothing. See 2 Kings 19:32-36.

The rich and powerful and those they controlled try to escape this fiery, cataclysmic event by hiding in the caves of the earth. "Our God comes and will not be silent; a fire devours before him, and around him, a tempest rages. He summons the heavens above, and the earth, that he may judge his people." Psalm 50:3, 4.

"Scream and wail, for the day of the LORD is near; it will come like destruction from the Almighty." Isaiah 13:6.

"Go into the rocks, hide in the ground from dread of the LORD and the splendor of his majesty! The eyes of the arrogant man will be humbled and the pride of men brought low; the LORD alone will be exalted in that day. The LORD Almighty has a day in store for all the proud and lofty, for all that is exalted (and they will be humbled). In that day men will throw away to the rodents and bats their idols of silver and idols of gold, which they made to worship. They will flee to caverns in the rocks and to the overhanging crags from dread of the LORD and the splendor of his majesty, when he rises to shake the earth." Isaiah 2:10-12, 20, 21.

"Then the kings of the earth, the princes, the generals, the rich, the mighty, and every slave and every free man hid in caves and among the rocks of the mountains. They called to the mountains and the rocks, fall on us and hide us from the face of him who sits on the throne and from the wrath of the lamb! For the great day of their wrath has come, and who can stand?" Revelation 6:15-17.

The mocking jokes have stopped. Lying lips are silent. "Turn back, turn back from your evil ways; for why will you die?" Says Jesus: "I called, and you refused, I stretched out my hand and no one paid attention; and you neglected all my counsel and did not want my reproof." Ezekiel 33:11, RSV; Proverbs 1:24, 25, NASB.

Jesus raises those from the dead who took part in torturing Him. They see the awesome glory of His return to Planet Earth. They see His face shining brighter than the sun. Nearly two thousand years ago Jesus had told them that in the future, "You will see the Son of man sitting at the right hand of the Power, and coming on the clouds of heaven." Matthew 26:64, NKJV. His prophecy has come true!

They laughed then at the idea that He was the king of the universe. In their ridicule they made a crown of long, piercing thorns for His head. They laughed as they beat those thorns into His head and watched the blood run down His face and His beard. Boastful King Herod, who had mocked Him, looks at Jesus, completely unable to say even one word now. Instead, he stands almost frozen, his only movements all involuntary. His whole body shakes as he stands there trembling in fear.

Those who ridiculed Christ remember their own words. "He saved others; but He can't save Himself! If He be the King of Israel, let Him come down now from the cross, and we will believe Him. He trusts in God. Let God rescue Him now if He wants him." Matthew 27:42, 43. Those who crucified Christ scream in anguish, "He really is the Son of God!" They all run as rapidly as they can, hoping to escape such intense heat as they have never felt before. In their fear, they hide in the enormous caves left when the mountains were ripped right out of the ground

The sight of Christ coming down through the sky causes everyone to tremble. We all cry out, "Who can stand?" Our guardian angels are absolutely silent. Everything and everyone is absolutely quiet. It is a period of awful silence. Then Jesus speaks. He says: "My grace is sufficient for you." Our faces light up with smiles of great joy. We hear the most beautiful music—the voices of angels. The beauty of it all is so amazing. It is indescribable in contrast to the sorrow we have experienced.

Christ calls all His children from their graves. They come out with the freshness and energy of eternal youth. They are forever young, strong, and vibrant! Forever! I look and notice that those from this last generation are so much smaller than our great grandparents, Adam and Eve. We will "grow up" until we are the normal height of man before he rebelled against God— the height of Adam, Eve, and the angels, much larger than people are now. See Malachi 4:2.

Angels, men, women, and children are now united as one family. Angels reunite family members. Angels carry babies and children to their mothers' arms and bring friends together again who had been separated by death. The trip we are taking is so very exciting! We travel together upward to the City of God, singing songs of joy.

Jesus Himself places the crown of glory on our heads. There is a crown for each of His obedient children. Each crown has a different name—our very own new name. Revelation 2:17. "To him who overcomes, I will give the right to sit with me on my throne, just as I overcame and sat down with my Father on his throne." Revelation 3:21. "He loved us, and washed us from our sins in His own blood, and has made us kings and priests for ever and ever." Revelation 1:5, 6

When we finally reach the gates of the Holy City, Jesus opens the gate wide and says, "Welcome home, children. Your difficulties are over! Come, my children, and inherit the kingdom prepared for you from the beginning of the world." I look and see the garden of Eden where Adam and Eve first lived.

We all gather about the great white throne, overwhelmed with happiness. Everyone is smiling, and many are singing. There are exciting reunions of those we have won for Christ, with many warm embraces, hugs, and smiles. Everyone is extremely happy—a happiness never felt before!

Jesus and Adam, our great grandfather, walk together through the garden. Adam is astonished to see the very trees from which he used to pick fruit in the garden of Eden. He looks in amazement at the grapevines that he himself had taken care of. And at his feet are the very flowers he had once enjoyed so much. Jesus takes Adam to the Tree of Life, with its dozen different fruits to choose from. Jesus picks one of those brilliantly colored fruits and gives it to Adam. Adam takes a bite and then looks at those around him, realizing this is his own family—his descendants—standing here in this beautiful paradise. Adam is overcome with emotion. He takes off his beautiful crown, dropping it at Jesus' feet. He throws his arms around Jesus' chest, hugging his Friend, Redeemer, and King.

Adam, the angels, and all God's people—you and I—join in singing: "Worthy, worthy, worthy is the Lamb that was slain, and lives again!" We "follow the Lamb wherever He goes." Revelation 14:4.

The Bible tells us: "These are they who have come out of the great tribulation; they have washed their robes and made them white in the blood of the Lamb. . . . Never again will they hunger; never again will they thirst. . . . He will lead them to springs of living water. And God will wipe away every tear from their eyes." Revelation 7:14-17.

The King of glory, Jesus, wipes tears away with His hand and speaks words of encouragement. Child of God, He is watching over you right now. He knows when you're unhappy. Be patient—He will make you happy again. You can experience some of that joy and happiness now. Then He will wipe away all your tears, all your pain, all your sorrow. He will flood your life with happiness.

This is time to celebrate! While waving palm branches with great enthusiasm, we sing songs of praise—clear, sweet, and harmonious: "Salvation to our God who sits upon the throne, and to the Lamb." And all the angels answer, singing: "Amen: Blessing, and glory, and wisdom, and thanksgiving, and honor, and power, and might, be unto our God for ever and ever." Revelation 7:10, 12, NKJV.

"God himself is judge." Psalm 50:6. The unfair judgments against God's children are forever over. We are no longer feeble, sick, persecuted, and scattered. From now on we will always be with the Lord. The crowns of earthly kings and popes don't even compare to the magnificence of the crowns we will be able to wear throughout eternity. Jesus has forever ended long stays in hospital beds and weeping at the graveyards of the world.

29

Solitary Confinement

The combination of the violent anger of the lost who are now totally controlled by the devil, and the anger of God in the seven last plagues, has killed all the unholy people of the earth—priests, the rulers, and every one who fought against His chosen people, whether they were rich or poor. The brightness of His glory blots them from the face of the whole earth. "At that time those slain by the Lord will be everywhere—from one end of the earth to the other. They will not be mourned or gathered up or buried, but will be like refuse lying on the ground." Jeremiah 25:33.

When Christ has taken His people to the City of God, not one living person is left on Planet Earth. "See, the LORD is going to lay waste the earth and devastate it; he will ruin its face and scatter its inhabitants—the earth will be completely laid waste and totally plundered. The LORD has spoken this word. The earth is defiled by its people; they have disobeyed the laws, violated the statutes and broken the everlasting covenant. Therefore a curse consumes the earth; its people must bear their guilt. Therefore earth's inhabitants are burned up, and very few are left." Isaiah 24:1, 3, 5, 6.

"I saw an angel coming down out of heaven, having the key to the bottomless pit and a great chain in his hand. He laid hold of the dragon, that serpent of old, who is the devil, and Satan, and bound him for a thousand

217

years. And he cast him into the bottomless pit, and shut him up. He set a seal on him, so that he should deceive the nations no more, till the thousand years were finished. But after these things he must be released for a little while." Revelation 20:1-3.

Have you ever talked on the telephone and said, "I'm sorry, but I can't come over. I'm all tied up"? I've said that before. Did I mean that my wife had gotten angry with me and tied me up in ropes or chains so that I was helpless to move or to physically come over? No! Of course not! I meant that I had another commitment. I had something else I was doing that I felt was more important than coming over to your house right now.

Will the devil be chained with literal "chains" made out of metal? Of course not! He will be chained with a chain of circumstances. He is isolated to Planet Earth—and now that this earth is "without form and void," it resembles a bottomless pit. Have you ever said, "That is really the pits"? It will indeed be "the pits" for the devil. With the righteous in heaven and the wicked dead asleep in the sleep of death on the earth, the devil and his angels have no one to tempt. Time will hang heavy upon them. It will drag slowly by for one thousand years.

Super stupendous! The devil will be put in prison. This is how it is expressed in the *Clear Word* Bible: "Then I saw an angel come down from heaven holding in his hand a large key and a huge chain which I was told symbolized his power to bind. The angel took hold of the dragon, that ancient serpent who is called the devil and Satan, and bound him to this planet for a thousand years. It was like throwing him into a dark pit from which he could not escape.

"The angel confined him to this desolate planet and he had no one to deceive until these thousand years were over. That's when the wicked will be raised to life, which is known as the second resurrection. Satan will then be free again but only for a little while." Revelation 20:1-3, CWB.

The phrase *bottomless pit* pictures the earth in a state of disorder and darkness. The Bible says that "in the beginning," the earth "was without form, and void; and darkness was upon the face of the deep." The Hebrew word here translated "deep" (Genesis 1:2) in the Septuagint (Greek) translation of the Hebrew Old Testament is the same word translated "bottomless pit" in Revelation 20:1-3. Revelation teaches that God will bring the earth back, partially at least, to this condition.

Looking forward to the great day of God, the prophet Jeremiah declares,: "I looked at the earth, and it was formless and empty; and at the heavens, and their light was gone. I looked at the mountains, and they were quaking;

all the hills were swaying. I looked, and there were no people; every bird in the sky had flown away. I looked, and the fruitful land was a desert; all its towns lay in ruins before the LORD, before his fierce anger." Jeremiah 4:23-26.

For a thousand years, Satan will travel back and forth in the devastated earth looking at the results of his rebellion against the law of God. During this time he will experience extreme pain. The Judgment of the lost takes place during this one thousand year period between the first and the second resurrections.

Judgment was given to God's children. "The Ancient of Days came and pronounced judgment in favor of the saints of the Most High." Daniel 7:22.

"And I saw thrones, and they sat on them, and judgment was committed to them. Then I saw the souls of those who had been beheaded for their witness to Jesus and for the word of God, who had not worshiped the beast or his image, and had not received his mark on their foreheads or on their hands. And they lived and reigned with Christ for a thousand years. Blessed and holy is he who has part in the first resurrection. Over such the second death has no power, but they shall be priests of God and of Christ, and shall reign with Him a thousand years." Revelation 20:4.

During the 1,000 years, the righteous will judge both unholy people and unholy angels.

"Do you not know that that the saints will judge the world? And if you are to judge the world. . . . Do you not know that we will judge angels?" 1 Corinthians 6:2, 3.

And Jude declares that "Angels rebelled against God, so He had to expel them from heaven and confine them to this world until the day of judgment when they will be destroyed." Jude 6, CWB. "The wicked remained dead and were not resurrected until these thousand years were over." Revelation 20:5, CWB.

30

The Eternal City

The Lord descends from heaven with all His holy angels, bringing His people with Him. His feet will touch the top of the Mount of Olives east of Jerusalem, and the mountain will split in two from north to south and leave a huge valley. "On that day there will be no cold or frost, neither will there be any more darkness. It will always be day, because even at night it will be light." The Lord will make it so. "The Lord will be King over all the earth. On that day everyone will worship Him as God and there will be one Lord and His name alone will be honored." Zechariah 14:4-9, CWB.

"The City was laid out in a square. Its length was the same as its width, and it measured fifteen hundred miles along each wall, with a height that was proportionate. Then the angel measured the wall, and it was two hundred feet thick. The wall was made of jasper, while the City itself was made of pure transparent gold, clear as glass."

Brilliant Colors

"The foundations of the City and its walls were made of all kinds of precious stones of varying colors. The first foundation was deep green made of jasper, The second was blue made of sapphire, The third was milky white, the fourth was bright green, made of emerald, The fifth was reddish pink, the sixth was reddish orange, the seventh was bright yellow, the eighth was deep blue, the ninth was pale blue made of topaz. The tenth was gold colored, the eleventh was red and the twelfth foundation was purple, made of amethyst." Revelation 21, *The Clear Word Bible*. The city was surrounded in brilliant color, with these twelve brilliantly colored foundations, and surrounded by a brilliant rainbow.

The City and its walls rests on twelve foundations, each having the name of one of the twelve apostles of Christ written on it. The City has twelve gates—three gates on each side. The city is always full of daylight due to the light, brighter then the sun, coming from God. The River of Life, clear as crystal, flows from the throne of God through the City. The Tree of Life, loaded with twelve different types of fruit, spans the river with part of its trunk on either side.

As the New Jerusalem, in its dazzling splendor, comes down out of heaven, it rests upon the place purified and made ready to receive it. Christ, with His people and the angels, then enters the Holy City.

Satan's Super-Army Attacks New Jerusalem

Christ speaks, calling all the lost who have ever lived back to life again. Satan thinks he has one last chance to succeed in His rebellion. He thinks, "If I could just train and equip all of these people, together with the angels that have followed me, I will have a super army. I will attack New Jerusalem, and I will achieve my dreams of being God."

Satan works with new energy. He works miracles and tells those who were raised from the dead, "I am God, and it was my power that brought you out of the grave. Look," he says, "at that beautiful city. That is my city. That is where you will live once we capture it back from the evil enemy." Satan puts on a real show. He makes the weak people strong and electrifies all with his enthusiasm. Everyone is excited and works hard building a mighty army. We don't know how long they work at this, but they prepare vast military weapons of war and lay plans on how to attack and conquer the beautiful city New Jerusalem.

General Satan lays his plans first with his angels and then with other generals who have fought great wars in their former lives. Big names are there, such as Napoleon and Adolph Hitler and Alexander the Great. We don't know all their names at present, but they are skilled military leaders. Military leaders and angels organize the lost billions into companies and divisions.

At last Lucifer gives the order to march, and his super army moves on. There has never been, in all of history, such a mighty army or one better equipped with military hardware. Putting together all the armies that have ever fought could not compare to this one army made up of Satan, his angels, and the billions that have chosen to rebel with him.

Kings, generals, soldiers, and the multitudes follow in vast companies, each under its chosen leader. With military perfection, they march over the earth's cracked and uneven surface to the City of God. Jesus then shuts the gates of New Jerusalem. The lost are shut out, and the saved are safely inside. Satan and his armies surround the city and prepare to attack.

Now Christ takes charge of the situation. Everyone sees Him. High above the city, on a foundation of shining gold, Christ sits on an elevated throne. His people are all around Him—the saved of all ages. A "great multitude that no one could count, from every nation, tribe, people and language standing before the throne and in front of the Lamb. They were wearing white robes and were holding palm branches in their hands." Revelation 7:9.

"I saw a great white throne and Him who was seated on it. Earth and sky fled from his presence, and there was no place for them. And I saw the dead, great and small, standing before the throne, and books were opened. Another book was opened which is the book of life. The dead were judged according to what they had done as recorded in the books. If anyone's name was not found written in the book of life, he was thrown into the lake of fire." Revelation 20:11, 12.

When the books of record are opened, Jesus looks at the wicked. All of their sins are fresh in their minds. They see just how far they drifted from the path of righteousness and holiness. They see just how far selfishness and rebellious choices carried them away from God's great law of love.

Then they finally realize how very unthankful they were for the numerous times God had protected them. It all seems to be branded on their minds in living fire. They see the hatred they showed for those who truly cared for them, the rejection of God's messages of warning, His messengers, and His mercy. It all appears as if written in letters of fire.

God Uses the Sky As a Giant Movie Screen!

A cross appears above the throne. We all look up, and every eye is focused on the cross. Like a panoramic movie with the sky as the movie screen, the scenes of Adam's temptation and fall appear in the sky. Next, we watch the actual scenes of the human birth of the King of kings in Bethlehem. We see Joseph putting straw and a blanket in a donkey's food box, preparing a place for the baby King to sleep. Mary wraps her newborn baby, gently rocking her baby. She nurses the newborn King and gently puts her newborn in the place prepared by Joseph.

Everyone continues watching, and we see the video scenes from Christ's simple, obedient childhood. As we look, we can see Him walking down to the side of the river talking with John the Baptist. John baptizes Jesus. We see Jesus holding the hand of John as John eases Christ down under the water of the Jordan River. Jesus is coming out of the water, and we hear the voice of God the Father saying, "This is My Son in whom I am well pleased." At that very moment, a form of a dove comes down from the sky, and we know this to be the sign of anointing by God the Holy Spirit.

Next we see miracles performed by Christ, and we hear His teachings. At last we see Him spending a night that begins in prayer in the garden and ends with being ridiculed and tortured in front of Herod and Pilate. We see Pilate's soldiers laughing at Christ and making a crown of long, sharp thorns for His head. Blood runs down His face and His beard as the soldiers laughingly beat the long, sharp thorns into His head. "So you are a King. How do you like the crown we made you? Ha, ha, ha."

He is being beaten and mocked by the crowds. They drag Him this way and that way. Next we see Pilate's soldiers using a whip with chunks of metal and bone in the ends of the whip. Blood is now streaming down His back. After this we see Christ lying down on the cross as the big Roman soldiers come with their hammers and drive nails through our King's hands and feet. The soldiers are lifting the cross together and letting it drop into the hole prepared for it. These soldiers seem satisfied as they see the extra pain they have caused in letting it drop into the hole. Christ's face is so full of pain, and with all the blood, He is hardly recognizable. All of the darkness, pain, and agony of the cross is revealed in living detail. Everyone sees that how they treated Christ in their dealings with others determines their destiny. "Whatever you did for one of the least of these brothers of mine, you did for Me." Matthew 25:40.

The whole wicked world stands beneath the great white throne accused of rebellion against God and His government. They now see that they are judged by how they treated Christ. And the law of God has everything to do with how we treat Christ. The first four commandments show us how to love Christ, and the last six how to love our fellow men and women. Jesus says, "Whatever you did for one of the least of these brothers of mine, you did for me." They are without excuse; and God orders the sentence of eternal death against them. Matthew 25:40.

"All this," the lost cry out in agony, "I might have had!" As if entranced, the wicked see Christ crowned with a crown of many crowns.

The Devil Will Be Burned to Ashes!

God considers the devil a defeated foe. In this scripture passage, He speaks of the future death ("reduced to ashes") of the devil as though it had already happened.

"Through your widespread trade you were filled with violence, and you sinned. So I drove you in disgrace from the mount of God, and I expelled you, O guardian cherub, from among the fiery stones. Your heart became proud on account of your beauty, and you corrupted your wisdom because of your splendor. So I threw you to the earth; I made a spectacle of you before kings.

"By your many sins and dishonest trade you have desecrated your sanctuaries. So I made a fire come out from you, and it consumed you, and I reduced you to ashes on the ground in the sight of all who were watching. All the nations who knew you are appalled at you; you have come to a horrible end and will be no more." Ezekiel 28:16-19.

"Every warrior's boot used in battle and every garment rolled in blood will be destined for burning, will be fuel for the fire." "The Lord is angry with all nations; His wrath is upon all their armies. He will totally destroy them. He will give them over to slaughter." "On the wicked he will rain fiery coals and burning sulfur; a scorching wind will be their lot." Isaiah 9:5; 34:2; Psalm 11:6.

Fire Turns Satan and His Rebels Into Ashes

Christ sends fire down from God to the earth. The fire from above the earth meets the fire from below the earth, and all the vast stores of coal and oil unite. The entire earth is one vast, seething fire. Everything is on fire except for the city of God. Fierce, hungry flames burst from every opening in the cracked surface of the earth. Even the rocks are on fire. The day that will burn as an oven has arrived. "That day will bring about the destruction of the heavens by fire, and the elements will melt in the heat." The earth's surface seems like a vast boiling lake of fire. "It is the time of the judgment and punishment of ungodly men." 2 Peter 3:12.

The wicked receive their just reward in the earth. They "will be stubble: and the day that comes will burn them up, says the Lord of hosts." Some die immediately, while others suffer many days. Each is punished "according to his deeds." Proverbs 11:31; Romans 2:6.

"The voice of a great multitude," "as the voice of many waters, and as the voice of mighty thunderings," shout: "Hallelujah! For our Lord God Almighty reigns. Let us rejoice and be glad and give him glory!" Revelation 19:6, 7, NIV, KJV.

While God wraps the earth in the fire of destruction, the righteous are safe in the Holy City. On those that had part in the first resurrection, the second death has no power. While God is a destroying fire to the wicked, He is both a sun and a shield to His people. See Revelation 20:6; Psalm 84:11.

"I saw a new heaven and a new earth: for the first heaven and the first earth had passed away." The fire that burns up the wicked sterilizes the earth. Every trace of the curse is swept away. No eternally burning hell will keep before the saved the fearful price of sin. Revelation 21:1.

One reminder alone remains: Jesus Christ will always have the wound marks of His crucifixion. The scars on His wounded head, His side, His hands and His feet, are the only reminders of the cruel work that sin has caused. The prophet Habakkuk saw into the future. He saw Christ in His glory and said: "His Splendor was like the sunrise; rays flashed from his hand, where his power was hidden." From His pierced side and hands had come the blood that reunited man to God. This is Jesus Christ's glory. This is "the hiding of His power." Habakkuk 3:4.

Christ is "mighty to save" those who accept His love, and He is strong to execute justice upon those who hate and hurt His children. The scars He received when He was tortured on the cross are His highest honor. Through the eternal ages, the nail and spear scars Christ received on the cross of Calvary will shout out to each individual in God's great universe: "God loves you!" and "God's power has saved you!"

31

Home at Last

God has finished His original purpose in the creation of the earth. He has finally made it the eternal home of the redeemed. "The righteous will inherit the land, and dwell in it forever." "No eye has seen, no ear has heard, no mind can imagine what wonderful things that God has prepared for those who love Him." Psalm 37:29; 1 Corinthians 2:9, NKJV.

In the new Earth, Jesus Christ leads His family to springs of living waters. The Tree of Life produces its fruit every month, and the leaves of the tree are for everyone's well being, making sure to prevent all illness. The streams are clear and pure and never dry up. Nature is more beautiful than ever, with no more deserts and no more weeds and blood-sucking insects and mean, wild animals. The animal kingdom is at peace. There is supreme beauty, prepared as a gift for those our Lord has rescued. The flower-covered plains rise into hills and mountains with majestic peaks of great beauty. It is among all this beauty that God makes a home for His children.

"My people will live in peaceful dwelling places, in secure homes, in undisturbed places of rest." "No longer will violence be heard in your land." "They will build houses" and live "in them." " They will plant vineyards and eat their fruit. No longer will they build houses and others live in them or plant and others eat. . . . My chosen ones will long enjoy the work of their hands." Isaiah 32:18; 60:18; 65:21, 22.

There, the wilderness and the solitary place will be glad for them. "The desert will rejoice, and blossom as the rose." "Instead of the thornbush will grow the pine tree and instead of briers the myrtle will grow." "The wolf will live with the lamb, the leopard will lie down with the goat, the calf and the lion and the yearling together and a little child will lead them. They will neither harm nor destroy on all my holy mountain." Isaiah 35:1, KJV; 55:13; 11:6, 9.

Pain will never be felt again. No one will ever cry again. No graveyards will ever exist again anywhere. "There will be no more death or mourning or crying or pain, for the old order of things has passed away." "No one will say, I am ill, and the sins of those who live there will be forgiven."

"God's home is with men, and he will live with them. They will be his people and God himself will be with them and be their God." Revelation 21:4, Isaiah 33:24, Revelation 21:3.

In the City of God, "there will be no night." No one will need or want sleep. No one will be tired in doing God's will and praising Him. No one will need to go to the emergency room, the hospital, or the drug store. Instead, we will all eat from the Tree of Life with its twelve different types of fruit, and we will eat its leaves as preventive medicine. "The leaves of the tree are for the healing of the nations." Revelation 22:2.

We notice something different! We are always feeling so full of enthusiasm. We are always feeling great—as fresh as a bright summer morning. "They will not need the light of a lamp or the light of the sun, for the Lord God will give them light." The light of the world is now our sun in the sky. Then God will be the light of the world, and His brightness will be far brighter than the sun. The light from God the Father and from Christ does not go out. It floods the Holy City with unfading daylight. The redeemed walk in the sunless glory of endless day. Revelation 22:2, 5.

The one thing we find so overwhelming is the fact that we now have the honor and joy of talking to God face to face. We will never be lonely again! Life now is just one wonderful adventure! We learn new things every day. It's all new to us, and we are having so much fun discovering worlds upon worlds that we knew nothing about when we lived on Planet Earth. It is thrilling being taught by Jesus about His universe and exploring it with angels and prophets and apostles whom we once only read about in the Bible. It is far better then my wildest dreams! Everybody treats others with kindness, cooperation, and love. We are all part of the same family now. We are all God's redeemed children forever and ever!

"I did not see a temple in the city, because the Lord God Almighty and the Lamb are its temples." "Now we see but a poor reflection as in a mirror; then we shall see face to face. Now I know in part; then I shall know fully, even as I am fully known." Revelation 21:22; 1 Corinthians 13:12.

On earth we saw just a reflection of God in His creation of nature and in His dealings with men. However, now we see Him "face to face." We stand in His presence and see the glory of His face. God is so happy to see how happy He has made us. We know everyone by name. Adam, Eve, Moses, Elijah, Peter, Paul, and Mary are all family. "The whole family in heaven and earth" will be united. Ephesians 3:15.

Not only are we growing larger physically, we are constantly learning new things, and our bodies and minds are never tired. We have boundless energy!

Space Travel Adventures!

Each day is a new adventure! We are constantly reaching out for what once was "the impossible dream." We discover that now all our "impossible dreams" are not only possible, but that we are actually reaching our dreams and our highest hopes. And the travel through space is so exhilarating! Wouldn't even Superman be jealous!

In our journeys to these worlds—worlds upon worlds of unfallen beings—we find complete openness. They are not proud and arrogant. They share the treasures of knowledge and understanding they have gained through ages upon ages in contemplation of God's handiwork. Love, reverence, and happiness increase moment by moment and year after year. We in turn share with them how merciful God was and is to us.

"Then I heard every creature in heaven and on earth and under the earth and on the sea, and all that is in them, singing. To him who sits on the throne and to the lamb be praise and honor and glory and power for ever and ever." Revelation 5:13.

32

The Four Horsemen of the Apocalypse

The four horsemen are the symbol of *Prophecy Made Easy*. Let's take a look at "the four horsemen of the apocalypse." Doesn't that sound fascinating?

Actually, the last book of the Bible is named "Revelation," but the term *apocalypse*—the Greek word from which it is translated—carries a fascination all its own. So . . . "the four horsemen of the *apocalypse*," rather than "the four horsemen of *Revelation*"!

In chapter 5 of Revelation, someone is holding a mystery book—the book of the future. This mysterious book has seven chapters, known as "seven seals." All the angels wanted to see inside this mystery book that deals with future events, but no one could be found who was worthy to open it. The angels were discouraged until Jesus, the only one worthy to open it, took the book and opened it.

Jesus opened chapter 1 of the book, "the first seal," and there was revealed a vision of a white horse. The rider had a bow in his hand and arrows strapped to his back. He was wearing the crown of a king. He galloped into the future to spread the gospel and to conquer the world for the

Lord. This represented the victorious church, following the death and resurrection of Jesus Christ.

The apostle Paul saw into the future. God revealed to him that the church
would compromise with the pagan world, and the world would walk right
into the church and take over. 2 Thessalonians 2:3-5. "Don't let anyone
deceive you in any way, for that day, the day of the Lord, will not come
until the rebellion occurs and the man of lawlessness is revealed, the man
doomed to destruction. He will oppose and will exalt himself over everything that is called God or is worshiped, so that he sets himself up in God's
temple proclaiming himself to be God." Paul here foresaw the rise of the
papacy. The apostasy of the papacy did not take God by surprise. He foretold it all. No wonder the Bible was hated by the papacy over its centuries
of rule. *(See the Appendix.)* Notice the words, "He will oppose and will
exalt himself." You probably remember that this was the very sin that got
the devil to rebel against God in the first place. Isaiah 14:13, 14.

The Four Horses: White, Red, Black, and Pale

The changes in the Christian church—its apostasies—are revealed in
the changes in the colors of the horses. The first horse is white. The second
horse is red. The third horse is black. And finally, the last horse is a pale
color—the color of death. Each of the four horses and the four horsemen of
Revelation deal with a different period of time. They deal with the first
four of seven segments of time from the death of Christ to the second coming of Christ.

The first horse and rider, white in color, represent the church going out
in victory, sharing the gospel. The time, however, eventually came where
the church actually became a persecuting power, pictured here as a rider on
a red horse with a sword in his hand. The church turned on its own members, killing over fifty million in a period of just over one thousand years of
rule. The crime of many who were killed was the "crime" of reading the
Bible. Most history books that told the truth about this have been carefully
destroyed. The one still available in bookstores today is *Fox's Book of
Martyrs,* written By George Fox over four hundred years ago. The apostate
church is pictured in Revelation 17:6 as "drunk with the blood of the saints,
the blood of those who bore testimony to Jesus."

The black horse is next. The rider of the black horse is seen holding the
scales of death. A voice screams out, "A quart of wheat for a day's wages."
There seemed to be a spiritual famine for the Word of God. The same voice
said, "Do not damage the oil and the wine!" Even though the established
Christian church rebelled against God, the Spirit of God and His graces were

not wholly extinguished. Through this period of time, God always had those who remained true to Him.

It was against the law even to own a Bible, another "crime" punishable by death. The "light of the world"—Jesus—was shut out, and darkness replaced the light of the gospel. It was the time of the black horse; we call it the "dark" ages. Superstition controlled daily life. The pale-colored horse of death came galloping forward, and the church was filled with spiritual death. The four horses are just the first four chapters of this mystery book of the future. There remain three more chapters in the book.

The fifth chapter deals with an appeal by those who had been killed by the church in persecution. It is as though they are saying, "God, please punish those who killed us in your name" This can be understood from the fact that their bodies are found "under an altar crying out for justice."

We live in chapter six of this mysterious book of the future. Remember, it has seven chapters. Chapter six opens with the earth shaking mightily, the sun being darkened and appearing black. Next, the moon looked as if it had been dipped in blood. And then the stars of heaven fell as thick and fast as late-ripening figs fall from a tree when shaken by a strong wind. "I watched as he opened the sixth seal. There was a great earthquake. The sun turned black like sackcloth made of goat hair, the whole moon turned blood red, and the stars in the sky fell to earth, as late figs drop from a fig tree when shaken by a strong wind. " Revelation 6:12, 13.

These are the opening signs announcing that Jesus would come again soon. First, the earth shook mightily. This was commonly called the Lisbon earthquake of November 1, 1755. It was the most terrible earthquake ever recorded. It involved most of Europe and Africa and even reached America, Great Britain, and Ireland. It covered more than four million square miles.

Next came the great dark day of May 19, 1780. Since the time of Moses, no period of darkness of equal density, extent, and duration has ever been recorded. Joel prophesied, "The sun shall be turned into darkness, and the moon into blood, before the great and terrible day of the Lord come." Joel 2:31. After midnight, the darkness disappeared, and the moon, when first seen, had the appearance of blood.

Next was a vision of stars falling as thick and fast as late-ripening figs fall from a tree when shaken by a strong wind. Read in history books about the fulfillment of this great meteoric shower of November 13, 1833. These were signs that the soon return of Christ was near. A couple hundred years have passed since these signs occurred, but in the light of eternity, that is a very short time. Jesus will come again soon.

Read about these events in history. Revelation chapter 6, verse 14 explains that these were only an early warning to the inhabitants of the earth of what is yet to come. The next vision is that of the sky seeming to disappear as if someone had rolled it up like a scroll. Mountains sink out of sight, and entire islands disappear. Kings, heads of governments, political figures, military commanders, the rich, the powerful, and all others, whether oppressed or free, who have turned against God, hide in the caves left by those disappearing mountains, shouting to the mountains and the rocks to help them hide from the coming One wrapped in flaming fire. Those who just a little while earlier were persecuting God's children now scream out, "The day of God's judgment has come, and who can stand?"

The second coming of Christ is also described in Psalm 50:3, 4: "Our God comes and will not be silent; a fire devours before him, and around him a tempest rages. He summons the heavens above and the earth, that he may judge his people." He will not keep silent while his children are mistreated. He will fight for His children, and He will win and bring His children—you and me—home to be with Him forever!

Are you ready for Jesus to come? Now is the time to prepare. When the mountains sink and the islands disappear, it will be too late. I believe the period of silence in heaven in chapter 7, "the seventh seal," is the silence left when all the angels leave heaven and travel with Jesus to Planet Earth. Jesus says: "The harvest is the end of the world; and the reapers are the angels." Matthew 13:39, KJV. This is one sight everyone will see and hear and feel! There will be nothing secret about this great and wonderful day!

Are you ready for Jesus to come? Why not invite Christ into your heart today? You can learn how to accept Christ into your heart by reading "The Secret of a Life of Super Power," located in the Introduction—or "What Did Jesus Do for Me?"—number 19 of the Appendix at the back of this book.

I invite you to join me in the beautiful New Jerusalem. And I encourage you to invite others. One way to do that is through the distribution of this life-changing book. Won't you share several with your family and friends? After Jesus Christ comes again, I plan to know each of you that are choosing to live with Jesus Christ in the beautiful earth made new. We will be friends throughout eternity! Today I'll be praying for you, and I thank you for praying for me. May God richly bless you, child of God!

****

Give a friend a copy of this book today!
They will be eternally grateful!
Send them this Internet address and
let them read this book online FREE:

www.prophecymadeeasy.com

Need a Speaker?

Does your church or organization need a speaker who understands God's great love from experience and from prophecy? Jesus promises us a triple blessing if we will seek to understand Revelation, the last book of the Bible. Revelation reveals God's great love to you as no other book can! It reveals God's love to you in all of history and prophecy.

In Revelation 1:3, Jesus says, "Blessed is the one who reads the words of this prophecy, and blessed are those who hear it and take to heart what is written in it, because the time is near."

The author of this book, Glen Walker, will take you behind the headlines. What is really happening on Planet Earth? He will share with you "the rest of the story"—the story that newspapers can't and don't talk about! Don't miss inviting Glen Walker to speak to your organization, church, or group. You will discover, perhaps for the first time, what the newspapers can't tell you!

What is the real story behind the movies "Left Behind," "Star Wars," and "Raiders of the Lost Ark"? What is "the ark," and what does it have to do with prophecy? And what is the real story behind the movie "Star Wars"? You will be amazed as you find the answers to these questions.

Discover the real story behind the television show "Touched by an Angel." Who are the angels? And who is the the devil? Is he real? You will discover for yourself whether the devil is real or just a made-up fictitious character invented to scare people. Does he really wear red pajamas? Does he really have horns, a tail, and a pitchfork?

Glen Walker has found the true meaning of life! What is actually going to happen the moment you die? What is the story behind the "mark of the beast"? Learn the true identity of the "beast" of Revelation and the true identity of its "mark."

God is real. He loves you and has an exciting plan for your life. Let Glen help you find a happy and secure future. The future is very bright for everyone who will invest time in preparing for it! If you have invested in the stock market, if you have invested in your future, and are unsure of what your future holds, invite Glen Walker as a guest speaker. The stock market may fail you, but Jesus Christ never will. Invest your time today! Invite Glen Walker to speak. It will prove to be the best investment you have ever made!

Get out your spiritual glasses, and we will have fun understanding the wonders of Jesus in Revelation.

Glen Walker is a graduate of California College for Health Sciences and Southern Adventist University. At the University, he was Prison Ministries Leader. He grew up in complete ignorance of Jesus, the Bible, and of the truths of the Bible. At the age of 19, he met a Christian who shared many of the truths that you now read in *Prophecy Made Easy*. He is currently a writer and lay evangelistic speaker. He is also a registered respiratory therapist. His area of expertise is in speaking on Christ in Bible prophecy.

Have you ever felt insecure wondering about the future? If you have, this seminar is for you! When you are alone in the dark, do you ever wonder about the day when you will die? Do you know what will happen the very moment you die? Do you really know what will happen the moment after you die? This seminar is for you!

Do you want real evidence and real answers? Discover the facts. You can know God. God has some fantastic, real answers to your future. God has an exciting plan for your life! Discover His plan for your future.

Invite Glen Walker to speak at your church or organization. It is exciting! It is beyond the imagination! Glen has the ability to make the truths of God's Word easily understandable. His goals are found in the Bible phrase that says, "Write the vision, and make it plain." Habakkuk 2:2. What he says is easy to understand, has a solid Bible foundation, and is exciting and encouraging.

Appendix

1. Exodus, chapter 20—the Ten Commandments

The papacy has made changes in the three longest of the Ten Commandments. They changed the fourth commandment from the seventh to the first day of the week. They removed the second commandment. And they divided the tenth commandment into two parts to give the impression that they still believed in the Ten Commandments. Without the second commandment, they only have nine left. See their catechism.

The papacy has divided the tenth commandment to read: "You shall not covet your neighbor's house" as one commandment, and "You shall not covet your neighbor's wife" as the other.

Below, the Ten Commandments are listed as they read in the Bible (Exodus 20:2-18, NKJV. The Bible does not number them, but this is the way they are numbered because of their order.

"I am the LORD your God, who brought you out of the land of Egypt, out of the house of bondage."

1. "You shall have no other gods before Me."

NOTE: The second commandment has been removed from the Catholic catechism!

2. "You shall not make for yourself a carved image—any likeness of anything that is in heaven above, or that is in the earth beneath, or that is in the water under the earth; you shall not bow down to them nor serve them.

For I, the LORD your God, am a jealous God, visiting the iniquity of the fathers upon the children to the third and fourth generations of those who hate Me, but showing mercy to thousands, to those who love Me and keep My commandments."

This is how the Revised Standard Version says it. "You shall not make for yourself an idol in the form of any likeness of what is in heaven above or on the earth beneath or in the water under the earth."

3. "You shall not take the name of the LORD your God in vain, for the LORD will not hold him guiltless who takes His name in vain."

4. "Remember the Sabbath day to keep it holy. Six days you shall labor and do all your work, but the seventh day is the Sabbath of the Lord your God. In it you shall do no work; you, nor your son, nor daughter, nor your manservant nor your female servant, nor your cattle, nor your stranger who is within your gates. For in six days the Lord made the heavens and the earth, the sea, and all that is in them, and rested the seventh day. Therefore the Lord blessed the Sabbath day and hallowed it."

Or, as the New International Version says: "Therefore the LORD blessed the Sabbath day and made it holy."

5. "Honor your father and your mother, so that your days may be long upon the land which the Lord your God is giving you."

6. "You shall not murder."

7. "You shall not commit adultery."

8. "You shall not steal."

9. "You shall not give false testimony against your neighbor."

NOTE: Commandment 10 is divided into two parts in the Catholic catechism.

10. "You shall not covet your neighbor's house. You shall not covet your neighbor's wife, or his male servant or his female servant, nor his ox nor his donkey, nor anything that is your neighbor's."

Definition of *covet:* "To desire enviously, to long for something belonging to another person."

2. According to the Bible, Which Day Is the Sabbath?

The fourth commandment says the seventh day is the Sabbath. Exodus

20:10, NKJV. "God said. . . . The seventh day is the sabbath of the Lord your God." Look at the calendar. Which is the seventh day? Saturday, of course. Every week on the calendar begins with Sunday, the first day, and ends with Saturday, the seventh day. Luke 23:56 says, "They went home and prepared spices and perfumes. but they rested on the Sabbath in obedience to the commandment." And Luke 24:1 says, "On the first day of the week, very early in the morning, the women took the spices they had prepared and went to the tomb." Everyone knows that Christ died on Friday. After His death, the Bible says, they "rested on the Sabbath day in obedience to the commandment." The day after Friday is Saturday. They obeyed the Sabbath after Christ's death "in obedience to the commandment." Christ rested in creation on the Sabbath, and He rested in redemption on the Sabbath.

Then Christ's followers came to the grave on "Easter Sunday." Now, we know that the day before Sunday is Saturday. Notice that the Sabbath was over when they came to the tomb on what we call "Easter Sunday." God's Sabbath commandment was obeyed after the death of Christ. There were no chapter divisions in the original language of the Bible. Luke 23:56 is the verse that comes just before Luke 24:1. According to this verse, Saturday was still recognized by the disciples as the Sabbath of the fourth commandment *after* the death of Christ. And the Sabbath day fell between the death of Christ on Friday and "the first day of the week"—Sunday. The day between Friday and Sunday is Saturday, the seventh day.

3. Was The Sabbath Day Created for the Jews?

No, the Sabbath was originally given, not to the Jews, but to everyone. No Jew was alive when the Lord gave the Sabbath day to the human race. We read in Genesis 2:2: "By the seventh day God had finished the work He had been doing; so on the seventh day He rested from all His work. And God blessed the seventh day and made it holy, because on it he rested from all the work of creating that He had done." At Creation, God did three things to set the seventh day apart. He rested on that day—what an example to us! God also blessed that day. And the third thing He did was to "make it holy."

4. Has God Changed the Fourth Commandment?

Some religious people and religious leaders say that God's law has been done away with. If you were to ask them point blank, "Has the commandment 'Thou shall not kill' been done away with?" they would say, "No—not that one." Well, what about the one that says, "Thou shall not steal"? They would also say No to that one. You could go through the commandments one by one, and they would say that each commandment still applies —until you come to the fourth commandment. It seems that the only commandment some religious leaders have problems with is the fourth commandment—the only one that says, "Remember."

God knew they would not like that one, so it is the only commandment that begins with the word *remember.* God knew people would be inclined to "forget" that one. What does God say about changing His commandments? He says in Malachi 3:6, "I am the Lord, I change not." Or, "I the Lord do not change." The problem with the seventh-day Sabbath is that it is not convenient to keep the seventh day holy when the rest of the world is observing another day. But Christ says, "Take up your cross and follow Me." Following Christ—being a Christian—means following Him when it is convenient and also when it is *not* convenient.

5. God Wants You to be a New-Covenant Christian

To the new-covenant Christian, God says, "This is the covenant I will make with the house of Israel after that time. I will put my laws in their mind and write them on their hearts. I will be their God and they will be my people. For I will forgive their wickedness and will remember their sins no more." When Paul speaks of Israel, he is speaking of spiritual Israel, the Christian church, Notice that John in Revelation says that all of the saved enter New Jerusalem through gates named after the twelve tribes of Israel. If you are saved at last, you will be part of spiritual Israel forever. God's purpose and plan is to put His ten, not nine, commandment law of love in your heart. God wants you to become a champion lover in the true sense of love. Hebrews 8:10.

6. The Pope As God on Earth

In a passage included in the Roman Catholic Canon Law, or *Corpus Juris Canonici,* Pope Innocent III declares that the Roman pontiff is "the vicegerent upon earth, not of a mere man, but of very God," and in a gloss on the passage, it is explained that this is because he is the vicegerent of Christ, who is "very God and very man." See *Decretales Domini Gregorii*

Papae IX (Decretals of the Lord Pope Gregory IX), liber 1, de translatione Episcoporum, (on the transference of Bishops), title 7, ch. 3; *Corpus Juris Canonici* (2d Leipzig ed., 1881), col. 99; (Paris, 1612), tom. 2, *Decretales,* col. 205.

The documents which formed the Decretals were gathered by Gratian, who was teaching at the University of Bologna about the year 1140. His work was added to and reedited by Pope Gregory IX in an edition issued in 1234. Other documents appeared in succeeding years from time to time including the *Extravagantes,* added toward the close of the fifteenth century. All of these, with Gratian's *Decretum,* were published as the *Corpus Juris Canonici* in 1582. Pope Pius X authorized the codification in Canon law in 1904, and the resulting code became effective in 1918.

For the title "Lord God the Pope," see a gloss on the *Extravagantes of Pope John XXII,* title 14, ch. 4, Declaramus. In an Antwerp edition of the *Extravagantes,* dated 1584, the words *Dominum Deum nostrum Papam* ("Our Lord God the Pope") occur in column 153. In a Paris edition, dated 1612, they occur in column 140. In several editions published since 1612 the word *Deum* ("God") has been omitted.

7. Papal Infallibility

On the doctrine of infallibility as set forth at the Vatican Council of 1870-1871, see Philip Schaff, *The Creeds of Christendom,* "Dogmatic Decrees of the Vatican Council," vol. 2, pp. 234-271, where both the Latin and the English texts are given. For discussion of the Roman Catholic view, see *The Catholic Encyclopedia,* "Infallibility," by Patrick J. Toner, vol. 7, p. 790 ff.; James Cardinal Gibbons, *The Faith of Our Fathers*, 110th ed. (Baltimore: John Murphy Company, 1917), chs. 7, 11.

For Roman Catholic opposition to the doctrine of papal infallibility, see Johann Joseph Ignaz von Doellinger (pseudonym "Janus"): *The Pope and the Council* (New York: Charles Scribner's Sons, 1869); and W.J. Sparrow Simpson: *Roman Catholic Opposition to Papal Infallibility* (London: John Murray, 1909). For the non-Roman view, see George Salmon, *Infallibility of the Church,* rev. ed. (London: John Murray, 1914).

8. Image Worship

"The worship of images . . . was one of those evils which slipped into the church silently and almost without detection. This evil did not, like other heresies, develop all at once, for in that case it would have met with decided condemnation and rejection: but, it began small under a disguise. It gradually grew to the point that the church removed the second commandment from their teachings and catechism.

"Images and pictures were first introduced into churches, not to be worshiped, but either in the place of books to give instruction to those who could not read, or to excite devotion in the minds of others. How far they ever answered such a purpose is doubtful; but, even granting that this was the case for a time, it soon ceased to be so, and it was found that pictures and images brought into churches darkened rather than enlightened the minds of the ignorant—degraded rather than exalted the devotion of the worshiper. So that, however they might have been intended to direct men's minds to God, they ended in turning them from Him to the worship of created things."—J. Mendham, *The Seventh General Council, the Second of Nicaea,* Introduction, pages iii-vi.

9. The First Sunday Law

The law issued by the emperor Constantine on the seventh of March, A.D. 321, regarding a day of rest from labor, reads thus: "All judges and city people and the craftsmen shall rest upon the venerable Day of the Sun.

"Country people, however, may freely attend to the cultivation of the fields, because it frequently happens that no other days are better adapted for planting the grain in the furrows or the vines in trenches. So that the advantage given by heavenly providence may not for the occasion of a short time perish."—Joseph Cullen Ayer, *A Source Book for Ancient Church History* (New York: Charles Scribner's Sons, 1913), div. 2, per. 1, ch. 1, sec. 59, g, pp. 284, 285. The Latin original is in the *Codex Justiniani* (Codex of Justinian), lib. 3,

10. Year-Day Principle

An important principle in prophetic interpretation in connection with time prophecies is the year-day principle, under which a day of prophetic time is counted as a calendar year of historic time. Before the Israelites entered the land of Canaan, they sent twelve spies ahead to investigate. The spies were gone forty days, and upon their return, the Hebrews, frightened at their report, refused to go up and occupy the

Promised Land. The result was a sentence the Lord passed upon them: "According to the number of the days in which you spied out the land, forty days, **for every day a year**, you shall bear your iniquity, forty years, and you shall know my displeasure." Numbers 14:34, RSV.

A similar method of computing future time is indicated through the prophet Ezekiel. Forty years of punishment for iniquities awaited the kingdom of Judah. The Lord said through the prophet: "After you have finished this, lie down again, this time on your right side, and bear the sin of the house of Judah. I have assigned you forty days, **a day for each year**." Ezekiel 4:6.

This year-day principle has an important application in interpreting the time of the prophecy of the "two thousand and three hundred days" (Daniel 8:14, NKJV) and the 1260-day period, variously indicated as "a time and times and the dividing of time" (Daniel 7:25), the "forty and two months" (Revelation 11:2; 13:5), and the "thousand two hundred and sixty days" (Revelation 11:3; 12:6).

11. Forgeries

"Among the documents that at the present time are generally admitted to be forgeries, the *Donation of Constantine* and the *Pseudo-Isidorian Decretals* are of primary importance. The *Donation of Constantine* is the name traditionally applied, since the later Middle Ages, to a document purporting to have been addressed by Constantine the Great to Pope Sylvester I, which is found first in a Parisian manuscript (Codex lat. 2777) of probably the beginning of the ninth century.

"Since the eleventh century it has been used as a powerful argument in favor of the papal claims, and consequently since the twelfth it has been the subject of a vigorous controversy. At the same time, by rendering it possible to regard the papacy as a middle term between the original and the medieval Roman Empire, and thus to form a theoretical basis of continuity for the reception of the Roman law in the Middle Ages, it has had no small influence upon secular history."—*The New Schaff-Herzog Encyclopedia of Religious Knowledge,* vol. 3, art. "The Donation of Constantine," pp. 484, 485.

The "false writings" referred to in the text include also the *Pseudo-Isidorian Decretals,* together with other forgeries.

The *Pseudo-Isidorian Decretals* are certain fictitious letters ascribed to early popes from Clement (A.D. 100) to Gregory the Great (A.D. 600), incorporated in a ninth-century collection purporting to have been made by "Isidore Mercator." The name *Pseudo-Isidorian Decretals* has been in use since the advent of criticism in the fifteenth century.

Pseudo-Isidore took as the basis of his forgeries a collection of valid canons called the *Hispana Gallica Augustodunensis,* thus lessening the danger of detection, since collections of canons were commonly made by adding new matter to old. Thus his forgeries were less apparent when incorporated with genuine material. The falsity of the Pseudo-Isidorian fabrications is now incontestably admitted, being proved by internal evidence, investigation of the sources, the methods used, and the fact that this material was unknown before 852. Historians agree that 850 or 851 is the most probable date for the completion of the collection, since the document is first cited in the *Admonitio* of the capitulary of Quiercy, in 857.

12. Purgatory

Dr. Joseph Faa Di Bruno defines purgatory: "Purgatory is a state of suffering after this life, in which those souls are for a time detained, who depart this life after their deadly sins have been remitted as to the stain and guilt, and as to the everlasting pain that was due to them; but who have on account of those sins still some debt of temporal punishment to pay; as also those souls which leave this world guilty only of venial sins."—Catholic Belief (1884 ed.; imprimatur Archbishop of New York), page 196.

13. The Church's Historical Hatred of the Bible!

The Council of Toulouse, which met about the time of the crusade against the Albigenses, ruled: "We prohibit laymen possessing copies of the Old and New Testament. . . . We forbid them most severely to have the above books in the popular vernacular." "The lords of the districts shall carefully seek out the heretics in dwellings, hovels, and forests, and even their underground retreats shall be entirely wiped out."—*Council Tolosanum,* Pope Gregory IX, Anno. chr. 1229. Canons 14 and 2. This Council sat at the time of the crusade against the Albigenses.

"This pest [the Bible] had taken such an extension that some people had appointed priests of their own, and even some evangelists who distorted and destroyed the truth of the gospel and made new gospels for their own purpose . . . (they know that) the preaching and explanation of the Bible is absolutely forbidden to the lay members."—Philip van Limborch, *History of the Inquisition,* "Acts of Inquisition," chapter 8.

The Council of Tarragona, 1234, ruled that: "No one may possess the books of the Old and New Testaments in the Romance language, and if anyone possesses them he must turn them over to the local bishop within eight days after promulgation of this decree, so that they may be burned lest, be he a cleric or a layman, he be suspected until he is cleared of all suspicion."—D. Lortsch, *Histoire de la Bible en France,* 1910, p. 14.

At the Council of Constance in 1415, Wycliffe was posthumously condemned by Arundel, the archbishop of Canterbury, as "that pestilent wretch of damnable heresy who invented a new translation of the Scriptures in his mother tongue."

The opposition to the Bible by the Roman Catholic Church has continued through the centuries and was increased particularly at the time of the founding of Bible societies. On December 8, 1866, Pope Pius IX, in his encyclical *Quanta Cura,* issued a syllabus of eighty errors under ten different headings. Under heading IV, we find listed: "Socialism, communism, clandestine societies, Bible societies. . . . Pests of this sort must be destroyed by all possible means."

14. Fox's Book of Martyrs

Readers of *Prophecy Made Easy* are encouraged to read what was once once of the most read books in the United States—*Fox's Book of Martyrs,* by John Fox (b. 1517 in England). Though not for the faint of heart, the events chronicled in this book are a true historical record of those persecuted and murdered for the "crime" of serving their God according to the Bible. Those with Internet access may read the book online at:

www.ccel.org/f/foxe/martyrs

15. Date of Decree to Rebuild Jerusalem

According to Jewish reckoning, the fifth month (Ab) of the seventh year of Artaxerxes' reign extended from July 23 to August 21, 457 B.C. After Ezra's arrival in Jerusalem in the autumn of the year, the decree of the king went into effect. For the certainty of the date 457 B.C. being the seventh year of Artaxerxes, see S. H. Horn and L. H. Wood, *The Chronology of*

Ezra 7 (Washington, D. C.: Review and Herald Publishing Assn., 1953); E. G. Kraeling, *The Brooklyn Museum Aramaic Papyri* (New Haven or London, 1953), pp. 191-193; *The Seventh-day Adventist Bible Commentary* (Washington, D.C.: Review and Herald Publishing Assn., 1954), vol. 3, pp. 97-110.

16. The Seventh Day in Ethiopia

Until rather recent years, the Coptic Church of Ethiopia observed the seventh-day Sabbath. The Ethiopians also kept Sunday, the first day of the week, throughout their history as a Christian people. These days were marked by special services in the churches. The observance of the seventh-day Sabbath has, however, virtually ceased in modern Ethiopia. For eyewitness accounts of religious days in Ethiopia, see Pero Gomes de Teixeira, *The Discovery of Abyssinia by the Portuguese in 1520* (translated in English in London: British Museum, 1938), p. 79.

17. The Last Three Persecuting Powers

Three powers work together to try and crush God's children just before Christ returns in glory. They are: a) the leopard beast, b) the lamb-like beast that speaks like a dragon, and c) the image to the beast of Revelation 13. Discover the identity of these three powers in chapters 14 to 16 of *Prophecy Made Easy*. Remember, God fights for His children! God Wins! And His commandment-keeping children, filled with the love of Jesus, win also! Isn't it wonderful to have God on your side? He loves you, and He will watch over you with tender loving care!

18. Let's Vote!

We could make all our decisions as the politicians do. We could take a poll to find out what is truth. We could vote on it. If there are six billion people on Planet Earth, and 5,999,999,999 of them all came to a decision of what truth is, it would not count with God. He has the veto. Bible truth has never been left to popular decision.

It was not popular in the days of the Flood, and it was not popular at the cross. The whole world voted against entering the ark. In the days of the Flood, everyone except eight people rejected the plan of salvation. They did not want to look foolish by getting on board the ark and then have nothing happen.

The crowd at Pilate's judgment hall cried out, "Crucify Him, crucify Him." They voted to kill Christ. God is calling for those who will not wait until truth is popular before accepting it. God is asking you to accept His Word as final authority no matter how the majority vote—no matter what the majority decides to do.

Jesus calls you, saying, "Enter through the narrow gate. For wide is the gate and broad is the road that leads to destruction, and many enter through it. But small is the gate and narrow the road that leads to life, and only a few find it." Matthew 7:13-15.

Stand with the few, the brave, and the victorious!

19. What Did Jesus Christ Do for Me?

Sometimes we read so quickly that we lose the significance of what really happened to Jesus Christ beginning in the garden of Gethsemane. Let's examine Christ's own words as He entered the garden of Gethsemane the night before His death.

Mark writes that He began to be deeply distressed and troubled. Christ said "My soul is overwhelmed with sorrow to the point of death." Mark 14:33, 34. People can get sad at the drop of a hat, but not Christ. He was usually cheerful, but not on this night—on the eve before His death on the cross.

In the garden of Gethsemane that evening, Jesus was deeply troubled, suffering pain, stress, and agony. There are different types of trouble and different degrees of pain. This was the worst trouble, the worst pain, the worst agony any person in history had ever faced. It was so bad that words cannot describe it. Notice how the Bible writer tries to describe it. Mark wrote, "He was troubled and deeply distressed." How deep was His stress? So deep that it forced blood vessels in His face to rupture. He experienced a deeper stress, a deeper agony than any person had ever before experienced or ever could experience.

Jesus Himself said that He was "exceedingly sorrowful even to death." Mark 14:34, NKJV. Jesus, the Eternal One, left the throne of glory as the King of kings and Lord of lords for the very purpose of coming into this world to carry the weight of the sins of the world—yours and mine. The result was that He went through a suffering no one had ever gone through before or ever would afterward.

Jesus was "exceedingly sorrowful even to death." He was full of sorrow, full of sadness, full of pain. He was not just full. He was "exceedingly" full, "even to death." He was so full of sorrow, sadness, pain, and agony that it was killing Him. He was dying in the garden of Gethsemane. What happened to Jesus Christ after the Last Supper with His disciples? What happened when He went to the garden to pray on the night before His death on the cross? What can we learn from the biblical account of Christ's last 18 hours of life?

Christ went to pray that night in the garden where so often before, He had prayed. But this night, He felt a pain, a sorrow He had never felt before. The guilt and weight of the sins of every person who had ever lived or ever would live was heaped upon Christ—a weight so great He would not survive it.

All the emotional garbage and mental pain of every sin ever committed by each of the billions of people who ever would live through all human history was compressed together and heaped upon Jesus Christ as He prayed there in the Garden of Gethsemane. The crushing weight caused Him to stagger and forced Him into the earth in prayer. The weight was so great that it ruptured small blood vessels in His face and forced drops of blood to run down His face and moisten the ground beneath Him in the garden where He prayed. He would have died right there on the spot in the garden, sweating great drops of blood, if an angel had not been sent to give Him the strength to delay His death until He reached the cross.

Later, when He was crucified, two thieves were also crucified—one on each side of Christ. The religious leaders wanted everyone off their crosses before sundown. The two thieves were still living, so their legs were broken before being removed. But Christ was dead already, so His legs were not broken. People usually survived the slow torture of the cross for days before finally dying. Why did Christ die so quickly?

It was not the nails through His hands and feet that killed Christ. It was not the Roman soldiers who killed Christ. It was not the religious leaders who killed Christ. It was your sins and mine that killed Him. You and I are responsible for the death of Jesus Christ. Everyone who has ever lived is responsible. It was our sins that caused His suffering and death. Jesus loves you so awesomely much that He was willing to take on Himself the death you deserve so that you can have the life He deserves! Jesus loves you that much!

Jesus had not been arrested yet. He had not been whipped yet. He had not been nailed to the cross yet. No one had touched Him yet, but He was suffering so much that blood was forced out of His face and fell in drops to the ground. You see, the death of Christ was not caused by the Jews, and it was not caused by the Romans. The actual cause of His death was the crushing weight of the sins of the world—your sins and my sins. We are guilty of His death. It was for us that He prayed, "Father, forgive them, for they do not know what they are doing"—as well as for the Roman soldiers and the religious leaders who wanted Him dead. The mental anguish, the mental pain that Christ endured was so much greater than the physical pain that He cried out, "My God, My God, why have You forsaken me?"

In the garden of Gethsemane, Christ could have even then refused to die in our place. It was not yet too late. He could have wiped the great drops of blood from His forehead and left us to die. He could have gone free. He could have said, "Let the guilty sinners receive the penalty of their own sin, and I will go back to My Father." He had that choice. He was innocent. He was sinless. He did not have to die. It was entirely His choice. He thought of you and me and made His final choice. He chose, if necessary, to be forever separated from God the Father. He made that choice for one reason and one alone. God loves you! It was love for those He made that guided His final decision.

Sin had brought death, and He, the Eternal One, chose to enter this world as a little baby boy, live a sinless life, and die in place of guilty sinners such as you and me.

His final decision is made. He will accept the baptism of blood and spit and sweat and tears and shame. He will save you at any cost to Himself. In submission He trembles and prays, "If this cup may not pass away from Me, except I drink it, Your will be done."

"And being in agony, He prayed more earnestly. Then His sweat became like great drops of blood falling down to the ground. O My Father, if it is possible let this cup pass from Me; nevertheless, not as I will, but as you will. . . . O My Father, if this cup cannot pass away from Me unless I drink it, Your will be done." Luke 22:44, Matthew 26:42.

Soldiers and religious officers from the chief priests and Pharisees came to the garden with lanterns and weapons. Jesus asked, "Who are you looking for?" They said, "Jesus of Nazareth." Jesus said to them, "I am He," and an invisible angel pushed the troops back, forcing them to the ground. They looked up at Christ as He asked again, "Who are you looking for?" and they answered again, "Jesus of Nazareth."

"I have told you that I am He," Jesus replied, "so let my friends go free." Peter drew his sword and cut off the ear of a servant. Jesus reached up and touched the servant's ear, and the blood stopped running down and the ear was healed. "Do you think that I cannot now pray to My Father, and He will send Me more than twelve legions of angels?" Jesus asked Peter.

Christ was taken first to Annas, Caiaphas's father-in-law, and then to Caiaphas, the high priest. Annas questioned Christ about His teachings. But Christ told him, "I spoke openly to the world. Why do you ask Me? Ask those who have heard me. They know what I said." When Jesus had said this, one of the officers standing by hit Jesus with his hand and demanded, "Do You answer the high priest like that?"

Next Jesus was taken to the palace of Caiaphas, the high priest. The chief priests and all the council tried to find people to testify against Jesus so they could have an excuse for condemning Him to death. Several spoke, but their stories did not agree. Through all of this, Jesus kept silent. The high priest tried to get Christ to condemn Himself and asked Him the all-important question, "Are You the Messiah, the Son of God?" In answering, Christ knew He was sealing His own death sentence, but He answered, "I am, and you will see the Son of Man sitting at the right hand of the Power, and coming with the clouds of heaven."

The high priest tore his clothing in mock shock, shouting, "Blasphemy—what do you think?" And they condemned Jesus to death. They blindfolded Him so He couldn't see and then spat in His face and beat Him. Others struck Him with the palms of their hands, saying, "Prophesy to us, Christ! Who is the one who struck You?"

One of Christ's best friends, Peter, was confronted three different times: "You also were with Jesus of Galilee." Each time Peter denied it, saying, "I do not know what you are saying. I do not know the man." And for emphasis, the third time he was accused of knowing Jesus, Peter cursed and swore as he denied it. Immediately, while he was still cursing, the rooster crowed. The Lord turned and looked at Peter. Then Peter remembered the words the Lord had said to him: "Before the rooster crows, you will deny me three times." So Peter went out and wept bitterly.

When morning came, the chief priests and elders and scribes and the whole council tied Christ's hands and led Him to Governor Pilate's palace. "Are you king of the Jews?" Pilate asked. "Yes, I am," Jesus replied. Pilate said to the chief priest and to the crowd, "I find no fault in this man." But the chief priests and elders shouted, "He stirs up the people, teaching throughout all Judea and Galilee." When Pilate heard of Galilee, he asked if Jesus were a Galilean. As soon as he knew that Jesus belonged to Herod's jurisdiction, he sent Him to Herod, who was visiting Jerusalem at that time.

Herod was exceptionally happy to see Jesus, thinking that He would work some miracles for him. He asked Jesus many, many questions, but Jesus didn't answer any of them. The chief priest and the scribes stood there shouting that Jesus deserved to die.

Herod felt very angry that Jesus would not answer any of his questions and would not perform miracles for him. He thought that Christ would do anything to obtain His freedom. He was hopeful that Christ would entertain him by performing miracles like a magician or like a clown at a birthday party. But Christ had nothing to say to the man who'd had John the Baptist beheaded. The very silence of Christ was the greatest rebuke that could have been given. Herod and his soldiers mocked Christ, dressing him in one of Herod's old kingly robes, and sent Him back to Pilate.

Pilate said, "Neither I nor Herod find any reason to put Him to death. I will therefore punish Jesus and release Him." It was a custom that one prisoner should be pardoned during Passover time. Pilate tried to take advantage of that custom and spoke to the crowd. "I have two prisoners, and I will release one of them and let him go free. I will give you a choice between Christ, your king, and Barabbas, the murderer. Which one should I set free?" They all cried, "Barabbas! Set Barabbas free and crucify Christ!"

Then Pilate's soldiers took Jesus into a building. They made a circle around Him and took off all His clothes. There He stood, completely naked. The soldiers took their whip, with pieces of metal embedded in it, and lashed His back until the blood flowed freely. Then they put a purple robe on Him. They twisted a crown of long, sharp thorns and jammed it down on His head—and placed a stick as a mock scepter in His right hand. They bowed their knees and mockingly worshiped Him, shouting, "All honor to you, King of the Jews!" Then they spit on Him and took the stick and struck Him on the head, driving the long, sharp thorns into His head, causing blood to run down His face and beard. Then they took the robe off Him, put His own clothes on Him, and led Him away to be crucified.

The soldiers stripped Him of His clothing again and, after crucifying Him, divided up His clothing among themselves. Christ lay down naked on the wooden cross. The soldiers drove nails through His hands and feet and then lifted the torture device, the cross, and let it fall into the hole prepared for it. This caused the most extreme pain to the Saviour of the world.

The wounds made by the nails tore the flesh in His hands and His feet as the cross thudded to the bottom of the hole prepared for it. The nail wounds gaped, and blood drops landed on the earth beneath the cross. Christ prayed, "Father, forgive them, for they do not know what they do."

Rulers, religious leaders, people, and soldiers passed by the cross, mocking

Him and saying, "If you are the Son of God, come down from the cross. You trusted in God—so let Him deliver Him now if He will save Him, for He said, I am the Son of God." Even the robbers who were crucified with Him said the same thing. "If you are the King of the Jews, save Yourself."

A sign was placed over Him—written in Greek, Latin, and Hebrew—that said: THIS IS THE KING OF THE JEWS.

The sun was shining at its brightest. It was 12:00 noon. One of the criminals who was dying on a cross next to Jesus said, "If You are the Christ, save Yourself and us." The other said, "Do you not even fear God?" He turned his head toward Jesus and said, "Lord, remember me when You come into Your kingdom." And Jesus said to him, "I say to you today, you will be with Me in Paradise." Notice the paradox. Here was a man who was helplessly dying. He could do absolutely nothing except to speak a few words before dying. Yet this man found the secret to a life of ALL POWER. And that secret removed his fear of death and filled him with a new freedom he never thought he would ever find in a million years.

All of a sudden the sun seemed to be blotted out of the sky. From noon until 3:00 p.m. there was a strange darkness over all the land. And about 3:00 p.m. Jesus cried out with a loud voice, saying, "My God, My God, why have you forsaken Me?" Psalm 22:1. Jesus cried out with a loud voice, "Father, into Your hands I commit My spirit." And then He breathed His last. Immediately, the veil of the temple was torn in two from top to bottom by the unseen hands of an angel. The leader of the soldier guard had heard Christ speak to the dying thief. He had watched as the sun was blotted out for three hours. He had just felt the earthquake that had thrown him to the ground, and he knew that this was truly the death of the King of kings. He felt he must share these feelings as he said, "This was truly the Son of God."

Christ's last cry on the cross revealed the real cause of His death. The mental pain of being separated from God the Father and carrying the mental and emotional pain of all the billions of people who would ever live was so much greater than His physical pain that it killed Him. He was killed by the weight of your sins and mine. The sins of the entire human race crushed out His life. He died of a broken heart and, without the additional strength from the angel in the garden, would have lost His life before reaching the Cross. He would have been crushed by sin while He was still in the Garden of Gethsemane sweating "great drops of blood." Christ took your pain that you might have His victory. He wants you to share His throne with Him forever. Revelation 3:21. "He who overcomes will receive the right to sit with me on my throne, just as I overcame and sat down with my Father on His throne."

Why did the King of the universe leave His home to come to Planet Earth? Why did He choose to become a human—a little baby boy—and then grow up with the religious leaders hating Him? Why did He allow His enemy, Lucifer, to bring Him pain and suffering? Why did He allow those He had made to spit on Him without retaliation? Why did He suffer the ultimate humiliation of dying naked on two pieces of wood—on "The Old Rugged Cross"—hanging between heaven and earth? It was out of love for you. And it was out of love for me. If you had been the only sinner who needed a bridge over "the valley of death," God would have done it for you, alone.

What would it be worth to you to have Jesus Christ in your home today? I mean to have Him really come walking up to your door and knock on it.

What would you do if Jesus Christ, who loves you personally so incredibly much, walked up to your door and offered you a crown? What if He said "_____," (and imagine here your name in the blank—because He knows you by name!) "I just stopped by to bring you this crown. It is a much finer crown than has ever been worn by any king. Also, I am inviting you to come to My house—to My mansion. I have a special place of honor for you."

"To those who overcome, I will give the right to sit with me on my throne, just as I have overcome, and now sit with my Father on His throne." Revelation 3:21.

"In My Father's house are many mansions." John 14:2, KJV.

What would you do? I know what I would do—I would shout with joy! I would be excited! If you accept Jesus as your Bridge over "the valley of death," He will one day be just that physically close. The Bible, God's Word, says that every person is a sinner. It says that sin is disobedience to God's Ten Commandment law. It also says that everyone must die because the just penalty for sin is death. There is a law that says that weight keeps an object on the ground. That law is the law of gravity. Yet we have discovered another law, the law of aerodynamics, that overcomes the law of gravity and allows very heavy objects, like airplanes, to fly through the sky.

Sin holds us down, just as gravity holds us down. The power that overcomes gravity is the power of aerodynamics. The only power that overcomes sin is Jesus Christ! People are trying every other option. Many of the other attempts to overcome sin have good-sounding religious names. But the only problem is that they don't work. The only one that works is Jesus

Christ. It was Jesus who said, "I am the way, the truth, and the life. No one comes to the Father but by me." If you want to go to California, you had better get on the right highway. If you want to have eternal life, Jesus Christ is that highway. If it is truth you are after, you will find truth when you choose Christ. If it is life that you want, you will find that in knowing Christ. It is Christ who says, "I am the way, the truth and the life."

Jesus says, "For God so loved_____[say your own name here] that He gave His only Son, that [by believing] in Him, you should not die but have eternal life." John 3:16.

When anyone offers you a gift, you have a choice. You can either take it or reject it. The thief on the cross chose to accept it. He asked Jesus to give him the gift of eternal life. If you have never asked for the gift of eternal life and want this wonderful gift, all you have to do is ask Jesus for it in prayer. Prayer is just talking to God as to a friend. God wants you to talk to Him every day. He wants to be your friend every day. To begin your friendship with God, you must invite Jesus Christ to be your Saviour from sin. You must ask Him for forgiveness for your past sin. He says, "Come now, let us reason together," says the Lord. "Though your sins are like scarlet, they shall be as white as snow; though they are red as crimson, they shall be like wool." "If we confess our sins, He is faithful and just to forgive us our sins and to cleanse us from all unrighteousness." Isaiah 1:18; 1 John 1:9.

Here is a suggested prayer. If you are alone, speak these words aloud to God. And if someone is with you and you cannot speak out loud, you may repeat this prayer in your mind. God will still hear your prayer.

Pray this prayer—and eternal life begins right now!

"Dear Father, forgive me for my life of sin. I invite Jesus into my heart to be my Saviour from sin. You promised that when I do this, you make me 'clean.' I believe You and thank Jesus for cleaning my life and coming into my life. In Jesus' name, Amen."

If you prayed that prayer and meant it, you have just become a "born again" child of God—you are accepted as part of the family of God. Now continue choosing Christ to be your daily Friend and Strength, and you will grow in strength, in knowledge, in peace, and in joy! Jesus tells us that "no one can see the kingdom of God unless he is born again." John 3:3.

Now that you have been "born again," let Jesus write His law in your heart. Hebrews 8:10. Continue following Him, and you will one day sit with Christ on His throne. Revelation 3:21. You have just begun a life of ALL POWER!

To maintain your life of ALL POWER, you must:

1. Let Jesus talk to you through daily Bible study.

2. Pray—talk to God as to a friend, regularly throughout the day.

3. Help others find what you have found—a life of ALL POWER with Jesus Christ, the King of kings. Begin sharing your new faith today. One good way to do that is to purchase extra copies of Prophecy Made Easy for family, friends, and others. This little book is like a little acorn. There is an oak tree inside every little acorn. Plant this little book in the minds of your family and friends by faith, and be amazed at the power you have released into their lives.

If you have further questions, please write me at the address below.

Your friend in Christ,
Glen Walker

To Order *Prophecy Made Easy*

For additional copies of *Prophecy Made Easy,* please send $12.99 + $2.00 shipping and handling to:

Glen Walker
Prophecy Press
P.O. Box 12221
Fort Wayne, IN 46863-2221

You may also order *Prophecy Made Easy* on the Internet, or read it online, at: *www.prophecymadeeasy.com*

We also recommend the colorful online Bible lessons at *www.amazingfacts.org/bibleschool/bibleschool.html*

FREE Focus on Prophecy Bible Guides

For an in-depth, chapter-by-chapter study of the Bible books of Daniel and Revelation, we recommend the *Focus on Prophecy* Bible Guides.

To receive your FREE Bible Guides, send your name, mailing address (including zip code and country, if outside the United States) in a stamped envelope or on a stamped postcard, to:

Focus on Prophecy
P.O. Box 53055
Los Angeles, CA 90053-0055